Reprints of Economic Classics

LIFE OF FRIEDRICH LIST

LIFE OF

FRIEDRICH LIST

AND SELECTIONS FROM HIS WRITINGS

By

MARGARET HIRST

[1909]

WITH AN INTRODUCTION BY
JOSEPH DORFMAN

AND THE ADDITION OF LETTER XII TO
Outlines of American Political Economy

REPRINTS OF ECONOMIC CLASSICS

Augustus M. Kelley, Bookseller
New York 1965

Library of Congress Catalogue Card Number
65 - 16266

FRIEDRICH LIST
AND AMERICAN ECONOMIC THOUGHT

The current intense concern of economists with industrial development has revived interest in those schools of economic thought whose theories are centered on this problem. Among these are the various branches of the historical school which stressed economic growth and comparative economic development; in particular, the German historical school. Of that wing, Friedrich List (1789-1846) has been among the most fertile theorists, and is now recognized as one of the first of the group. It has been well said that "List's approach . . . was highly dependent upon a dynamic theory of economic development." [1]

While German economists and policy makers neglected this creative native son during his lifetime they began in the 1850's paying ever increasing homage to him, especially since the rise of the powerful German Empire after the Franco-Prussian War and Bismark's adoption of a policy of protective tariffs to industrialize the nation.

The Germans have periodically published multivolume editions of List's writings, set up archival libraries to further the investigation of his life and

---

[1] Lloyd A. Metzler, "Tariffs, The Terms of Trade and the Distribution of National Income," *The Journal of Political Economy*, February 1949, p. 26.

work, and even erected monuments in his honor. But in the Anglo-American world, very little was known about List and his work until the twentieth century. To be sure his most famous book, *Das nationale system der politischen Oekonomie* (1841) was translated in the United States in 1856 under the title *National System of Political Economy;* almost thirty years later as the economic power of Germany began to be felt, came a translation in England which became the standard one.[2]

Short memoirs and sketches, based on the early German accounts, were prefixed to both translations. They suffered, however, not only from their briefness but also from the fact that the German biographies relied heavily and rather uncritically on List's own reminiscences. Furthermore, there was only scant recognition of his activities during his sojourn in the United States from 1825 to 1831.

Margaret E. Hirst's *Life of Friedrich List*, although published in 1909, is still the best and most comprehensive account in the English language. She had the equipment for the task through her training at Cambridge University; she also had the help of her brother, Francis W. Hirst, the editor of the famed London *Economist* and a noted biographer of Adam Smith. Miss Hirst performed an important service not only in giving a careful, detailed discussion of his American

---

[2] There is as yet no complete translation of the work. The American translation omits the preface; the British translation gives extracts from the preface but omits the introductory chapter which gives a summary of his theories. A British translation of the introduction is given below pp. 287-318.

INTRODUCTION

period,[3] but also in reproducing his two pamphlets published in Philadelphia in 1827, *Outlines of American Political Economy*, and *Appendix to the Outlines of American Political Economy*. These publications, as her annotations point out, contain all the essential ideas elaborated in *The National System of Political Economy* which was issued fourteen years later. They were composed of eleven of the twelve articles that List originally wrote for a leading protectionist newspaper, the Philadelphia *National Gazette*, from August 18 to November 27, 1827. The twelfth and last article which Miss Hirst was unable to locate, has since been discovered and has been added in this reprint of her book.[4]

The two *Outlines of American Political Economy* are important not only for an understanding of List's system but also for indicating that the United States was beginning to pay back the large intellectual debt it owed to Europe in the field of economic theory. List's thought was guided by the much earlier American literature. Miss Hirst building on her own researches

---

[3] Miss Hirst's account should be supplemented by William Notz, "Frederick List in America," *The American Economic Review*, June 1926, pp. 249-265, and Michael J. L. O'Connor, *Origins of Academic Economics in the United States* (New York: Columbia University Press, 1944) pp. 32-35. See also Joseph Dorfman, *The Economic Mind in American Civilization*, 5 vols. (New York: Viking, 1946-59), II, pp. 575-584.

[4] That Miss Hirst could find no trace of the last article was partly due to the fact that she translated the title of the newspaper from List's reference as the "Philadelphia National Journal," instead of the "Philadelphia National *Gazette*."

The articles were directed against the influential free trade treatise, *Lectures on the Elements of Political Economy* (Columbia, South Carolina: P. E. Sweeney, 1826) by Thomas Cooper, President of South Carolina College (now the University of South Carolina). On Cooper, see Dumas Malone, *The Public Life of Thomas Cooper, 1783-1839* (Columbia, S.C.: South Carolina University Press, 1926; reprint with additions, 1961).

and that of American and Italian scholars, shows that List, before he came to the United States, was a "theoretical free trader" of the Adam Smith—J. B. Say variety, and that in formulating his system of state aid and regulation for developing an industrial nation, he owed much to American publications which presented a "national system of political economy" for the United States.[5]

These writings included Alexander Hamilton's *Report on Manufactures* (1792), the pamphlets of Mathew Carey and Tench Coxe, Hezekiah Nile's *Nile's Weekly Register*, and Daniel Raymond's *Thoughts on Political Economy* (1820) which was expanded into the two volume *Elements of Political Economy* (1823). Raymond had much earlier than List developed such key propositions as the distinction between national wealth and individual wealth, the notion of the nation as an organic unity, the concept of the manifold development of productive powers, rather than an immediate accumulation of goods, and the danger of oversaving (or underspending in modern terminology).[6] Furthermore, "The idea of historical stages in the economic development of a nation and the necessity of governmental policies appropriate to each" which some have declared "to be the most important part of

---

[5] As Miss Hirst put it, List while in his native Würtemberg "pleads for the abolition of all internal customs [between the German states], and advocates import duties [on the goods of non-German countries] only as a means of retaliation against foreign countries until they shall have adopted the principle of European free trade." (See p. 111 below).

[6] A detailed comparison of Raymond and List is in Charles P. Neill, *Daniel Raymond: An Early Chapter in the History of Economic Theory in the United States* (Baltimore: Johns Hopkins University Press, 1897) chap. 4.

INTRODUCTION

List's theory" was stated twenty-three years earlier
in Coxe's *Essay on the Manufacturing Interest of the
United States.*[7] In other words, the *Outlines* so clearly
show the influence of the American writers "that there
can be little reasonable doubt that American conditions
and ideas were predominant, if not decisive, in the
development of List's economic theories."[8]

It could even be added that what has been hailed as
List's "greatest single contribution . . . to modern
[military] strategy; [namely], his elaborate discussion of the influence of railways upon the shifting
balance of military power," stems in good part from
his American experiences. "He first became interested
in railways during his residence in America, when he
was one of the promoters of the Schuylkill Navigation,
Railroad and Coal Company, a forerunner of the
present Reading System."[9] More significant for the
purpose in hand, the idea of the military importance
of the railroad was common in the United States, even
before his arrival.

During this time, railway promoters seeking federal
aid, often used the argument that the railways were
vital for the speedy movement of troops and military
supplies. In fact as early as the War of 1812, John
Stevens, who was also prominent in the development

[7] Harold Hutcheson, *Tench Coxe: A Study in American Economic Development* (Baltimore: The Johns Hopkins Press,
1934) p. 199.

[8] E. M. Earle, "Adam Smith, Alexander Hamilton, Friedrich
List: The Economic Foundations of Military Power," in *Makers
of Modern Strategy: Military Thought from Machiavelli to
Hitler,* edited by E. M. Earle *et al.* (Princeton, N. J.: Princeton
University Press, 1943), p. 141.

[9] *Ibid.,* p. 148.

of the steamboat, was showering the country with pamphlets along these lines. It was not uncommon for railway companies to petition for and secure the services of the army engineers to make the necessary surveys and even to direct the construction on the basis of the military importance of their roads.

Miss Hirst recognizes that List was no mere borrower; her presentation of the merits of his work may seem somewhat over cautious, and her characterization of him as a high class journalist rather than a theorist would not be accepted today. But it should be remembered that she was writing at a time when British economists still believed that the area of government interference in economic affairs was very narrowly limited; in fact economists supporting protective tariffs were held to be either poor theorists or no theorists.

To sum up: as the case of Friedrich List illustrates, there was a much greater interchange of ideas between the United States and Europe than has generally been realized, and the borrowing was by no means all one way.

JOSEPH DORFMAN

Columbia University
November 1964

LIFE OF
FRIEDRICH LIST

AND

SELECTIONS FROM HIS WRITINGS

BY

MARGARET E. HIRST

LATE SCHOLAR OF NEWNHAM COLLEGE, CAMBRIDGE

WITH AN INTRODUCTION BY

F. W. HIRST

LONDON

SMITH, ELDER & CO., 15, WATERLOO PLACE

1909

PRINTED BY
WILLIAM CLOWES AND SONS, LIMITED,
LONDON AND BECCLES

PREFACE

Some time ago the suggestion was made to me that, as the writings of Friedrich List, apart from the "National System," are little known in England and America, an annotated reprint of his letters on the "Outlines of American Political Economy" (written in 1827, during the early Protectionist controversy) might be of interest. The two pamphlets —for Letters IX.-XI. form a separate Appendix— are rare, but the British Museum possesses copies.

As the work progressed its scope insensibly grew, and to complete it translations of two other writings by List have been included. The memorial addressed to the German Federal Council in 1819 expounds his economic views before he experienced American conditions, and the Introduction to the "National System" (omitted in Mr. Lloyd's translation) gives his own summary of his later theories. An important collection of List's papers and manuscripts is preserved among the municipal archives in the tower of the Marienkirche at Reutlingen, his native town. The Alice Hopkinson Memorial Studentship (open to former students of Newnham College) was awarded to me in 1907, and I availed myself of the opportunity to visit Germany, and to examine such of the Reutlingen papers as related to List's English and American experiences. Neither Häusser nor Jentsch, his German biographers, deal at much length with these episodes, and from the papers and from other sources I have been able, I believe, to give a more complete account of them than any which has yet appeared. I have also made use of material which I found during my researches in the University Library of Tübingen and the Royal Library at Stuttgart.

It is a pleasant task to record my thanks to those, whether in England, Germany, or America, who have so freely helped me: at Tübingen, to Herr Ober-Bibliothekar Dr. Karl Geiger and to the late Professor von Schönberg, for my ready admission to the University Library, and to the former for much assistance there; at Reutlingen, to the Oberburgermeister and municipal officials, for facilities granted me in regard to the List-Archiv. Herr Oberfinanzrat Dr. Losch of Stuttgart, who is an authority on all matters relating to List, was good enough to give me valuable information, and to lend me books which I could not otherwise have obtained. I am under a similar debt to Dr. Max Höltzel of Stuttgart and Professor F. W. Taussig of Harvard University. To Mrs.

Hopkinson, the donor of the studentship, I am also grateful for the constant and helpful interest she has shown in my work. My brother, besides contributing the Introduction, has helped the progress of the book in many ways.

M. E. H.

April, 1909.

CONTENTS

INTRODUCTION

By far the greatest name in the short but rich and fruitful annals of economic science is that of its founder, Adam Smith. Very high among his successors, if our touchstone is to be influence upon national policy, stands Friedrich List — a romantic figure, displaying, through all the disappointments and vicissitudes of a most disappointing and vicissitudinous career, dauntless courage, heroic energy, and unquenchable enthusiasm.

Whether the man of action or the man of thought is the more enviable, admirable, or powerful, is a question of taste which every one must answer for himself. In the art and science of public finance as well as in the larger sphere of political economy there is plenty of scope for both—for the pure theorist and for the statesman who is the practical interpreter, perhaps the mere instrument, of other men's ideas. Between these two types — between, say, a Ricardo and a Goulburn — there are many intermediates; and it might well be disputed in what order five contemporaries — Bastiat, Mill, Cobden, Gladstone, and List—should be ranked by the discriminating historian of political economy. If Adam Smith illustrates very well the superiority that is usually assigned to the life of philosophic study and discovery, Friedrich List may equally be cited by those who regard an active participation in public affairs not only as necessary to happiness, but as a positive aid and stimulus to political genius. Both views may be true. Probably there are such differences and distinctions among minds of the highest order that in the very same temperature, soil, and environment, which bring one plant to perfection, another will wither and decay. The sauntering or sedentary life of a private tutor, a university professor, and a customs official suited Adam Smith and gave him twenty years of golden leisure in which to revolve, and ultimately to revolutionize, economic thought and commercial policy. But such a life would never have satisfied Friedrich List. What is one man's food is another man's poison.

For reasons which, if not obvious, are discoverable, List—though his influence on commercial policy and perhaps even on public finance in general, may almost rival that of Adam Smith— is comparatively neglected in the universities of Europe and America. He may perhaps be described as the Cobbett of Tariff Reform. Reading List for Cobbett and Adam Smith for Paine, a critic may be tempted to adapt a famous passage in one of Hazlitt's sketches. List, with vast industry, an active imagination and lively pen, never seems to build upon a perfectly scientific foundation or to complete any of the work to our full satisfaction, whereas Smith seems to clear every problem that he chooses to handle from all controversy— past, present, and to come. List provokes us to criticism. Smith reduces us to silent consent. Smith takes a bird's-eye view of things, though when occasion requires he can make good use of the microscope. List is always eyeing current controversies, fighting on one side or the other with the acrimony of a party journalist. The muse of history is his slave rather than his teacher. Like Cobbett, he sticks close to whatever business he has in hand, inspects its component parts, and "keeps fast hold of the smallest advantages they afford him." Perhaps, too, we may say that he is a pleasanter writer; or at least, that the task of reading him is lighter; for he appeals freely to our natural prejudices and combative instincts, is more desultory, less consistent; and seems to be urged upon his path rather by an urgent opportunism than by the logical necessities of a wide comprehensive and scientific argument. Hazlitt says of Cobbett: "He is therefore tolerated by all parties, though he has made himself by turns obnoxious to all, and even those he abuses read him. The Reformers read him when he was a Tory; the Tories read him now that he is a Reformer. He must, I think, however, be *caviare* to the Whigs."

Similarly almost every type of economist can find something to abuse and something to praise in Friedrich List. He must, I think, be *caviare* to Mr. Balfour. An industrial Protectionist loves him as a protector of manufacturers, if a rural Protectionist loathes him for refusing protection to agriculture. An English Tariff Reformer is pleased with his denunciations of Adam Smith; American and German Tariff Reformers enjoy explaining that if List were now alive, he would consider a policy of free trade to be no less wise for the United States or Germany now, than it was in his opinion for England in the forties. Not that List's political career, or his economic opinions, present the almost ludicrous changes and conversions of Cobbett. It is rather that the groundwork of argument on which List had to found one part of his brief, was difficult to reconcile with what was required for the other part. When he was growing up to manhood, and began to throw himself into politics, Germany was divided into a great number of states, some large like Austria and Prussia, some of moderate size like Saxony, Bavaria, and Württemberg, others mere petty principalities or dukedoms or free towns, but all claiming and exercising the right to surround themselves with customs houses and to tax one another's products and manufactures. It was against this paralyzing system of commercial feud that List directed his first energies as an organizer and pamphleteer. In talent, courage, and public spirit he was not inferior to Cobden. Constantly distracted, as Cobden was also, by pecuniary anxieties, and exiled, as Cobden happily was not, from his own home by the tyranny of a reactionary Government, he had to live somehow by his own exertions, and by the ceaseless activity of his wits and his pen. If he was at heart a German patriot, his greater Germany embraced not only Austria, but in moments of expansion the Low Countries and even Denmark. And he was a cosmopolitan, a citizen of the world. At one time he seemed likely to settle in England. At another he almost became a Frenchman. The first draft of his principal work was written in French. With a little more encouragement at Washington he might probably have remained in America to inscribe another distinguished name on the great roll of American citizens. In modern Germany or modern America, he might have made a great fortune in some financial house; for his versatile and enterprising mind had a natural bent toward the flotation of financial schemes. He might have been, in fact, a prince of company promoters, but he lived a little before his time. His ideas were always too large for his age; and instead of laying up wealth, he laid up fame. He did not leave a fortune, but he left a reputation.

Yet List, considering the extraordinary interest that attaches to his writings as well as to his dramatic career, has been strangely neglected. To the Free Trader he is a type of reactionary, though he was one of the founders of a great free trade movement—a movement for the consolidation of Germany, which eventually destroyed more customs houses and more obstacles to trade than had been swept away even by the political whirlwinds of the American and French Revolutions. By the modern bureaucrats and official professors of his native land he is remembered as a rebel against their own class, a rash and dangerous champion of free speech, a believer in democratic institutions, and a Tariff Reformer whose doctrines would be altogether subversive of the so-called "scientific" tariff of modern Germany. If List had had his way there would have been free trade from Rotterdam to Memel, and from Memel to Trieste. This great territory he would indeed have surrounded by a temporary tariff for the purpose of protecting manufactures (but not agriculture) until its "infant" industries were able to resist the competition of their stronger rivals in

England. When the time came, and the industries reached the stage at which they could export and compete successfully in neutral countries, the protective tariff would be removed, and the consumers who had been taxed during this period of probation in order that the productive capacity of the nation might be nursed into life and vigour would be relieved of their burdens and allowed to enjoy the blessings, not only of cheap food (of which List would never have deprived them), but of cheap clothing and boots and tools, and of all the other conveniences of life. This idea of the tariff as a nursery grew upon List during his stay in America. Had he lived another half-century to see the American tariff on worsteds and woollens raised higher and higher until the natural cost of warm clothing was doubled for the whole American people, he might have begun to question the working value of his theory. Instead of tariffs falling as industries grow, colonial, American, and European experience tells us that the reverse is usually the case.

The economic contradictions of List are the natural consequence of the part he played as controversialist and propagandist. As controversialist he was eager at all costs to differ from Adam Smith. As propagandist he thought that the manufacturers with whom he worked could be induced to concede internal free trade for the sake of an enlarged home market only if they were guaranteed against French and English competition. The true answer to this theory is that free trade, by keeping the cost of production at the lowest point, gives all the industries which suit a country best, the best chance of success. Moreover, if an industry anywhere is likely to pay, capital will be found; and capital flows most readily to countries where living is cheap and cost of production low. A protective tariff is, on the whole, an obstacle to investment. Money naturally flows to the places where its purchasing power is highest. Nor can vigorous industries be swamped by the removal of protection; for the imports from abroad have to be paid for by those things which are most cheaply produced at home. Every reduction of a tariff increases the purchasing power of the home consumer and reduces the cost of production. And every increase of imports has to be paid for by a corresponding increase of exports. It must often have occurred to List that if free trade between Prussia, Saxony, Holland, and Austria were beneficial, as he stoutly maintained it would be, free trade with Switzerland, Denmark, France, and England must also be beneficial. In the case of France, he could answer with some appearance of reason that free trade is of no use unless it is mutual and reciprocal. We often hear now that "one-sided" free trade is a great mistake. But when List wrote his principal book, England was already throwing open its ports, so that he had to fall back upon the infant industries argument, an argument that was equally applicable to the case of a Bavarian or Swabian manufacturer, who stood to be ruined by some more powerful Saxon or Bohemian competitor.

Probably, his real reason for desiring a moderate protective tariff for a greater Germany was an idea that this, together with internal free trade and a national system of railways and a national post, would help to consolidate the race. Every patriotic German felt at that time the need for unification. Without political unification Germany would remain what it had been for centuries, weak, poor, and distracted, the seat of domestic jealousies and civil war, an easy prey to the greed and ambition of foreign potentates. If the promise of a protective tariff would help the states of Germany to sink their differences, pull down their customs houses and coalesce, a German economist might easily be induced to acquiesce in a moderate measure of temporary protection. List himself sometimes opened out a larger view, as when he said: "If the whole globe were united by a union like the twenty-four states of North America, free trade would be quite as natural and beneficial as it is now in the union."

The poet Heine, whose friendship List enjoyed

during his three years' residence in Paris, revisited
Germany in the autumn of 1843, and celebrated the
journey in a masterpiece of imaginative satire.
There is one incident in the piece that may have
been suggested by his talks with List. At any
rate, it serves to give us a glimpse of Germany
in the making. Heine had come to the Prussian
frontier—

> "Said a fellow-passenger of mine :
> The Fatherland goes better ;
> See, there is the Prussian Zollverein,
> The mighty Douanenkette.

> "The Zollverein's encircling band
> Will fasten our people together,
> And save our distracted Fatherland
> From all political weather.

> "It gives us an outward visible ark,
> A bond materialistic ;
> The inward grace is the censor's mark,
> The union idealistic.

> "The censorship makes of our national life
> A single unanimous whole,
> We need a Germany free from strife,
> United in tariff and soul."

It is not too much to say that most of the ideas
which underlie modern tariffs, both in the old
world and in the new, were originated or formulated by List ; and whatever may be our individual

opinions of commercial policy or of the functions
of a tariff, we may agree that no satisfactory view
of the subject can be gained without some study of
his career and writings.   Hitherto, American and
English readers have had no adequate memoir of
his life, though the "National System" was translated by Samson S. Lloyd in 1885, and republished
in 1904 with an introduction by Professor Nicholson.   It is, perhaps, to be regretted that List's
theories·have been so little discussed by English-
men.   Among foreign critics Rabbeno, in his
"American Commercial Policy," devotes a chapter
to our author, and summarizes the "Outlines of
American Political Economy."

These remarkable Outlines are now for the first
time republished with some other (translated)
pieces which lend important aid to the interpretation of List's ideas and aims.   My sister's
researches in the List Archiv at Reutlingen have
enriched this biography, and the new material
(particularly that which relates to List's stay in
the United States) will, I hope, more than justify
her labours.   To form a right opinion about tariffs
is one of the chief functions of a sound education
in political economy.   In the heat of fiscal controversy no text-book can be more useful than one
which, alike by its virtues and defects, stimulates
the mind to further reasoning and research.   If
List's arguments are sometimes inconsistent, if

his logic is sometimes defective, if some of his forecasts have proved wrong, if some of his historical illustrations are false, so much the more reason for studying with a fresh, active, and critical intelligence the life and writings of one whose influence has moulded for more than half a century the commercial policy of two out of the three greatest industrial nations of the world.

F. W. H.

London, 1909.

LIFE OF FRIEDRICH LIST

CHAPTER I

WÜRTTEMBERG, 1789–1825

FRIEDRICH LIST was born at Reutlingen in Württemberg on August 6, 1789. The little town lies
in the pleasant valley of the Echaz overshadowed
by the green slopes of Achalm, an outlying spur
of the Swabian Alb, whose range of volcanic
limestone runs across the state from east to west.
Two of its peaks, Hohenstaufen and Hohenzollern,
are famous in history as the cradles of those
Imperial Houses whose rival claims divided and
distracted mediæval Germany. Reutlingen itself,
with its fine thirteenth-century church, ancient
houses, and remnants of massive wall and tower,
is still quaint and interesting; in former days,
small though it was, it played a gallant part in
German history.

A free imperial city, it remained loyal to the
house of Hohenstaufen, and withstood an attack
from their enemies in May, 1247. A hundred
years later it entered the confederacy of Swabian

towns, formed to resist the encroachments of the Württemberg rulers. Uhland has immortalized the Fight on Achalm in which the forces of Ulrich, Duke Eberhard's son, were routed. Under the favour of the Emperor Maximilian I. (whose statue adorns the fountain in the market-square) the town received many privileges, and when in 1519 another Duke Ulrich carried it by storm, it was freed again by its allies of the Swabian Bund. The novelist and poet Hermann Kurz (himself a Reutlinger) has given a picturesque description of the primitive simplicity and good fellowship of the townspeople at the end of the eighteenth century. Then the circuit of the walls still stood, the gates were shut each evening, and the unwary traveller who entered by night plunged with his horse into the swift tributary from the Echaz which occupied the middle of the main street.[1] Even the bitter fact that in 1802 (when List was twelve years old) Napoleon, as he coloured the map of Europe at his pleasure, handed over the gallant little town to Württemberg, could not make its children forget their proud memories. In this free atmosphere Friedrich List passed his earliest years.

His father, a prosperous tanner, held municipal office first in the old free city, and then under the Württemberg *régime*. Our hero, Georg Friedrich, the second son and youngest child of a

[1] " Schillers Heimath-Jahre," by Hermann Kurz.

large family, was educated at the "Latin School," which, notwithstanding its title, was unable to make him a good classic. His chief talent lay in the writing of German essays, and in these he showed the first promise of that lively and nervous style which was to gain him so many readers in later years. At the age of fourteen he entered his father's tannery, where he was put under the charge of his elder brother. But the young Friedrich found tanning a distasteful trade. Why, he asked, should it not be carried on by machinery, the power for which could easily be supplied from the river close at hand? At every opportunity he played truant, escaping to the garden and devouring tales of travel under a shady tree, or to a pond where he had made an old trough into a clumsy boat. His evil example infected the other workmen and apprentices, and in despair his father and brother were converted to his own view, that his vocation was not the tanning of hides. What his vocation was did not seem so clear; but at last his family decided the point, and at seventeen years of age, as a "Schreiber," or clerk, he entered the ranks of the Württemberg bureaucracy. First a learner in Blaubeuren, then, after passing his Assistant's examination, Taxes and Warehouses Commissioner in Schelkingen near Ulm, he came in his twenty-third year to a post at Tübingen. Here he took occasion to improve his education by attendance at University lectures and by wide reading. At this time Schlayer, afterwards a reform Minister in the Württemberg Government, was a student at the University. With him, and in a lesser degree with his teacher the jurist Malbranc, List formed an intimacy which was perhaps more profitable than lectures. Schlayer and Malbranc had rooms opposite one another in two of the picturesque old many-storied houses whose gables overhang the steep and narrow streets of Tübingen. Here it was their favourite pleasure of an evening to discuss knotty points of law through their open windows. If worsted in the dispute Malbranc would shut his window with an ironical compliment to "his Excellency the future Minister of Justice." Of List he thought less favourably. "He wanders at will and reads as he likes that dreamer Montesquieu, Abraham Smith, John Adam Say, or even the mad Schanschak (Jean Jacques) and such empty-headed folk. Actually he said the other day that the German Michel,[1] with his Roman code of law, seemed to him like a meagre boy who is dressed for Confirmation in his fat old grandfather's wedding coat. Yes, List is a good-for-nothing, and he will never be a lawyer." The Professor's acquaintance with even

[1] The typical German peasant, corresponding to John Bull or Brother Jonathan.

the names of writers outside his own sphere of work was evidently hazy, but there is no reason for doubting this account of List's studies.

In an autobiographical passage List relates how once in answer to a question from a teacher he asserted that Rousseau had not evolved the theory of the Social Contract from his own brain, but deduced it from the constitutions of the German imperial cities, or perhaps from his own town of Geneva, where the annual day of oath-taking was simply the renewal of a social contract for the course of the coming year. He adds an interesting refutation of the charges of revolutionary ideas made against himself, saying that he always took existing facts as the basis of his proposed reforms, and that on the summit of his ideal commonwealth stood a King or an Emperor. He wished Germany to adopt those institutions to which England owed her strength and greatness, without the blots by which they were marred in England.

At the moment, however, it seemed probable that List would disappoint Malbranc's gloomy prophecy. A successful examination raised him to a higher grade of clerkship, and he obtained a post in the Chancery department. The reformer Wangenheim,[1] then Minister, found a kindred

---

[1] Born at Gotha in 1773. He was curator of Tübingen University, which may have brought him into contact with List. In 1816 King Friedrich of Württemberg died, and was succeeded by his son Wilhelm. The change of rulers gave a temporary impetus to reform.

spirit in the eager young official; he was made Secretary to the Ministry in the Local Government Department, and in 1816 Chief Examiner of Accounts and a member of the Court of Audit.

List the elder had died in 1813. The subsequent loss of mother and brother incensed Friedrich against the existing system of administration. In 1815 his mother had been publicly insulted by an overbearing official for some trivial breach of regulations committed by one of her household. His brutal words about her "himmels-sakramentischen reichsstädtischen Hochmut" wounded her deeply, and she died within a few weeks. List's brother, wishing to marry, sought exemption from conscription. He was harried to and fro between Reutlingen and Stuttgart in search of a document needed for some petty formality. On one of these rides his horse stumbled; he was thrown, and received fatal injuries. Friedrich felt the blow keenly, and could never speak of his brother's end without fierce indignation. In 1816 he was appointed to act as Secretary for a Commission to inquire into the complaints against the bureaucracy and to make proposals for reform, and annoyed his senior colleagues by presuming to insert some of his own ideas and suggestions in the report. In 1817 it was his duty to inquire into the case of seven hundred inhabitants of the

lower Neckar valley, whom the weight of taxes
and the oppression of officials had driven to plan
a combined emigration to America. Perhaps the
remembrance of this experience may have influenced
him in his own later difficulties, but its immediate
effect was to increase his zeal in the furtherance
of Wangenheim's reforms. His first piece of
literary work appeared in the "Württembergisches
Archiv"[1] at this time—an essay on Local Government with the motto, "Let the village and the
town learn self-government under the guidance of
the ruler." Wangenheim was anxious that civil
servants should have some opportunity of instruction in the theoretical principles of government.
With this aim he founded a Chair of Administration
and Politics (Staatspraxis und Staatswissenschaft)
at Tübingen, and appointed as first Professor List,
who had already supported the idea in a Memorial.[2]
The pamphlet depicts in vivid colours the retro-
grade state of the administration, and throws light
on the subjects that were already occupying List's
thoughts. "No one in our University," he says,
"has any conception of a national economy. No
one teaches the science of agriculture, forestry,
mining, industry, or trade." Again, "the legislature, in regard to administration and finance, is

[1] "Württembergisches Archiv," Band II. Heft 2.
[2] Häusser II., Gesammelte Schriften, pp. 1-14. "Gutachten
über die Errichtung einer Staatswirthschaftlichen Fakultät." 1817.

so entirely unscientific, the forms of government are in such a truly barbarous state, that if an official of the seventeenth century rose again from the dead he could at once take up his old work, though he would assuredly be astonished to find the advances that had been made during the interval in the simplest processes of manufacture."

As an example of the financial chaos, List points out that the estimates were made for ten years in advance and could only be revised at the end of that period. The young Professor, with all his talent, was scarcely ready for the post, as he himself admitted in later years. He threw himself, however, with characteristic energy into his duties, publishing an interesting little introduction or syllabus to his lectures under the title, "The Theory and Practice of Administration in Württemberg."[1] In it he defended the new and unpopular suggestion that bureaucrats needed theoretic training. "The question whether it is better to introduce civil servants to public administration through a course of teaching or by actual experience of affairs, seems to me just like the question : do we learn about a country from

[1] "Die Staatskunde und Staatspraxis Württembergs in Grundriss zur näheren Bezeichnung seines Lehrfaches und als Leitfaden für seine Zuhörer : entworfen von F. List ordentlichen Professor der Staatswirthschaft und in besondere der Staatspraxis auf der hohen Schule zu Tübingen, 1818."

a map or by travelling? ... He who really wishes to know a land can only enter upon a journey with profit if he has studied the map first." (Preface.)

The growing importance of corporations is emphasized. " Up to the present the slight attention paid to the nature of corporations or guild-organizations has been a great gap in political theory, for through them alone can true freedom and order be preserved. A great indivisible state without any organization is a French chimera, either an aberration of liberty or an attempt to introduce an Eastern despotism according to the proverb *Divide et impera*" (p. 31).

The appendix is noteworthy, in view of List's later writings, for some sentences directed against cosmopolitan theories. "The idea that the whole world can be joined in a union of citizenship is wholly unnatural. For the wars of independent nations are just as much outbreaks of primitive human nature as are the combats of individuals." A quarter of a century later, in the introduction to the *National System*, he described such a union as the " highest imaginable."

His lectures were frankly propagandist, supporting Wangenheim's reforms and panegyrizing the modern constitutional state in contrast with more antiquated forms of government. With the same end in view he and some like-minded friends founded a paper, the *Volksfreund aus Schwaben*, which advocated important political reforms— genuine representative government, ministerial responsibility, local self-government, trial by jury, and freedom of the Press. In the preface to the *Staatskunde* he had already eulogized the Press. "Thoughts are free of duty, and since the Press began no human power can keep them outside its boundaries, either by a military cordon or a Great Wall of China." The paper at first was under official favour, but after Wangenheim's fall it was suppressed, and its founders all, at different periods, visited the fortress of Asperg as political prisoners. "In the *Volksfreund*," wrote List later, "I made my first attempt to humanize the official aristocracy, to attack the conservative idealists (Altrechtler), and to spread correct ideas of the nature of constitutional monarchy." The early pages of his "Preface to the National System" tell how in this year of journalism and teaching his first doubts regarding the universal validity of Free Trade, and his first conception of a difference between cosmopolitan and national political economy arose; how, too, he came to realize that the true commercial interest of Germany lay in the abolition of the various state tariffs and the formation of a national customs union. Some attributed the fall of the *Volksfreund* to the influence of Metternich; but the first modest reform proposals of Wangenheim met with a storm of opposition within Württemberg itself, and at the end of 1817 he was forced to resign. Even List and his lectures fell under suspicion; and in May, 1818, he addressed a memorial in his own defence to the King. A guarded answer was returned, pointing out that young men were too apt to translate innocent speculation into rash action, and that it was List's duty to watch against this danger. At the same time the new reactionary Ministry made secret inquiries from the Senate of the University about the character of List's lectures. He heard of this by chance, and naturally asked what report his colleagues had made, but his curiosity was rebuked as "extremely strange." In the Easter holidays of 1819, however, his activity was diverted into new and more congenial channels. (See note, p. 28.)

During the first thirty years of the nineteenth century Germany was just beginning to realize the causes of her economic and political poverty. Never was a great country most obviously intended for unity so hopelessly weakened and divided by artificial barriers. There was a multitude of states; and every state, nay almost every subdivision of each state, had its special tax-system. Each town was cut off by customs duties from neighbouring towns and from the surrounding countryside. Prussia alone could show within its boundaries sixty-seven different tariffs, levied according to districts, some on persons, and some on goods. No fewer than 2775 articles were liable to taxation, and the dues were collected by an army of eight thousand officials. As a foreign observer[1] remarked, the Germans were prisoners who could only hold intercourse with one another through iron bars.

On the other hand, there were few external taxes. The Napoleonic Wars had almost stopped foreign trade; the Berlin Decrees while ruining many industries had forced some into life, and in the intervals of battle landowners and manufacturers had enjoyed such prosperity as accrues from a season of artificially inflated prices. But after Waterloo this accidental protection disappeared, and English goods especially found a ready market. Their superior quality and cheapness (owing to the recent marvellous advance in mechanical production) made them dangerous rivals to home manufacturers, hampered as the latter were by their makers' prejudice against new inventions and by the network of internal tariffs which prevented the development of a home market. At the same time Germany's natural exchange to England—agricultural produce—was largely blocked by the English Corn Law of 1815, which amounted to practical prohibition. Bavaria (1807),

[1] De Pradt.

Württemberg (1808), and Baden (1812), had already tried to improve their home trade by the removal of all taxes to the boundary, but their action had less influence than Prussia's. That state took the first step towards reform in 1818. Free intercourse was established within the country, and all customs duties were transferred to the boundary. Prussian trade at once improved, but the step only aggravated the difficulties of other states, and especially of her numerous small neighbours. For twenty-eight states lay along her 1073 miles of boundary. List had already been struck by the idea of a commercial union between the German states, and had pressed it in letters to the Freiherr von Cotta, the Stuttgart publisher, and other influential men. Now, in April, 1819, on a holiday journey to Göttingen he visited Frankfurt-on-Main at the time of Easter Fair, when the town was thronged with merchants and manufacturers from all parts of Germany. A petition to the Federal Diet for the promotion of trade and industry, was on foot among them, and largely through List's influence it took the form of proposals to abolish internal customs, to include the whole of Germany within a single customs boundary, and to establish a system of retaliation against foreign tariffs. The idea of common action on behalf of German trade was not original. In 1816 at the Leipsic Fair, Ernst Weber, of Gera (one of List's chief supporters at Frankfurt), had urged a meeting of traders and manufacturers to draw up a memorial and to rouse the conscience of the Federal Diet over the question. List himself had small hope that the Diet, after two years of inaction, would take any practical steps, and trusted more to the traders' own efforts.

During his professorship List had married Caroline Neidhart, daughter of Professor Saybold of Tübingen, a young and beautiful widow.[1] She was to prove a faithful comrade through all the years of changing fortune that lay before them, and he wrote to her now in the first flush of success (April 14). "I am head over ears in work; I have founded a Union of German Merchants, and drawn up an address to the Diet advocating freedom of trade. About one thousand merchants will sign it to-day. The day after to-morrow it will be presented. This may have great results." The Handelsverein was not formally constituted till April 18, when at a meeting in the *Goldenes Ross* the "Union of Merchants and Manufacturers for the purpose of promoting

[1] She had by her first husband one son, Karl Neidhart, who became a physician and settled in America. He died in Philadelphia in 1895. List's own children were Emilie, b. 1818, d. 1902; Oskar, b. 1820, d. 1840; Elise, b. 1822, m. Herr Gustav Pacher von Theinburg of Vienna, d. 1891; and Caroline, b. 1829, still living in Munich, widow of Herr August Hövemeyer, the historical painter.

German trade and industry"[1] came into being. The Committee consisted of members from the merchant bodies of the Rhine, Old Prussia, Bavaria, Saxony, Württemberg, Hesse-Meiningen, Hesse-Darmstadt, Nassau, and Baden. Invitations to join were sent to the trading communities of Hanover, Brunswick, Leipsic, and the Hanse Towns. List himself was absent (on a journey along the Rhine to collect signatures for the memorial); but he was appointed Organizer or "Konsulent" of the society, and entrusted with the task of framing its constitution. At the end of April he formally notified the King of his action, and of the new work which he had undertaken. He considered it, he said, important and, beneficial to Germany as a whole, and to his native state in particular. The Ministry replied that a public servant should not take up a post unconnected with his office, especially in a foreign ("auswärtig") state, without express permission from his superiors. List must give a full defence and explanation to the Ministry of the Interior. In answer to this he asked permission to resign, but was told that before this request could be granted he must make his defence. This he did with spirit in a document dated May 20. The Handelsverein, he argued, was not a public but a

[1] "Zum Zweck der Beförderung des deutschen Handels und Gewerbes."

private association, and the post was not incompatible with his Professorship. In fact, an attempt to invigorate the depressed industries of Germany was a task well suited to a Professor of Political Economy, and he had undertaken it from disinterested motives, as the office was an honorary one. The statement that he had accepted a post in a "foreign" state completely ignored the existence of the German Federation. According to Federal Law, in all matters of common interest (and by the 19th Article of the Act of Union trade and tariffs fell under this head) Germans were considered citizens of a single state. Was a Württemberger not also a German? Had an official fewer rights than a private citizen? The latter could join such a union unhindered. An irresistible impulse had urged him to the relief of the oppressed, to a movement by which Governments might learn under what burdens their citizens suffered. Personal enmity, he feared, was the true cause of the Ministry's action, but he assured the King that the most loyal and devoted subjects were those of a constitutional monarch.

These outspoken remarks secured his dismissal, and he was free to follow the path he had chosen, and to work towards the union of Germany in a closer bond than any afforded by the Federation. "I need hardly say," he wrote later, "that my first thought in founding the Handelsverein was a political one. Though at that time the Prussians spoke so much about the historic growth of constitutions and regarded youthful hopes as folly, yet I wished to try whether a seed could not be planted out of which a constitution might grow." His whole time and strength were devoted to the work. The question of the Frankfurt memorial had been raised in the Federal Diet by von Martens, a deputy from Hanover; but the reply was not encouraging. The proposals, in the view of the Diet, were theoretically desirable, but it was difficult to unify the customs and abolish internal dues in a country consisting of different provinces. France had so found it in the eighteenth century; and though the Revolution had accomplished the task, such a price would be too costly for Germany to pay. Retaliation against foreign tariffs, though desirable, also involved many difficulties. The merchants must look for help to the state Governments. When it was clear that the Diet would take no action, a meeting of the Handelsverein at Nuremberg (July, 1819) decided to follow its advice, and send a deputation to the various German Courts. At the same time the *German Industrial and Commercial Magazine*[1] was founded, edited, and largely written by List. In its columns he advocated many reforms, some of which—such as an Imperial Postal System and

[1] *Organ für den deutschen Handels- und Gewerbestand.*

C

an Imperial Patent Law—were not accomplished until more than twenty years after his death. The deputation was well received at the South German Courts, at Carlsruhe in particular, where Nebenius had already been working in the same field. · In the autumn Weber and two companions went to Berlin. Maassen, the author of the Prussian financial reforms, was a strong Free Trader, and disapproved of the retaliatory part of the Handelsvereins proposals. But as his own tariff for revenue had not given satisfaction in Prussia, he told the delegates that he would gladly replace it by another, embracing if possible the whole of Germany. He promised to help forward their work to the best of his ability. In January, 1820, List, Schnell, and Weber proceeded to Vienna to press the matter on the Emperor and the Austrian Ministry. The Congress of Representatives from eight German Governments, whose meetings at Carlsruhe in the preceding year had been adjourned, was now reassembled in Vienna. List's every hour was crowded with activities — memorials, petitions, and visits to leading statesmen. In an audience with the Emperor Francis on March 6, he explained his views and was heard with attention. But the Congress was engrossed in other business, and was incapable of entertaining this grand idea of a unified Germany. To a petition it returned the curt reply (May 22) that the matter had already been considered by the Diet, which had expressly refused to recognize the Union's claim to represent German mercantile opinion. The Union itself found the far-reaching projects of its organizer somewhat overwhelming. A misunderstanding with Bauerreis the treasurer and a charge of financial maladministration drew an indignant denial from List. But his "castles in the air"— plans for a pan-German industrial exhibition or for a society to export German manufactures— frightened cautious men of business, not yet accustomed to think in terms of a greater Germany.

In September, 1820, a Commercial Congress met at Darmstadt with representatives from all the South German States, Prussia, and Saxony. It was the first definite result of List's work, but another deputy was chosen by his own Union to attend it. Although he visited the Congress in his private capacity he soon withdrew. The movement, to which he had devoted so much energy, progressed too slowly to please his eager spirit. Yet his work had not been thrown away. Between the years 1820 and 1825 negotiations were carried on between the Governments of several South and Middle German states, the most important being a conference at Stuttgart in 1825, in which Bavaria, Württemberg, Baden, Hesse Darmstadt, and Nassau took part. Ultimately, in the year 1828, two "Zollvereins" were formed, the one between Württemberg and Bavaria, the other between Prussia and Hesse. The formation of the Mid-German "Handelsverein" in the same year was due chiefly to the jealousy felt by the smaller states towards Prussia; but this combination had little vitality and soon went to pieces. The three Unions, however, by their very deficiencies prepared the way for transition to a wider system. In 1829 the Bavaria-Württemberg Union made a commercial treaty with Prussia and Hesse, which established practical free trade between the four states. List's friend and publisher, the Freiherr von Cotta, was an active worker in the cause of unification. Saxony was the chief obstacle to any further advance; and for some time longer, on political grounds, it refused to enter into any treaty with Prussia. At last, on January 1, 1834, a German Zollverein was formed between Prussia, Nassau, Württemberg, Bavaria, Saxony, and the Thuringian states; these were joined in the course of the next two years by Baden, Nassau, and the city of Frankfurt. "The elder generation," said a later writer, "can still remember how joyfully the opening hour of the year 1834 was welcomed by the trading world. Long trains of waggons stood on the high-roads, which till then had been cut up by tax barriers. At the stroke of midnight every turnpike was thrown open, and amid cheers the waggons hastened over the boundaries which they could from thenceforward cross in perfect freedom. Every one felt that a great object had been attained."[1]

In these fourteen years List had gone through many vicissitudes. On retiring from his post of Consulent he plunged into the politics of his native state. The people of Reutlingen had suffered from the arbitrary action of Government officials, and List had several times advised them in their difficulties. On July 6, 1819, the town elected him its deputy to the representative assembly of Württemberg, but as he was just below the statutory age of thirty his election was disallowed. Shortly afterwards the district of Waldsee offered him a seat, and asked him to publish some statement of his political views for the benefit of the electors. List drew up a "Catechism," of twelve questions and answers, his main theme being a complaint against the heavy taxation from which Württemberg at that time suffered. The Ministry considered that such a publication was likely to foment popular discontent and disaffection, and List incurred official censure. At the end of 1820, after his resignation of the post in the Handelsverein, Reutlingen elected him for a second time.

[1] Gustav Fischer, " Ueber das Wesen und Bedingungen eines Zollvereins." Hildebrand's "Jahrbüchern für National Oekonomie und Statistik," Bd. II., S. 375.

The Ministry which commanded a majority in the Chamber was reactionary, and he naturally joined the Opposition. He took his seat on December 7, and characteristically began his parliamentary career by bringing forward three proposals in quick succession : first, that the Chamber should take steps to revive and support the depressed industries of Württemberg; second, that the Finance Committee should accommodate the burden of taxes to the circumstances of the country; and third, that the Upper House should meet every year, and that annual Budgets should be introduced. These suggestions met with little response in the brief time before the adjournment of the House. List spent the Christmas holidays in drawing up a petition on behalf of his Reutlingen constituents, which contained a damaging if somewhat overstrained indictment of the existing *régime* in Württemberg, with some bold proposals for financial, administrative, and judicial reform. The petition had just been lithographed when List's house (where he lay ill in bed) was entered by a police officer; the newly printed copies and the manuscript were seized, and the author put on his trial for sedition. When the Chamber re-assembled it became known that List was debarred from attending. This was the interpretation put by the Ministry on a paragraph in the royal rescript by which the constitution had been established. According to this clause, any deputy against whom a criminal action was pending *ipso facto* lost his seat. List and his friends protested against such a confusion between political and criminal offences. The Chamber appointed a Commission, among whose members was the poet Uhland, to inquire into the terms of the rescript. Before their report appeared List had obtained permission to defend himself in the Chamber, which he did on February 17 in an able speech. The majority of the Commission reported that in its opinion the prohibition was only meant to apply to cases of gross non-political crime. But when the question, "Should List leave the Chamber?" was put to the full House it was carried by fifty-six to thirty-six votes. A supplementary question, whether he could re-enter the Chamber after the conclusion of his trial, was agreed to by the ministerial party, but opposed by his friends on high constitutional grounds.

Meanwhile the process continued, with many petty casuistries and quibblings, for more than a year, at a ruinous cost to List and his household. On April 6, 1822, judgment was pronounced: ten months' imprisonment with hard labour in the fortress of Asperg, and payment of eleven-twelfths of the cost of the action. The sentence, as List complained in a memorial to the King, destroyed all civic rights. He determined to appeal against the decision, and meanwhile to leave the country. On April 15, he reached Strasburg where he remained some months, pleased with the place and people, but harassed by "eternal want of pence;" for his efforts to gain money by literary work met with small success. The difficulties of his wife and family, whom he had left behind in Stuttgart, were also a constant anxiety. In a letter to his friend Cotta he gives detailed reasons for his flight (May 1, 1822) :—

"Had I any choice? Should I have allowed myself to be chained to a clerk's desk on Asperg amid the delight of all my enemies the Government clerks? Even if as a private man for the sake of my family (whom this action has involved in difficulties) I might have borne such a disgrace, yet should I have been worthy ever again to come forward as an advocate of constitutional freedom? I, who when it was possible to escape had surrendered myself to a judgment which insulted both the representative system and the dignity of a representative? Now the die is cast. . . . Should they drive me hence I will go to London, to Madrid, nay, I will go to America, in order to escape this outbreak of passion and to vindicate myself before the world."

List was soon to receive a more definite impulse towards America. In the mean time, as pressure had been put upon the Strasburg authorities by the Württemberg Government, he took refuge in Baden, where his family joined him. But at the end of December he heard that the Court of Appeal at Esslingen had upheld the decision

against him, and at the same time the Baden
Ministry showed that his presence in the country
was not desired. A visit to Paris early in 1823
brought him into contact with Lafayette, from
whom he received much kindness. The General
was planning a visit to the United States in 1824
as the "guest of the nation," and invited List to
go with him. But his friends dissuaded him from
so momentous a step, and instead he crossed the
Channel to England in the hope of establishing
a journalistic connection in London. There is
curiously little record remaining of this visit.
Häusser barely mentions the fact. There is a
passing allusion by List (in a speech at Philadelphia) to kindness shown him by Richard Rush,
then American Ambassador in London. But he
certainly travelled in several parts of the country,
for he more than once makes the statement that
he first became acquainted with railways in England, and at that time rail traction was only
employed at a few of the mines of the North
and Midlands. Again, in a letter written two years
later from Metz he describes the place as "more
regularly built than any old town I have seen
in Germany, France, or England."[1] He was not
to revisit the country until a few months before
his tragic end.

[1] See preface to the "National System," p. 12, and "Nord und
Sud," Band III., 1877, p. 71. List's letter is dated April 18, 1825.

Disappointed in his hopes of work in England, List turned to Switzerland, visiting Basle, Aarau, and other towns. At this time he published a petition to the King of Württemberg and a voluminous account of the proceedings at his trial in a number of *Themis*,[1] a political periodical which he had set on foot. Wolfgang Menzel, the critic and historian, in his "Reminiscences" has given an account of an expedition to Fluelen, which illustrates List's vehement and fiery character. "As we crossed the lake, List told us his experience and burst into a storm of curses against the Württemberg 'scribblers.' As he stood up in his anger with outstretched fist, gnashing his teeth and shouting, 'Those wretched clerks!' ('O Schreiber! Schreiber!') he made the boat rock, stumbled, and would have been drowned had we not seized him. He was the most impetuous man I have ever met; still young,

[1] *Themis, eine Sammlung von Staatswissenschaftlichen Abhandlungen Übersetzungen, und in die Politik einschlagenden Rechtsfällen.* Zweiten Bändchen. "Friedrich Lists, Mitglieds der Württembergischen Deputirter-Kammer ehrfurchtsvolle Denkschrift an Seine Majestät den König von Württemberg, einen von den königlichen Gerichtshöfen an seiner Person und an der Verfassung des Landes begangenen Justizmord betreffend ; oder Aktenmässiger Beweis der Verwerflichkeit des *heimlichen Kanzlei-Inquisitions-Gerichts* und der *Unentbehrlichkeit* des *Geschwornen-Gerichts* und der *Gerichtsöffentlichkeit* in konstitutionellen Staaten. Jacta est Alea. Gedrückt in Strasburg. In Kommission des Gersnerischen Buchhandlung in Zurich, 1823." Its first number had consisted of a translation of Aighan's "History of the Jury System."

but already corpulent. Any one who had once seen him, would assuredly always remember him, for his short squat body was crowned by a disproportionately large and lion-like head. His eyes sparkled, thunder played round his fine brow, and his mouth was as fiery as the crater of Vesuvius."

List had hoped to make Basle his home, but he got embroiled with the town authorities and was sentenced to twenty-four hours' imprisonment upon a diet of bread and water. A medical friend lightened the punishment by sending him the useful "prescription" of a sausage and bottle of wine. After this experience the wanderer returned to Aarau. His customary optimism led him to suppose that the official resentment against him in Württemberg had by this time evaporated. According to his biographer, Häusser, friends encouraged him in this opinion. Menzel, on the contrary, declares that they strongly dissuaded him from return. It is certain, at least, that he despatched a letter to the King begging for the revocation of his sentence, and without waiting to hear the result returned in May, 1824, with his family to Stuttgart. He was at once arrested and despatched to Asperg. The "literary hard labour" consisted of monotonous copyist work for the governor of the fort, lists of soldiers' accoutrements, descriptions of foreign arsenals, and the like. A report on the state of the French artillery evoked this ejaculation in his diary: "We pay great attention to the arts of destruction as practised in foreign lands. If only we gave the same heed to the condition of their laws and industry!"

From the few records which remain of this period, it seems that List was released for a short time under police supervision, and then again imprisoned, but on what pretext does not appear. From his letters it is plain that he hoped for a final release in December, 1824, after which he might spend some time in preparations for departure. For he had at last decided to accept Lafayette's invitation and to sail for America in the following April. But it was not until January, 1825, that he was brought from Asperg to Stuttgart. There he was told that a passport would be given to him, and that he must leave the country in three days. He went to Alsace, only to find that he was not allowed to settle either there or in Paris. Returning to the right bank of the Rhine, he waited with impatience until his family could join him.

NOTE.—Robert von Mohl, who was a student at Tübingen during List's professorship, gives an account of the difficulties that beset List in his academic life (" Lebenserrinerungen," pp. 93, 94). In his Latin inaugural address he perpetrated some false quantities, and this mishap combined with his inexperience as a lecturer to lose him the confidence of the students, while his colleagues regarded him with suspicion as an upstart favourite of Wangenheim. Fulda, indeed, the Dean of the Faculty of Politics, made secret complaints against him to the Government. The matter is fully discussed in Dr. Köhler's recent book, " Problematisches zu Friedrich List," pp. 51–55.

CHAPTER II

A LETTER from Lafayette (dated Richmond, Virginia, January 22, 1825, and received by List in the following March) urged him to come to the new world, adding stories of other German fugitives who had found successful careers awaiting them. List's own letters to his wife show that (as ever) his hopes rose high. "When Madame M. speaks of the dearness of living in America, she judges merely from what she saw in her own surroundings. Living in America is costly and luxurious, but in America it is also cheap and simple. The Americans are knavish, cheating, avaricious folk—but the Americans are also generous, high-spirited, and hospitable. This is as much as to say that America is a large country, that there are a great many Americans, that men and districts differ from one another yonder even more than with us, since America is ten times the size of Germany." (Rastatt, March 14.) A chance meeting with a Sontheim innkeeper, lately returned from America, increased his eagerness.

" The fellow has suffered from fever for six months, and scarcely spoke unless spoken to. But when I mentioned America his whole being became animated, and he commended our resolve. As you know, he was there for six years, and only came back to look after his property, but during his visit home he married, and then could not induce his wife to return with him. Now he is homesick for North America twelve months of every year, and whenever any one begins to speak with him on the subject his dragon of a wife (otherwise a worthy woman) becomes quite venomous in the fear that, though she is very well off, he may some day slip away from her. I consulted him especially about the accusations which various people have brought against the country, and he declared that they were all infamous lies. The people are good, industrious, honest, and kindly. He had, he said, travelled in the States for at least twelve months, and the country folk who entertained him as a guest at their well-spread tables, had never asked or accepted the smallest sum from him. More than once they had wished to provide him with capital to establish himself in business—purely out of friendship. Respectable people can find help and friends everywhere, but the land is so flooded with European adventurers that people wait to find out what manner of man you are before they trust you far. We shall, he was convinced, find ten times more culture and pleasant qualities among the middle class there than in Europe, and for a German life is far pleasanter in Pennsylvania than in Alsace. Customs, language, character, kindliness—they are all as in Germany. As to the value of freedom, no one can judge of it (his very words)—no one can judge of it unless they have lived there. In a word, the man has heartened me so much that I consider everything that has happened to us for a real piece of good fortune. Madame Rosch bustled about impatiently during our conversation, and as we were leaving she accompanied us out of the house. There she said to me, ' I am not angry with you for talking about America to my husband as you are going there yourself. I am only afraid, if you talk much more to him, that he will slip out of my hands.' We laughed heartily." [1]

After meeting with many petty annoyances from the Württemberg Government the family of List joined him, and they left Germany on April 15, 1825.

"At break of day," wrote List to a friend, "we started, encumbered with luggage in true emigrant fashion and at a funereal pace, as if we feared to reach the German boundary too soon. We elders sat in gloomy meditation : to-day we must leave Germany and so much that is dear and precious to us. Ah ! we must leave it, perhaps for ever, and cross the wide ocean ; perhaps we shall see one of our darlings buried in the waves, perhaps we shall die apart from them with the bitter anxiety of leaving them alone in a strange land. So we sat, each with his own sorrow, no one dared to look up for fear of betraying his thoughts to the other. Then the children began the song—

> ' Auf, auf, ihr Brüder und seid stark ;
> Wie ziehen über Land und Meer nach Nordamerika.'

We could restrain our grief no longer. My dear wife was the first to regain her composure. 'You

[1] Quoted by Roscher, "Zur Erinnerung des Friedrich List" ("Nord und Sud," Band III., 1877).

have nothing with which to reproach yourself, you have acted like a man ; we are not leaving because of our ill deeds. In God's Name, let us compose ourselves. He has watched over us, He will guard us. Now, children, we will sing with you !'

"It was one of the most beautiful spring mornings I have ever seen. The sun was just spreading its first beams over the lovely meadows of the Pfalz country, and the sight poured healing balm into our sore hearts. Soon we were singing merrily every one of Schiller's songs that we could recollect, and finally Uhland's jesting—

"'So hab' ich denn die Stadt verlassen.'

The people who met us must have taken us for the family of some Bavarian official, who had been transferred to a higher post, rather than for a band of exiled emigrants."

After two days' rest in Paris they reached Havre on April 21, sailing thence on the 26th.[1] List's letters during the journey give a lively description both of the country through which they passed, and the inconveniences of travelling by diligence eighty years ago. It is amusing to find the man, who three years later became one of the earliest advocates of railways, now almost

[1] From the papers at Reutlingen it appears that the boat was the *Harry* (Captain Kemp), belonging to the firm Larne and Palmer, and that the cost of the voyage for the whole family (himself, his wife, and four children) was 2300 francs.

awestruck by the speed of a "caravan" of ten diligences conveying about one hundred and fifty passengers from Paris to Havre.[1] The sight of a prosperous manufacturing town in Normandy (Bolbec) called forth some characteristic comments. "When will the sight of such manufacturing prosperity bring the obstinate worshippers of Adam Smith into the right road? However much this teacher of national economy may have been of service to the world from other points of view, all his services cannot compensate for the incalculable mischief which he has caused by instilling the dream of so-called 'free intercourse' into the minds of some of our theorists. Smith's initial error is in attributing a productive power to capital; whereas labour alone, with the help of a greater or less amount of capital, is productive. Of course I have already opposed this theory in my earlier writings for the Handelsverein, but the subject demands a special study in order to overthrow the special arguments of the founder of the school.

"I hope that the United States will afford me a fine example in proof of my assertion. They followed Smith's theories till their whole industry lay in ruins, and then began to follow the system which the theorists abhor. We shall see how they fare under it. In truth, I am beginning to believe

[1] Roscher, "Nord und Sud," p. 71.

D

myself that I am undertaking a *literary* journey to the United States." (His passport declared that his journey was for purposes of research.)

The boat entered New York harbour on June 10, and List immediately went to Philadelphia. There he met with a cordial reception from Lafayette, who invited him to be his companion during his triumphant journey through the States. List thus had the privilege of being introduced under the best auspices to many leading politicians, amongst them Henry Clay, and of seeing American life under the most favourable circumstances. He was present at the famous Fourth of July celebration on Bunker's Hill, and recorded some impressions in his note-book. "The soldiers marched without stiffness, but in good order, and with the bearing of free men who do not fear the rod. In monarchical states the public festivals revolve round the monarch; here the festival is general, happiness and rejoicing beam on every face. It all reminds me of my own free imperial city—this public rejoicing of young and old, the thunder of cannons, platoon-firing, flags, and processions. . . . As far as elegance is concerned, I do not know whether I could give the preference to this company of statesmen over the *levée* of some great monarch, but I am certain that in this assembly there is a greater movement of profitable ideas, a greater display of honourable sentiments than

there is among all the royal *levées* in the world.
I do not see here those hungry faces and loafing
figures which are in the majority at any European
festival." Later, he expressed his general opinion
of the nation: "Anything new is quickly introduced here, and all the latest inventions. There
is no clinging to old ways, the moment an American
hears the word 'invention' he pricks up his ears.
All matters concerning the people as a whole,
public order, legislation, holidays, newspapers, and
so forth, are excellently managed, and the experience must broaden the mind of any European.
But if he penetrates into their private life he finds
it dull, monotonous, and stiff." This drawback
List put down to democracy, because in a monarchy
the aristocrat's rank is assured, and he need not
always consider his dignity; in America a man's
superiority is not taken for granted, hence he
feels he must continually assert it by his behaviour.

These months of travel, though full of interest,
had not brought him any means of livelihood. In
the autumn of 1825 he began to look in earnest
for the "little property"—the haven of rest to
which his thoughts had turned during the last
few troubled years. In his search he visited
Pittsburg, Harmony, and Economy. This last-
named town was the most successful of the com-
munistic settlements founded by the Württemberg
Secretary Rapp, where he and his followers lived

in expectation of the speedy second coming of Christ. Another less fortunate settlement—New Harmony—was bought by Robert Owen in 1824, but only met with another failure under his guidance. The German atmosphere naturally appealed to our exile—"The vesper bell rings there as in my Swabian home,"—but for some reason he did not settle there. A little farm— ten acres of land and a house—was purchased in the neighbourhood of Harrisburg, and the family moved thither from Philadelphia in November, 1825. The enterprise, as might have been fore-told, proved unsuccessful; List had much zeal, but little practical knowledge of farming, and came off badly in his dealings with shrewder neighbours. The situation of the house was damp, and the health of all the family suffered. In a few months' time, after a vain attempt to dispose of his purchase, he was forced to leave it un-occupied and take up a less speculative, if not very remunerative employment—the editorship of *Der Adler*, a German-American paper in the little town of Reading. List himself declared later (in the introduction to the "National System"[1]) that this episode had been of great educational value. During his exile from Württemberg, he said, he had read widely in Economics, History, and kindred sub-jects; but "when Fate led me to America I left

[1] "National System," edited by Eheberg, pp. 10, 11.

all books behind me; [1] they would only have led me astray. The best book on political economy which one can read in that country is life itself."

"Here before one's eyes wildernesses become rich and powerful states. Here it first became clear to me that nations pass through different stages of economic development. A process, which in Europe would require many centuries, takes place here under our very eyes—I mean the transition from a state of nature to pastoral cultivation, from that to agriculture, and from that to manufacture and commerce. Here we can observe how rent gradually grows from zero to an important sum. Here a simple farmer by practical experience has a better understanding of the means by which agriculture and rent can be advanced than the keenest intellects of the old world—he tries to attract manufacturers and artificers into the vicinity. Here the contrast between agricultural and manufacturing nations shows itself in the clearest manner and causes the most violent agitations. Nowhere so well as here, can we learn the true value of means of transport and their influence on the intellectual and material life of the people. I read this book with eagerness and industry, and sought to bring the lessons I learned from it into harmony with my former studies, experiences, and reflections."

For the first twenty years of their history as a separate nation the inhabitants of the United States were almost exclusively engaged in agriculture. The immediate necessities of life, tools, shoes, homespun cloth, and so forth, were indeed made in each locality, either by members of the

[1] This is not literally correct. Several lists of books in his handwriting, made during these years, survive, and show that especially in English his reading was wide.

farmer's household, or by independent artisans and craftsmen. But the American colonies had been compelled to import the chief varieties of manufactured goods from England, and though the force of coercion had been removed, economic necessity led the young republic to continue in the same path. Alexander Hamilton in 1792, when Secretary to the Treasury, had presented to Congress his famous Report on Manufactures, in which he advocated temporary protection as a measure of self-defence against the high tariff systems of Europe, and gave a forcible and lucid exposition of the two main arguments of later Protectionists—the importance of developing a home market, and the claim of "infant" industries to support and shelter. Yet, although the preamble to the first Tariff Act, in 1787, stated that among its objects were "the protection and encouragement of manufactures," the rates of the early tariffs were quite moderate. Many were, no doubt, protective in intention, but they only averaged from 5 per cent. to 15 per cent. *ad valorem.*[1]

The Embargo Act of 1808, the Non-Intercourse Act of the following year, and the subsequent war with England, by destroying for the time all

[1] Cp. Taussig, "Tariff History of the United States," pp. 15, 16, and Harrower, "Alexander Hamilton als National Oekonom," pp. 46–50.

commerce with Europe, forced American manufactures into activity and afforded them for a time complete protection of the results. One example may suffice; the estimated number of spindles in cotton mills rose from 8,000 in 1808 to 31,000 in 1809, and 130,000 in 1815.[1] The close of the Napoleonic Wars and the treaty of peace between England and the United States in 1815 removed this protection; English manufacturers hastened to avail themselves of the new markets thrown open to them, and America began again to exchange her raw materials for cheap English goods. Prices fell. Consumers were relieved. Farmers benefited. But a demand for protection arose among the industries which had sprung up during the years of non-intercourse and now were endangered by the tide of foreign competition. As a result, the tariff of 1816 was considerably higher than any preceding one, though part of the increase was explained by the necessity of meeting the heavy interest on the war debt. In 1819 land speculation and a disordered currency brought on a severe crisis; the prices of land and agricultural products fell rapidly, while good harvests in Europe and the effect of the Corn Laws in England had cut off the foreign demand for American grains. Meanwhile the manufacturers having tasted

[1] Taussig, *op. cit.*, pp. 16, 17, 27-29. See also James, "Studien über den amerikanischen Zolltariff," pp. 9-15.

prohibition were not content with a moderate
measure of protection, and became more and more
persistent in demanding more tariff support for
their infant industries.   The agricultural interests
were less organized, and while some of the farmers
are said to have been won over by promises of
a larger home market for their own products,
more were bought by promises of protection.   In
1820 a bill for a general increase of duties passed
Congress, and was rejected in the Senate by one
vote only.   The debates on this measure show
both the strength of the protective movement and
its local character.   Its stronghold was in "the
Middle and Western States of those days—in
New York, New Jersey, Pennsylvania, Ohio, and
Kentucky."[1]   The New England states, interested
in shipping and importing, were on the whole
strongly opposed to the movement, with the
natural exception of the cotton and woollen manufacturers, already an important body.   The South
had supported the bill of 1816; but in 1820 its
opposition was vehement and was continued during
the ensuing ten years.   "They had grasped the
fact that slavery made the growth of manufactures
in the South impossible, that manufactured goods
must be bought in Europe or in the North, and
that, wherever bought, a protective tariff would
tend to make them dearer."[2]

[1] Taussig, *op. cit.*, p. 71.   [2] Ibid. p. 73.

The Tariff of 1824 was distinctly protective, though its duties were chiefly levied on articles produced by the Middle and Western States (iron, wool, hemp, etc.). The duties on cotton and woollen goods were also increased, but in the case of the latter this advantage was offset to the manufacturer by an increased duty on raw wool, which was imposed to gratify the sheep farmers. The English duty on imported wool was reduced this year from 1s. per pound to 1d., thus enabling Yorkshire manufacturers to sell more cheaply and adding to the difficulties of American makers. Various efforts were made in the following years to gain increased protection for the American woollen industry, but in 1827 these particularist efforts were merged in a wider protectionist movement. Since 1819 the country had been deluged with petitions and pamphlets on the question, one of the most active agents on behalf of Protection being the "Pennsylvania Society for the Promotion of Manufactures and the Mechanic Arts," which had been founded (as the "Philadelphia Society for the Promotion of National Industry") by Alexander Hamilton. Its President at this time was Matthew Carey, an Irish refugee, the founder of an important Philadelphia publishing house, with a branch at Boston managed by his more famous son Henry C. Carey. Carey the elder was a prolific anti-English and

Protectionist pamphleteer; his colleague, the vice-president of the society, Charles Jared Ingersoll, was also a strong Protectionist and a leading citizen of Philadelphia. These two politicians and the society which they led took a very prominent part in the agitation, and apparently originated the suggestion that a "national convention" of Protectionists should be called to bring forward proposals for the new tariff. The idea became popular in the various protectionist states; meetings were held to appoint delegates, and the Convention was summoned for July 30, 1827, at Harrisburg, the capital of Pennsylvania.

Ingersoll had made the acquaintance of List during the latter's visit to Philadelphia, and was so much impressed by his ability that he begged him, not only to attend the Harrisburg Convention, but also to prepare the ground by drafting a popular pamphlet in support of Protection and in confutation of Cooper, a Free Trader and individualist, as well as a writer of repute and author of a leading American text-book of political economy. List wished to bury Cooper in German, but Ingersoll persuaded him to make a more superficial attack in English. The author's own account of the matter is given in the Preface to his "National System."[1] "When in the year 1827 the American

---

[1] Pp. xi and xii Eheberg's edition. It is odd that List twice gives Ingersoll the title of *President* of the society.

manufacturers were hard pressed over the tariff
question by the adherents of Free Trade, Mr.
Ingersoll urged me to enter into the controversy.
I did so with some success; the twelve letters in
which I expounded my system not only appeared
in the *Philadelphia National Journal*, but were also
reprinted in more than fifty provincial papers, and,
under the title, "Outlines of a New System of
Political Economy," were published as a special
pamphlet by the Society for the Promotion of
Manufactures, so that many thousand copies were
disseminated. Besides this, I was congratulated
by the most distinguished men of the country,
for instance the venerable James Madison, Henry
Clay, Edward Livingstone, and others."

The Convention met on the day when List's
concluding letter was written.[1] It consisted mainly
of wool-growers and manufacturers; but other
interests—iron, glass, hemp, and flax—were also
represented. Resolutions demanding high protection for manufacturers and producers were
passed, and were embodied in an address to Congress. List himself delivered a lecture to the
delegates in the Representative Hall, which is
referred to in terms of praise by Ingersoll in a
private letter. Some report of it has survived
in an unfriendly speech by a Free Trade member
of Congress.[2] A letter from Richard Rush,

[1] July 30, 1827.   [2] *Vide post*, p. 51.

Secretary to the Treasury, who had formerly been American Ambassador in London, and in that capacity (probably at Lafayette's request) had shown List some kindness in 1823, has been preserved at Reutlingen. Rush courteously acknowledges the gift of List's pamphlet, adding that he had already been interested by some of the letters when they had appeared in the Press. Their arguments may have influenced his annual Report to Congress, for he took up the question of Protection, and "claimed that, as the land laws of the country protected agriculture, at least a like amount of protection should be given to industry."[1]

So great was the success of the pamphlet that the Pennsylvania Society entertained List to a complimentary dinner in recognition of his services to the cause. It was held at the Mansion House, Philadelphia, on November 3, 1827. A printed account of it survives, as a preface to List's speech,[2] which shows that it was an occasion of some political importance. According to the fashion of the day, there is a portentous list of set toasts or "sentiments," some of which are interesting as tokens of the popular feeling. One coupled "the memory of Alexander Hamilton and

[1] Lalor Cyclopædia of Political Science, *art.* "Tariffs."

[2] Account of the dinner given to Professor List by the Pennsylvania Society for the Encouragement of Manufactures and the Mechanic Arts, at the Mansion House, Philadelphia, November 3, 1827.

the success of Richard Rush in perfecting their plans of national industry." Matthew Carey, avoiding grammatical pitfalls, made a great hit by his toast of "Henry Clay, the able and successful advocate of the protection of that portion of American industry which furnishes 'a domestic market, the best of all markets,' according to the sound doctrine of Adam Smith, 'for the rude produce of the soil.'" This skilful quotation was greeted with "rapturous applause." List himself gave the health of "Philadelphia and her Society for promoting Manufactures. This metropolis, not enjoying the commercial supremacy of her great sister city, will take hold of the banner of internal industry, and this patriotic society will inspire the whole Union with its praiseworthy zeal." Part of the speech proposing this toast—a remarkable piece of eloquence for a man speaking in an alien tongue—is included in the present volume.

The eighteen set toasts were followed by eighteen more "volunteers" or impromptu sentiments, among which some wit produced the following scintillation. "May this society be never List-less of their true interests." The perpetration of a pun so appalling throws some doubt over the reporter's statement that "the company adjourned at an early hour, impressed with the most pleasant sensations, after a day spent in *moderate*, but cordial festivity." But the society showed its appreciation of its new helper in more practical fashion ; for the Committee, at a meeting on November 21, 1827, passed the following series of resolutions :—

"Whereas it has appeared to the society that great and important interests of the United States have suffered and are suffering much, for want of a sufficient dissemination of the true principles of Political Economy, and whereas the enemies to the American system are ceaseless in their exertions to cause to be republished and disseminated in large numbers the inapposite maxims of Smith, Say, and other writers, which, however sound they may be as abstract principles in cosmopolitan economy, experience has fully proved them inapplicable to the present state of the commercial world. And whereas Professor Frederick List has proved himself a man of profound knowledge in the science of Political Economy, and has opened new and fundamental principles, clearing away the errors and removing the prejudices which have hitherto made a mystery of that science, and has thereby rendered it plain and comprehensible to every capacity ; and whereas this society are very desirous that Professor List should proceed forthwith to publish and disseminate his new and fundamental views of that important science for the use of schools, and also in a full and extended treatise. Therefore, *Resolved* that this society do earnestly call on Professor List to prepare and publish as soon as may be, an elementary work for the use of schools, and also an elaborate treatise on Political Economy adapted particularly to the situation in the United States. *Resolved* that this society do recommend the said Professor List to the members of the Congress of the United States, the legislature of the State of Pennsylvania and other legislative bodies, the several universities and public seminaries of learning, and to their fellow-countrymen generally for their aid in enabling him to accomplish this desirable object. *Resolved* that this society will subscribe for fifty copies of each work and will do all in their power, individually and collectively, to procure subscribers, and in every way to aid Professor List in his laudable undertaking."

An animated series of letters from Ingersoll preserved among the Reutlingen papers shows that List was employed by the society to answer the host of pamphlets, memorials to Congress, and speeches published in opposition to the new tariff proposals. A fragment of a letter (not from Ingersoll, but possibly from Matthew Carey) addressed to List at this time says, "I am glad you are going to answer the Boston memorial. It is very able and will require a cool, profound, and deliberate answer." [1]

List himself, in the " Mittheilungen aus Nordamerika," [2] mentions the answer as one of his contributions to the tariff controversy, and it seems at all events probable that the pamphlet "Examination of the Boston Report," published by the Pennsylvania Society and generally attributed to Matthew Carey, was in reality written by List. [3]

[1] For the authorship of this letter, see p. 62.

[2] " Mittheilungen aus Nordamerika," p. 3.

[3] To the kindness of Professor Taussig of Harvard University, the following information is due : " The copy of the Examination of the (Boston) Report published in Philadelphia in 1828, which is in our University Library, is stated on the title-page to be 'by a Pennsylvanian.' A pencil memorandum on our copy has added

Another letter from Ingersoll shows that List had not yet given much study to the history of economic theory. The Pennsylvania Society, says Ingersoll, was not in error when it mentioned France as the birthplace of the science of political economy and Scotland as the home of its disciple. The allusion was, not as List supposed, to Adam Smith and J. B. Say, but to Smith and Turgot ; the " Essay on the Formation of Wealth " having no doubt suggested to Smith " The Wealth of Nations."

These letters reflect the variations of hope and anxiety felt by the Protectionists during the tortuous manœuvrings in Congress over the bill of 1828. On April 16 of that year Redwood Fisher—the secretary of the society—informs List that " from present appearances it seems most probable that we shall get no tariff this session of Congress." The actual outcome of the agitation, however, was unexpected. The Convention had brought forward proposals for a general system of protection to agricultural products and manufactures, and especially for new duties on wool and woollens. These latter were so heavy as to amount to practical prohibition.[1] By this time what may be called the

' Matthew Carey.' I find also that Sabin's Dictionary of Books relating to America, usually a safe guide, ascribes it to Matthew Carey. Glancing through the pages, however, I confess it does not look like Carey's work, or at least as if it were all Carey's work."

[1] Taussig, *op. cit.*, p. 83.

"territorial" divisions over the tariff question
were complicated and crossed by political divisions
arising out of the coming presidential election.
John Quincy Adams and his followers were on
the whole Protectionist, while Andrew Jackson's
supporters in the South were bitterly opposed to
a high range of duties, and yet on most points
were willing to work against the "Adams men" in
conjunction with the Northern (and Protectionist)
"Jackson men." These cross-currents were at
play the whole session, and resulted in a piece of
diplomacy so elaborate that it over-reached itself.
The Tariff Bill was "to contain not only a high
general range of duties, but duties especially high
on those raw materials on which New England
wanted the duties to be low. It was to satisfy the
protective demands of the Western and Middle
States, and at the same time to be obnoxious to
the New England members. . . . When the final
vote came, the Southern men were to turn around
and vote against their own measure. The New
England men and the Adams men in general would
be unable to swallow it, and would also vote
against it. Combined they would prevent its
passage . . . and yet the Jackson men would be
able to parade as the true 'friends of domestic
industry.'"[1] This ingenious scheme failed, since
fear of the coming election induced a certain

[1] Taussig, *op. cit.*, p. 83.

E

number of New England members (including Daniel Webster, the Free Trade orator of 1824) to vote for the bill, and it passed both House and Senate by small majorities, becoming the famous "Tariff of Abominations." The circumstances of its passage gave point to John Randolph's pungent sarcasm that "the bill referred to manufactures of no sort or kind except the manufacture of a President of the United States."[1]

The debates upon the bill in the House of Representatives abound in allusions to the Harrisburg Convention, its "first inception,"[2] to Matthew Carey, Hezekiah Niles, and other leading Protectionists. List himself is referred to on at least two occasions. McDuffie of South Carolina (of course an opponent of the tariff), after reading a passage from the address to Congress presented by the Harrisburg Convention, ridiculed its style. "The Harrisburg Convention stands much more in need of a Professor of Rhetoric than they do of a Professor of Political Economy. . . . The writer of this address, who is a mere instrument in the hands of designing men, understands nothing of the political and economic bearing of American System."[3] Whether List was the author of this address or not, McDuffie apparently attributed it

[1] "Congressional Debates," vol. iv. p. 2471.
[2] Ibid. p. 2435.
[3] Ibid. p. 2391.

to him. We owe to this speaker also a more
definite allusion to him, and the only existing
quotation, as far as I can find, from his lecture
at Harrisburg. There is, McDuffie tells us, "a
certain German Professor of Political Economy
and Necromancy, in Pennsylvania, who has recently
been introduced to the American public by a
member of the Harrisburg Convention. And I
must do him the justice to say, that no one could
have been selected of more eminent qualifications
to lecture from the text of the Harrisburg Address.
I quote from a lecture of Professor List, delivered
in the Representative Hall of Pennsylvania—

"'If this country would succeed in raising in the course of
time its manufacturing industry like France, then the property
(land) of Pennsylvania would increase from 7 to 66 dollars per
acre, or from 210 to 2046 millions, which would be an increase
of 1836 millions. This sum would bring an interest, at 6 per
cent., of 110 millions, and the interest of the interest would
make 6½ millions ; which is certainly more than we consume,
at this moment, of foreign merchandise. To buy cheap
manufactures is, consequently, not the primary interest of the
farmer, but to increase the value of their produce, and, above
all, the value of their lands. It is not, therefore, well done if
they buy cheap goods, as the merchants say ; on the contrary,
the cheaper the worse, if they cannot exchange the produce of
their land. I venture to say, the worst of all things would be,
if they could get their goods for nothing ! because the English
would in that case indemnify the Americans only for the
interest of the interest of that sum which they would give if
they would make them themselves.'"

McDuffie's comment is, "An addition of 1836 millions made to the wealth of the nation by excluding 6½ millions of foreign merchandise and paying a higher price for the domestic substitute! This beats the celebrated scheme of British finance by which the National Debt was to be paid off without any taxes at all, by the mere mathematical power of compound interest. . . . Professor List is no doubt a legitimate descendant of the Rosicrucians who once figured in Germany; and I cannot but congratulate the Harrisburg Convention in having supplied the desideratum which they so much lamented by a Professor of Political Economy who bids so fair to be the discoverer of the philosopher's stone."[1]   The next day (April 19) his colleague Hamilton, carrying on the sarcasm, remarked that "we appear to have imported a professor from Germany, in absolute violation of the doctrines of the American System, to lecture upon its lessons—to convince Adam Smith of stupidity and Ricardo of error."[2]

In the mean time (December 22, 1827), List, with his usual hopefulness, had published a large advertisement of his unwritten work on Political Economy, headed by the Resolutions of the Pennsylvania Society.   The book was to be entitled, "The American Economist, by Frederick

[1] "Congressional Debates," vol. iv. p. 2394.
[2] Ibid. p. 2432.

List, of Pennsylvania, formerly Professor of Political Economy, and Counsel of the General Society of German Manufacturers and Merchants for obtaining a German system of Political Economy," and its aim would be to render "that important science which the works of Adam Smith and John Baptist Say covered with mysteries, with confusion and contradiction . . . what it ought to be in every free country, *truly* and *thoroughly popular* and *practical*. The author will endeavour not only to impart all important truths laid down by the principal writers of the old school, or by great statesmen and ingenious writers of this country, but to reveal the errors and imperfections of that system of which Napoleon said: *If an empire were of granite it would be ground to dust by following its precepts.*"

Protectionist sentiment was so strong that no doubt many subscribers could have been found for this frankly partisan work if the two volumes had ever been published as contemplated, in eight numbers at a total cost of five dollars. But no number ever appeared, and only the introductory chapter ever reached the printer.[1] In the autumn

[1] Preface to "National System," ed. Eheberg, p. xii. A fragment of four pages among the Reutlingen papers, entitled, "Chapter I. Survey of the History of Commerce and Commercial Supremacy," is no doubt a part of this introduction, which seems to have covered much the same ground as Chapters II. and IV. of the "National System" (on "The Hansards" and "The English").

of 1830, when List was approaching President Jackson with a view to a mission in Europe, he sent to him a rough proof of this introduction, accompanied by an interesting letter. After speaking of "the many years' labour and reflection which I attempted to concentrate within the space of these eighty pages," he says—

" My principal aim was to show how and by what means England, from being as it were a colony of the Hanseates, grew up to be the first naval, commercial, and manufacturing Power of the globe, and thus to point out the tracks in which this country has to step, in order to arrive at the point of her great destination. . . . In the second chapter I shall treat in a similar way the history of the science of political economy from De Witt and Stuart down to Malthus and McCulloch. . . . The aim of men as philosophers must be eternal peace. Their practical aim is to amass the greatest quantity of power and prosperity within their own nation. Eternal peace and freedom of trade throughout the world go hand in hand."

The Pennsylvania Society entered heartily into the project, and its secretary employed an agent to collect subscribers in the neighbourhood, among the names forwarded to List being those of Ingersoll and Carey. But as time passed and no signs of the book were forthcoming, Ingersoll apparently lost patience, and his letters contain pointed inquiries about its progress, to which List could give no satisfactory answer. His energies had been diverted (as he confesses in the Preface to the

" National System ") to the pursuit of more personal
and profitable interests.

During an expedition into the mountains near
his home he had discovered a rich coal-mine in
the Little Schuylkill valley and bought it, together
with a tract of the surrounding country. Anxious
to introduce his coal to the widest and most
profitable market, he turned his thoughts to the
new means of transport—railroads. A company
with a capital of 700,000 dollars was formed under
the name of the " Little Schuylkill Navigation
Railroad and Canal Company," to develop the
mine and to connect it by rail with the Schuylkill
Canal at Port Clinton. In a later account of the
enterprise,[1] List tells us that he had already
become acquainted with railways on his brief visit
to England in 1823. He goes on to say, however,
that before his stay in America he had only understood the importance of means of transport as it
can be learnt from the theory of value ; he had
observed the effect of transport arrangements only
in isolated cases and with regard to the extension
of markets and lowering of prices. " Now, for the
first time, I began to consider it from the standpoint of the theory of productive power and in
its combined operation as a national transport
system, consequently in its influence on the whole
intellectual and political life, social intercourse,

[1] Introduction to " National System," p. xii.

productive power and material strength of the country."

There is no doubt that List was one of the first to see what railways would do for industry and commerce. The "English 'railways" he mentions were mere horse tramways a few miles in length, though since 1809 Stephenson and others had been working at the development of iron roads and carriages drawn by locomotives. In May, 1823, the first rail of the Stockton to Darlington line was laid, but it is unlikely that List journeyed so far north when he visited England. The line from Liverpool to Manchester was opened on September 15, 1830.

In America the adoption of railway transport was slow and hesitating. Here also the first lines, like List's own venture, were tramways for the transport of minerals or stone to some neighbouring canal or river. The Baltimore and Ohio, the first line of importance, was not begun till 1828 (the year of List's discovery), and its first section of 14 miles was opened in 1830. Even in 1835 Pennsylvania with 318 miles of railway possessed nearly one-third of the mileage in the United States. Unlike those in England, the American lines were built for the moment, not for futurity. "They were rude and unsubstantial structures involving a heavy outlay for repairs, and were very inadequate to the service even then required

of them. The superstructure of the lines first
constructed was a longitudinal sill, the rail or
strap of iron laid upon it serving to prevent the
abrasion of wood rather than to support the train.
The change from wood to iron was a very gradual
one."[1]   In the "Mittheilungen aus Nordamerika,"
as well as later in his pamphlet "Ueber ein
sächsisches Eisenbahn-System" (1833), List re-
commends these wooden lines to German imitation.[2] He says in the former, "Where there is not
much transport wooden rails are preferable to iron,"
and in the latter pamphlet he quotes the arguments
of an American engineer in their favour.

The Little Schuylkill Railroad from Tamaqua—
the site of the mine—to Port Clinton was opened
on November 18, 1831.   List was not present, but
at the celebratory dinner Dr. Hiester, the chief
mover in the enterprise, spoke of him in enthusiastic terms, remarking that he was now on his
way home from Europe where he had at his own
expense spent the last year for the purpose of
introducing American coal, and a toast was drunk
with enthusiasm. "*Professor List.* His exertions
to introduce anthracite into the European markets
deserve our thanks."[3]   Dr. Hiester was apparently

---

[1] Encyclopædia Americana, *art.* "Railroads."

[2] "Mittheilungen aus Nordamerika," p. 41. "Über ein sächsisches Eisenbahn-System," pp. 59, 60.

[3] *Schuylkill Journal*, December 3, 1831, from the "Pennsylvania Intelligences."

the originator of the enterprise, though List says he himself founded the Little Schuylkill Railroad.[1] He certainly threw himself into the project with enthusiasm, for among his papers are many copies of deeds, share allotments, and letters concerning the construction, and there is evidence that in this, as in other undertakings, he met with his full share of difficulties and misunderstandings. In another passage[2] he remarks that the Little Schuylkill Canal, from the mouth of the Little Schuylkill to the coal-mines, has been given up in favour of a railroad. Perhaps Dr. Hiester was already interested in the canal project, and List was chiefly responsible for the change of plan. But List said of himself with truth, "Germany and the return to Germany always lie in the background of my plans," and almost at the moment that the idea of a railway crossed his mind it assumed the proportion of a national movement.

"In the midst of the wild Blue Mountain country I dreamt of a German railway system. It was evident to me that only through such means could the Commercial Union attain full efficiency. These thoughts made me unhappy in the midst of my good fortune. Of necessity the effect on the financial position and national economy of Germany must be all the greater,

[1] "Über ein sächsisches Eisenbahn-System," p. 18.
[2] "Mittheilungen aus Nordamerika," p. 38.

the more imperfect the means of transport had
been before, in comparison with culture, numbers
and industry of the nation."[1]   Already in the
year 1827 he had entered upon an animated
correspondence with Josef von Baader, Chief
Manager of Mines for the Bavarian Government,
who was anxious to introduce railways in that
State. In this correspondence (printed in the
Allgemeine Zeitung) and in a continuation of it sent
to his friends Weber and Arnoldi and published
under the title of "Mittheilungen aus Nordamerika"[2] he drew freely upon his American
experience for details of railway construction and
railway statistics, and especially exerted all his
influence in favour of railways as against canals.
The union of the Danube and the Main by a
canal was then under consideration, but List
poured scorn on the project. "*Union of the North
Sea with the Black Sea* has a fine sound, but when
you look into the matter, there is nothing behind
the phrase. The North Sea has long been united
with the Black Sea by a great natural canal, which
passes Gibraltar and Constantinople, and with

[1] Häusser, p. 165.
[2] "Mittheilungen aus Nordamerika von Fr. List. Herausgegeben von Ernst Weber und E. W. Arnoldi. Erstes Heft.
Über Canäle und Eisenbahnen, 1829; und Nachtrag zum ersten
Hefte enthaltend eine weitere Entwickelung der Vortheile I.
Eines Eisenbahnsystems in Innern Bayern. II. Einer bayerischer-
hanseatischen Eisenbahn, 1829. Hamburg: Hoffman und Comp."

which a waterway passing many hundred miles along the Danube by mountains and through uncivilized lands, then through a troublesome seventy miles of canal, and finally through the hundred river tolls and royal privileges of the Main and the Rhine, can never compete." Baader agreed with this view, but the Canal (which had been begun centuries earlier by Charlemagne) was carried through, owing to the personal influence of King Ludwig.

The Bavarian railways, in List's mind, were to be merely the prelude to a pan-German system; in 1833 he advocated a Saxon system to attain the same end. With fine imagination he paints the future of steam transport and the influence which the new invention would exercise on Germany's intercourse with neighbouring lands. The old trade routes to the East would be opened up, Venice and Hamburg would be brought near to one another, and the post from Calcutta to London would have to come through Germany, for the sea-voyage round the Cape could not compete with the railway route over the Continent. In this last prophecy List could not foresee that the Suez Canal would provide a shorter sea-route more serious as a competitor than the one by the Cape.

List pays a tribute to the individual enterprise of the Americans. "If in the United States all had

to be done by the Government, not the tenth part
of what actually is done could be accomplished, nor
would it be half so well done as it is now. Most
of what is accomplished here is done by those who
are really interested in bringing it to pass."[1] As
to the effect of railways on population, "Why," he
asks in the "Mittheilungen," "do the American
towns grow so visibly, so inconceivably fast that
often one can, after the lapse of a few months,
scarcely recognize their suburbs ? Some time ago,
when I visited Philadelphia after a six months'
absence, I found whole new streets, nay whole
new districts. The cause is the extraordinary
increase of agricultural production, and the resulting demand for manufactured goods, promoted
by the manifold means of communication both
natural and artificial."[2] List's own enterprise was
a striking example ; two small towns, Tamaqua
and Port Clinton, sprang up on ground belonging
to the company at each end of the proposed line,
and when his family visited the district before their
return to Europe in 1831, they found that several
other villages had arisen.[3] List's financial interests
in the mine and railway were enough to relieve
him from pecuniary anxiety. He had before made
some efforts to obtain an academic post, but

[1] Häusser, p. 172.
[2] "Mittheilungen Nachtrag," p. 23.
[3] " Über ein sächsisches Eisenbahn-system," p. 18; also
Häusser, p. 164.

apparently in vain. The following letter among the Reutlingen papers has lost its signature, but the writer was probably Matthew Carey, President of the Pennsylvania Society, since Fisher and Ingersoll were respectively the Secretary and Vice-President.

"Philadelphia, January 21, 1828.

"Mr. Fisher has communicated to Mr. Ingersoll, and Mr. Ingersoll to me your letter of the 18th. I have conferred in it with Mr. Ingersoll. We cannot understand what you expect to do with a Professorship of Political Economy. If I am not mistaken the Franklin Institute may establish one, and appoint a Professor without the special authorization of the Legislature. But when that is done, who will pay the Professor? Will the Legislature found a salary? I presume they will not. What then will be the object of memorializing?"[1]

Andrew Jackson obtained the Presidency in 1830. List was a friend of his Secretary of State, Edward Livingstone, with whom he used to correspond on economic questions—slavery, commerce and so forth.[2] Through his friendship he now hoped to obtain a diplomatic mission to the Continent. Two chief inducements seem to have influenced him: one, his longing to return home, and especially to advocate a German railway system; the other, his desire to promote his own interests

[1] This letter contains the allusion to the Boston Report, which has been dealt with on p. 43.

[2] *Zollvereinsblatt*, No. 11, March 17, 1846. "Die Nordamerikanische Sklavenfrage."

and those of American trade by the introduction of anthracite coal to the European market. With this object he not only addressed letters to President Jackson and other leading men, but visited Washington to press his claims in person, as is shown by the bill of the National Hotel, October 18–23, which still exists among the Reutlingen papers. A letter to the President (October 21) sketches out a suggested course of action in the event of his appointment to a diplomatic mission in France.

In general, he would continue to write on economic questions and in opposition to the English monopoly, and would be on the watch to notice and report to America any technical inventions and improvements in the new means of transport (railways and steamers). His special aim would be to improve the commercial intercourse between the United States and France, and promote the importation of anthracite coal by the latter country; to induce the French Government to take in hand a railway between Havre and Strasburg; to advocate a system of railway communication between South Germany and the North Sea, in particular along the Weser; and finally to look after the better organization of German emigration to the United States. Häusser, List's first biographer, remarks that these proposals were characteristic of the man who always thought in terms of the Universal. He used the modest proposal of developing a market for American coal as a foundation stone on which to build a series of towering projects, each of which would have required his whole energies. The United States Government probably was less hopeful about the results likely to be attained than List himself, but it accepted the offer of his services, arranging that after he had done what he could to carry out his plans in Paris he should proceed to the American Consulate in Hamburg. The patent was signed on November 8, 1830, List started immediately and landed on December 20, at Havre. It was a "new man" who returned to the old world, says Häusser, "one to whom, after his experience of the political liberty and economic prosperity enjoyed by Americans and their eagerness to use natural forces and mechanical inventions, the bureaucratic and unenlightened Governments of the German states were peculiarly hateful. He regarded England's economic and political position with a mixture of admiration and envy, and set before himself as one of his main aims the support of German manufactures and their advancement to a point at which they would be independent of British supremacy."[1]

He proceeded at once to Paris to begin his work. During his stay there he heard that the

[1] Häusser, p. 179.

United States Senate had refused to ratify his
appointment to the Hamburg Consulate, apparently
from a reluctance to displace Mr. Cuthbert, the
holder of the post, who supported himself and some
poor relations on the salary. List had already
determined not to oust the unfortunate man, and
a letter containing his resignation crossed with
one from Van Buren informing him of the Senate's
decision. In the event it proved that he could
not in any case have held the post, for a pro-
test (inspired, List suspected, from Württemberg)
was sent by the Hamburg Government to the
Senate, on the ground that he was a "dangerous
political fugitive." An attempt to obtain a revision
of his trial and gain permission to settle in
Württemberg was discouraged by his friends there,
and an official intimation was given that it would
be well for him not to enter the country. As he
wrote bitterly, "The return to Europe soon cures
one of home-sickness." In spite of disappointment
he worked actively in furtherance of his projects.
Belgium had just established her independence,
and he pointed out to Mr. Rives, the American
Ambassador in Paris, how the new State provided
a route for American trade from Antwerp to the
Rhine, alternative to that from Havre. He also
urged the idea upon leading Belgians whom he
met in the French capital. Mr. Rives was so
struck by List's arguments that he suggested

F

Brussels as the place where his services would be most valuable to the United States Government. At the same time List was urgent in advocating a railway system for France, and published several articles in the *Revue Encyclopédique* under the title " Idées sur des réformes économiques, commercielles, et politiques, applicables à la France." In these he laid especial emphasis on the growing importance of railway communication, and on the advantages which would accrue from a more extensive trade between France and America. But the time—immediately after the Revolution of July— was not propitious, and his views made little impression on the ministry, the opposition, or the general public. The chief result of his stay in Paris was an amended expropriation law to facilitate the acquirement of land for public purposes. Perhaps, however, it was by List's influence that in 1832 young Michel Chevalier was despatched by the Government to America to inquire into systems of communication there. In 1836 Chevalier published the results of his inquiry, under the same title as List's work, " Letters from North America."[1]

At the end of October, 1831, List re-crossed the Atlantic to bring his family back to Europe,

---

[1] A visit to England was followed by another book, " Material Interests in France : Public Works, Roads, Canals, Railways " (1838).

and returned with the promise of the United States Consulship in Leipsic. This post was practically unsalaried, but gave him the definite advantage of an assured position as an American citizen, and he thought—rightly as it proved—that the town was a good centre in which to start a movement for a national railway system. The ill-health of his wife, however, detained him in Hamburg for a year, during which he was untiring in his advocacy of railways, but found that the leading merchants looked on his proposals as mere wild speculations.

In the summer of 1833 List removed to Leipsic, where for the next four years most of his energies were divided between his literary work for the *Staats-lexicon* and his activities on behalf of a Saxon (or rather a German) railway system.

Before describing these it will be convenient to give some extracts from his official communications to America, which throw light on his political and economic opinions at this time. A thin folio volume in the Reutlingen Archiv contains copies of his official correspondence for the month of December, 1834. Probably other letters are preserved at Washington, but these seemed to have been considered by List as of special importance. They are, of course, written in English, and the following quotations are literal. In a letter to the Secretary of State (John Forsyth), dated

December 12, List suggests that it would be well for the Government to appoint a Consul-General as Representative to the German Customs Union, and proposes himself for the post, Leipsic being an excellent centre. He supported his suggestion by a second letter, giving a full account of the position of the Zollverein. "Austria, the Hansea towns, Hanover, Brunswick, and the Duchies of Mecklenburg have not yet joined this Union. But the latter three states, it is believed, will soon do so. This event will to a certainty take place on the death of the present King of England. . . . Even Austria seems to be inclined to treat on [? for] the reception of her German provinces, if we can rely on the assertion of the King of Bavaria contained in his last speech to the estates of the Kingdom. Thus we may expect that all Germany, with more than thirty-three millions of inhabitants, will form after a short time, in respect to their foreign relations, only one commercial power. But even as it is, it comprises above twenty millions of inhabitants, and is important enough to attract the attention of England, France, Belgium, and Holland, as you will probably have heard from the English and French newspapers."

Another letter deals with a still more interesting subject, though one in which List's suggestion bore no fruit. He sets forth (rather oddly, when we remember his activities of 1827–28) that "by the reduction of the tariff in 1833 the United States have contributed more than any other country of the civilized world to introduce into practice that great principle, by which the welfare of mankind will be more promoted than by any other, that is to say, the Liberty of Commerce." Unluckily the example has not been followed in Europe. Some countries, for instance Russia, have even strengthened their prohibitive system, while their exports to the States have increased on account of the above-mentioned measure. This policy has its roots not so much in the ignorance of Governments as in individual interests and prejudices. A change in public opinion is required. "Nothing would contribute so much to work such a change than (*sic*) a congress of representatives of the principal nations, the task of whom would be to discuss in common the hindrances of the liberty of commerce and the means to approach by-and-by to that much-desired object. They would not have to conclude treaties or to make particular propositions; they would only have to elucidate the principle that the concession of every nation to promote the general free intercourse must depend on the concessions of all other free nations, and thus to prepare public opinion for such changes, and to support the Governments in their propositions to the representatives of the nations." France would almost certainly join in such a

project, and England very probably, " as the repeal
of the Corn Laws must become soon one of the
principal objects of a reforming Ministry, in which
they will have to encounter powerful personal
interests and prejudices." He suggests that the
proposition should be made by President Jackson
in his next message to Congress, and concludes
with a necessary explanation. "These propositions are in full accord with the opinions I have
pronounced on former occasions. For at all times
I have been an advocate of the Liberty of Commerce, provided that the principal nations are
approaching that object in the same true and
right spirit. I only contended that no nation,
without injuring the foundations of its prosperity,
could walk that way alone." The extension of the
Zollverein, however, which meant the breaking
down of so many customs barriers, showed that
the age was tending in that direction, and the
next step of most continental nations "will be to
ask England to abolish her Corn Laws and moderate
her tariff. Thus the old continental system of
Napoleon will be revived, but on a more favourable
basis and with a great deal more efficiency."

A third letter described List's services to the
United States during his stay in France. He had
suggested to Van Buren a Commercial Treaty
with France and the reduction of the duties on
French wines, with the double aim of increasing

the trade between the two countries and of
inducing the French Government to acknowledge
the American claims for compensation arising out
of the Napoleonic war. He had discussed the
matter with Mr. Rives in Paris, and had published
articles in the *Revue Encyclopédique.* "The
circumstance that I opened these discussions by
the suggestion of a general system of railways
throughout France, is to be ascribed to our intention to disguise the real object of the essays and
to attract to them public attention." He also
attempted, in the interests of the Southern States,
to get the French Government to substitute an
import duty on tobacco for their monopoly, and
pointed out to Mr. Rives the advantage of Belgian
independence as opening up a rival route to
Germany against that from Amsterdam. "In the
course of the three latter years I have, in want of
another employment, turned my attention to the
introduction of a system of railroads throughout
Germany, and so far have been very successful."
In spite of his diplomatic phraseology there is no
doubt that List's advocacy of railroads was at
least as keen as his interest in questions of
American trade.

CHAPTER III

LIST during his enforced stay in Hamburg was not solely occupied with his railway projects. He had long cherished the plan of an encyclopædic work on all departments of politics and political economy, which might play the same part in spreading new ideas through nineteenth-century Germany as the "Encyclopédie" in eighteenth-century France. In Paris he had already corresponded with German publishers upon the matter, and now his proposals were accepted by the firm of Hammerich in Altona. He secured as his colleagues in the work Rotteck and Welcker, two distinguished professors at the University of Freiburg in Baden, an institution noted among German seminaries for its support of the Liberal and national movement. Indeed, Rotteck (the author of a "Universal History") had carried his enthusiasm so far that a Liberal paper which he edited, *Der Freisinnige*, had just been suppressed, and he had been deprived temporarily of his Professorship. Both men entered heartily into

List's plans, and in fact the chief editorial responsibility lay with them, while List, although he contributed important articles, took a share in the business management of the enterprise and in the negotiations with booksellers. In this work fortune involved him, as usual, in many difficulties and disputes.

The "Staatslexicon" appeared at intervals during the next twenty years (Welcker continuing it after Rotteck's death) and gained a high position among German works of reference. List's contributions are contained in the first, second, and fourth volumes. The most important is that on railways and steam transport, which he reprinted in 1838 as a pamphlet under the title "Political and Economic Aspects of the German Transport System."[1]

The year in Hamburg ended before his work for railways had met with any success. "The spirit of enterprise," he wrote, "is dead here." He also visited Denmark without result, but found some response among the merchants of Lübeck. In the spring of 1833 he settled at Leipsic, having come to the conclusion that the German railway system could be initiated best by a line between Leipsic and Dresden. Leipsic, he saw, was the central point of Germany's internal trade, and

[1] "Das deutsche National-Transport-System in Volks- und staatswirtschaftlichen Beziehung."

especially of the trade in books and manufactured goods. But even here his ideas at first made little headway. The average German of that day looked upon railways much as most of us have regarded airships—they would never be other than dangerous and impracticable. One or two short stretches of line between neighbouring towns had, indeed, been planned or opened; but these were scarcely more than tramways, and List's scheme for a systematic network of rails throughout Germany was thought wild and visionary. A friendly bookseller, who met him at this time, may represent the impression he left even on his supporters. "List has acted here in a most honourable way. His knowledge, his active intellect, and his personal charm filled me with admiration and respect. But from the first moment of our acquaintance I realized that he was an inveterate visionary, who foresaw glittering and successful results for all his schemes. His expectations are always exaggerated, and since only the future can prove them false we must perforce be silent."

At last, however, List gained the interest and support of some young business men, among them Gustav Harkort, whose more famous brother, " der alte Fritz," had a few years before written articles on the possibilities of railway transport, and had even made tentative experiments in Westphalia.

Thus encouraged, List busied himself with a survey of the ground between Leipsic and Dresden, made inquiries concerning existing traffic, and collected information about the cost of materials and the wages of labour. The result of his investigations was published in pamphlet form under the title "Thoughts on a Railway System for Saxony, as the Foundation of a System for the whole of Germany, and in particular on the building of a Line from Leipsic to Dresden"[1] (1833). The arguments of the pamphlet were liberally supported by illustrations drawn from his American experience, and he appended a scheme for raising the necessary capital by means of a joint-stock company. On the last page, beneath the map, "das deutsche Eisenbahn-System," is a rough sketch of an extremely primitive type of train which illustrates a practice occasionally resorted to in those days of low speeds. Two parties of travellers are voyaging luxuriously in their own open carriages placed on railway trucks; the public carriage is a most unwieldy omnibus with a second tier of seats on the roof. Whether this pattern was actually adopted by the Leipsic engineers or was merely a flight of fancy on the part of the draughtsman, it looks at least more comfortable than the cattle trucks

[1] "Ueber ein sächsisches Eisenbahn-System, als Grundlage eines allgemeinen deutschen Eisenbahn-Systems und inbesondere über die Anlegung einer Eisenbahn von Leipsic nach Dresden."

which were at first the lot of English third-class passengers.

The accompanying map is a noteworthy achievement of scientific imagination, for in it List's prophetic hand outlined practically the whole of the present German railway system. Lines from Prague to Leipsic and Dresden, Berlin to Leipsic, to Breslau, Danzig, Stettin and Hamburg, Hamburg to Lubeck and Bremen, Bremen to Hanover, Brunswick and Magdeburg, Leipsic to Gotha, Gotha to Nuremburg and Munich, Minden to Cologne, Basle to Carlsruhe and Frankfort, Carlsruhe to Stuttgart, Ulm, Augsburg and Munich, Augsburg to Lindau —these and their connections are all traced at a time when even England could only show a few isolated railways. And it was largely owing to List's untiring work that before two decades went by the prophecy became an accomplished fact.

Copies of the pamphlet were sent to the King of Saxony, to members of the Court and the municipality, and to other leading men. Its reception was sufficiently favourable to encourage the supporters of the line to hazard the enterprise. After much negotiations the doubts of the Government and the general public were partly overcome. The former gave its sanction to the scheme, and in May, 1835, the company was floated. The first section of the line was opened on April 24, 1837.

As soon as the permission was given, List

hurried to Berlin to persuade, if possible, the
Prussian Government to grant concessions for
lines between Berlin, Magdeburg and Hamburg.
He urged their strategic importance, but for some
time no definite result was achieved. Meanwhile
he busied himself with projects for other lines, and
in the winter of 1835, founded a paper with the
imposing title, *The Railway Journal or National
Magazine of Inventions, Discoveries and Progress
in Commerce, Industry, Public Undertakings and
Public Institutions, and of Statistics, National
Economy, and Finance.*[1] Almost the whole of its
contents were written by List, including a lively
attack on an English engineer, Elliot, who had
explained to the people of Hamburg that a German
railway system was impracticable. "We respect
and admire the English," declared List ; "they seem
to us the ideal of a nation, especially in economic
matters, and we are always advising our countrymen to follow in their footsteps. But when they
bring us presents, whether of money or good
advice, then we fear these Greeks *et dona ferentes.*"

The paper soon stood high among the technical
journals of the day, but at the end of its first year,
for no apparent reason, an official prohibition shut
it out from Austria, and List thus lost a large

[1] *Das Eisenbahnjournal oder National-Magasin für Erfindun-
gen, Entdeckungen, und Fortschritte in Handel und Gewerbe, in
offentlichen Unternehmungen und Anstalten, so wie für Statistik
Nationalökonomie und Finanzwesen.*

proportion of his subscribers. The paper had to be dropped, and on this blow followed another when the financial crisis in America seriously reduced List's means. Other troubles embittered these years. Difficulties arose over his status as American representative in Leipsic, difficulties for which (he constantly affirmed) he had to thank his old enemies in Württemberg, and even his work for railways was spoilt by quarrels and misunderstandings. According to List (in the preface to the "National System") and Häusser (in the biography) the committee of the Leipsic-Dresden railway, who had promised "not to treat him as Yankees would," nevertheless behaved with much unfairness and even dishonesty. The main grounds of complaint appear to have been three : that List was not a voting member of the committee, which was restricted to natives of Saxony, but was co-opted as an expert ; that he received many affronts from the members, though by neglect of his advice the line was both more costly and less useful than it should have been ; finally, that he received an informal promise of remuneration (some shares in the company and a position in its management) which was never fulfilled.

Another version of the matter is given, with less invective, in the life of Fritz Harkort.[1] Harkort also, as a member of another state, had to serve

---

[1] "Der alte Harkort," von L. Berger Witten. 1891.

on the committee by co-optation. Much of the
disagreement between List and the local directors
was due to the difference in their aims. They were
working for the success of the single line, while he
regarded it merely as a link in the future German
system. Hence they could not fall in with all his
suggestions, and his optimism often led him astray.
For example, he was confident that the line could
not cost more than a million thalers, whereas it
proved that more than five times this sum was
required. The committee had a complete answer
to the charge of dishonesty, but forbore to publish
it at the time when Häusser's "Life" appeared, out
of pity for his tragic end and respect for his surviv-
ing relatives. It is hardly possible at the distance
of seventy years to sift out the actual facts from the
conflicting stories of interested persons. It seems
probable that List in his proposals did not make
sufficient allowance for existing conditions, that
hence quarrels arose, and that after the rupture he
had some reason to complain of his treatment.
But in almost every undertaking in which List had
a share he sooner or later became involved in
quarrels, so that we may conclude he was unfortunate either in his temperament or in his colleagues,
or perhaps in both. He was certainly a man of
great impetuosity, and too prone to measure
German enterprise by American standards. List
twice received a gift of 2000 thalers from the

committee, with a vote of thanks for the services he had rendered; but this was small compensation for his American losses, although these ultimately proved to be less ruinous than he at first feared.

The general opinion of the Leipzic public seems to be expressed in a report sent from the Prussian Consulate there to Vienna, and dated July 17, 1835. The writer says—

"Although the experience he acquired in America, and the additional knowledge he gained by two years of work and study devoted to railway affairs, have enabled Herr List to be of much service to the undertaking, yet he has always gone to work with such sanguine expectations and views that the committee have been forced to hold him in check. This is especially true of the Railway Reports he composed, which had always to be modified by the committee after disputes with their author. Every one recognizes the good intentions of Herr List, his enthusiastic activity, and his expert knowledge, but every one is careful not to put unqualified faith in his schemes. Herr List's means are at present reduced, which fact made him wish for the position of a paid agent in the company. Owing to his quarrel with the committee he has been disappointed in this expectation, and he probably considers the two thousand thalers voted to him by the present directorate as an insufficient return for his labours. With this view I myself agree, since it is generally considered (and admitted by some of the directors) that he has given the most effective and powerful impulse to the Leipzic-Dresden railway, and through it to German railways in general, and by the advice he has given here, and especially by his talent for influencing public opinion in the matter (which talent has been recognized by the authorities concerned), he prepared the way for the success of the enterprise."

This letter is reproduced with other correspondence in an essay upon List by Dr. Max Höltzel of Stuttgart.[1] He shows how keenly Metternich and his agents in Germany watched List's movements after his first activity in Württemberg, and how anxious the Austrian Minister was at this time to put pressure on Saxony and the United States with the help of the Württemberg Government and to deprive the exile (whom he describes as "the most active, wary, and influential of the German revolutionaries") of the protection of office. The Saxon representative at Stuttgart even asked the Württemberg Government in September, 1834, whether it objected to List's co-option as an expert on the railway committee, and permission was graciously given on the express ground that the business would keep him away from Württemberg.

Yet in January, 1836, he visited Württemberg and met with great cordiality. "I have had a wonderful reception," he wrote, "friend and foe met me with open arms. The whole country seems to beg my forgiveness for the wrongs I have suffered. . . . Privy Councillor K. seized hold of me and danced round the room crying,

---

[1] " Preussische Jahrbücher," 1903.

'List is back! List is back! Now there will be a
little life in Württemberg again.'" But when,
after a vist to Carlsruhe, he returned in March
to put forward a plea for restitution of citizenship,
the King's answer was that he must be regarded
as a foreigner whose stay in the country was con-
ditional on his good behaviour. He would not
remain in his native country on these terms, and
returned to Leipsic. His troubles there, however,
determined him on a new departure. In the later
autumn of 1837, he left Germany for Paris by way
of Belgium, accompanied by his daughter Emilie
and his only son, Oskar. The latter, a boy of
seventeen, he settled in a technical school at
Brussels. List himself found a friendly welcome
in that town, King Leopold promising to recommend him to his father-in-law, Louis Philippe. At
Ostend, whither he went for health's sake, he met
Dr. Kolb, a former pupil at Tübingen and editor
of the well-known *Augsburger Allgemeine Zeitung*.
List had already contributed some articles to the
paper; he now became one of its permanent
correspondents, and many of his ablest essays
gained wide publicity in its columns. In Paris
the King and Ministers were friendly, but he was
soon diverted from the advocacy of a French
railway system to a new interest. The Academy
had just offered a prize for the best essay on the
following topic: "Lorsqu'une nation se propose

d'établir la liberté du commerce ou de modifier sa legislation sur les douanes, quels sont les faits, qu'elle doit prendre en considération pour concilier de la manière la plus équitable les intérêts des producteurs et ceux de la masse des consommateurs?" In spite of the short time which remained before the date fixed for delivering the essays, List determined to compete. A letter to his wife (January 1, 1838) shows with what energy he threw himself into the work. "We have celebrated the New Year right merrily and only got to bed at four o'clock this morning. I am through with my work. You can imagine what it is like when I tell you that it would fill two moderately stout printed volumes. This has all been written, translated into French, and annotated in six weeks. I have worked from one or two o'clock in the morning until ten, then to the library till three, work again till five-thirty, then dinner, and bed at seven or eight. I have never worked better in my life or been in better health. For the last few days I have not even gone to bed, but only slept an hour or two on the sofa. . . . Meanwhile I had to put everything on one side, King, Ministers, friends, correspondence; I could not waste a moment. There was no question of theatre-going or newspaper reading. I hardly know what has happened in the outside world."

The immediate result seemed an inadequate

return for such excessive labour. The Academy awarded no prizes, although the judges commended three essays, among them List's, as *ouvrages remarquables*. List attributed his comparative failure, not to the difficulties of writing under high pressure in a foreign tongue, but to the prejudice of his judges, since two of them (Blanqui and Rossi) belonged to the "school" of Adam Smith, whose theories he was combating.[1]

But he turned the failure to good account. He felt the necessity of systematizing his economic theories, and of extending and strengthening his historical knowledge before he could venture to draw trustworthy conclusions. Looking over the printed introduction to his projected American book, he found its historical basis "pitiable." Hence, on September 6, 1838, he wrote to Cotta—

"For many years I have been collecting ideas and materials for a new system of National Economy, and I have now decided to begin the work. The subject for a Prize Essay of the Academy—'Free Trade in International Commerce'— instigated me to submit in answer the main arguments of my unwritten book, and though I could not spend more than three weeks on the essay, yet it was named as the most remarkable of twenty-seven.[2] The Academy did not award

[1] See his preface to the "National System," p. 17.

[2] This double inaccuracy only a few months after the event about which List writes is puzzling. In the preface to the "National System" the actual six weeks spent over the essay have dwindled to "about a fortnight."

the prize for reasons which I consider worthless, but they framed a new question out of my essay, without acknowledging the source. 'On the importance of the German Zollverein and the application of its principles to other countries.' This was already answered in my essay. A man of standing assured me that the Academy was a 'den of thieves,' and I had no desire to provide these gentlemen with materials for their own books. So I intend to re-cast my essay as a book, complete in itself but also serving as an introduction to a larger work, that is to a new system of political economy. This book, with the title 'International Free Trade, and the Union of States under International Law,' will show how far free trade is desirable in theory and can be attained in practice, and will explain that as nations advance in industry and trade, in knowledge and culture, in political institutions and mechanical inventions, what we now call international law will become the common law of federated states. My aim will be practical rather that theoretical. You remember how some years ago, in the *Allgemeine Zeitung*, I urged the President of the United States to propose an international congress on trade. Secretary Van Buren, with his mole-politics, could not grasp the idea; but now the nation is ripe for it, and I hope they will force the Government into action. In France theorists and practical men, administrators and manufacturers, merchants and producers, hold sharply opposed views, and none of them have hit the nail on the head. England is content with her system, except that the Corn Laws depress industry and the labouring population for the benefit of the landed aristocracy. In Germany, too, we are astray; in spite of Nebenius the Handelsverein has no firm basis. Nebenius is too much hampered by his admiration of Adam Smith, he has thought and reflected much, but has seen little and has had no experience. Besides, his crabbed sentences make wearisome reading.

  " You see that such a book, if well written and to the point, must win publicity and influence. You must judge whether mine will fulfil these requirements from the contributions which I send to your Quarterly as specimens."

The next three years were devoted to historical research. French politicians, especially Thiers, were so much interested in his theories that at one time he thought of writing his book in French, and gave up the idea with some reluctance. In his spare time he contributed articles to the *Allgemeine Zeitung*, some on "The English Theory of Free Trade before the Judgment Bar of History" to the *Constitutionel* (1839), and an important series, based on his French Essay, to the *Deutsches Viertel-jahrschrift* (1839-40). These last, "Free and Restricted Trade," are reproduced in many passages and chapers of the "National System." Writing on "English Corn Laws and German Protection" (*Allgemeine Zeitung*, 1839), he blamed English landlords for insisting on heavy duties at the close of the Napoleonic War. "Like a two-edged sword, the Corn Laws inflicted a double wound on English trade; they set bounds to the growth of English manufactures, and they called into life the protective systems of the United States, Germany, and Russia, which have nourished manufactures in these lands to become serious competitors of England."

These busy years were passed in the Rue Navarino, not far from the Rue des Martyres where Heine lived, one of the few Germans with whom List held much intercourse during his stay in Paris. His chief pleasures, after the arrival of his wife and the other children in 1838, were found in his own family circle. "Our father was then in good health," wrote his daughter Emilie later of those days, "and when that was the case we needed nothing more to make the house cheerful and happy. He always came home in good spirits, told us what went on abroad, and understood to perfection the art of entertaining and instructive conversation. I do not think that there can ever have been a more indulgent and loving father." A note to his youngest daughter, a child of twelve, written in 1841, when the family were in Italy, gives us one of the rare glimpses of List in his gentler mood. "I am writing to you to-day, since my last letter was from you, and I will send you a good long letter in spite of the shortness of yours. Your tiny note contained more excuses than I liked. You tried to justify its shortness by the plea that nothing new had happened. It is not merely the new that interests me, I like to know the old as well. You can tell me what people you see, how you like them and what they think of you, who are your companions in the house and what you know about them, what your servant is like, and how you spend your day, how your rooms are furnished, and how you get on with Italian. All this would give you the means of writing more than *one* long letter. And you would be rewarded for your pains, since it is only practice that makes a good writer."

This happy life was rudely broken by a great loss. His son Oskar had long cherished a wish to become a soldier, and at last gained his father's consent. He entered the French Army, showed promise of rising in his profession, and was sent to Algiers. There, in 1840, he died of malarial fever. List was heart-broken, nor did he ever fully recover from the blow. A suggestion from Thiers that he should enter Government employ was refused, for his thoughts turned homeward. In the summer of 1840 he left France, going first to Leipsic to settle some outstanding matters connected with the "Staatslexicon." He found a fresh railway agitation on foot, into which he threw himself with all his old energy.

The towns of the beautiful Thuringian district (Gotha, Weimar, Jena and the rest) were not included in the route of a proposed railway from Halle to Cassel and Frankfort. List poured forth a series of articles over the pseudonym of the old patriot "Justus Moser"; in them, and in personal interviews, he fought for the longer route with all its political and financial advantages. The scheme was accordingly revised in harmony with his suggestions; he gained the reward of an honorary doctorate from the University of Jena, and a money gift from the Thuringian Railway Company. The latter inspired his jest that each of the three Duchies which the company declared he had "saved," must be worth merely 33⅓ louis d'or. His hopes of a more satisfactory recognition for his services led him to bring his family to Weimar, but he was disappointed. After this he made a temporary home in Augsburg, where he had the pleasure of intercourse with Kolb and other friends. He worked quietly at his book, and it appeared in May, 1841, under the title "The National System of Political Economy: International Commerce, Commercial Policy, and the German Zollverein." [1]

It bore the same motto as his essay for the Academy, " Et la patrie et l'humanité."

In the same month he visited Württemberg, partly in the hope that through his old friend Schlayer, now Minister, he might get a post in the State railway department. On the journey he broke his leg and was laid up for some time at Cannstatt, near Stuttgart. This mishap brought about a reconciliation with Menzel; the two men had had a literary quarrel some years before. "The news came to me," Menzel wrote in his

---

[1] "Das nationale System der politischen Oekonomie. Der internationale Handel, die Handelspolitik und der deutsche Zollverein."

reminiscences, "one Saturday. I hurried to him at once. He lay there with bandaged foot, and turned that familiar Titanic head, little changed with years, to gaze at me. '*You* have come? What a pleasure! You are the first who has given me a thought.' From that hour we were good friends again, and I visited him almost daily until his recovery. He always came to see me afterwards, on his journeys from Augsburg to Stuttgart, and he remained my firm friend up to his death."

When convalescent he went to recruit at Wildbad in the Black Forest—alone, for his family were at this time in Italy, where his daughter Elise was training as a singer. Returning to Stuttgart he made another vain attempt for the revision of his sentence. A new literary project met with greater success; the reception of the "National System" (a second edition had been called for within four months of its publication) induced Cotta to look with favour on List's proposal to found a weekly journal in support of the Zollverein. The Congress of 1842, at which representatives of the different states belonging to the union met to discuss the arrangement of the tariff, showed clearly that List's book had made its mark on many minds, though at the same time the supporters of free trade still enjoyed considerable authority and influence. List firmly believed, or at least asserted, that the German free trade party was encouraged by English statesmen for their own sinister ends, and when the first number of the *Zollvereinsblatt* appeared in January, 1843, he used it as a medium for some fiery attacks on English policy. The paper carried on an untiring agitation for a "national" commercial system, and its arguments were set forth with a wealth of illustration, a variety of treatment, and a flow of eloquence unknown till then in German economic discussion. List was peculiarly fitted for the post of editor. A born journalist and agitator, he had the double gift of collecting material from all possible sources and of presenting it in new and attractive guise. A well-known passage in an early number paints in glowing phrases the benefits of a national mercantile marine.

"The sea gives strength to nations as to individuals, refreshment to their members and life to their minds. It fits them to undertake great projects, accustoms their physical and mental vision to distant views, and cleanses them from all those stains of Philistinism which are so great a hindrance to national life and national progress. From time immemorial salt water has healed national ills; it clears away pretence and windy, unpractical philosophy, the itch of sentimentality, the palsy of printed words, the obstructions of learned pedantry, and eradicates academic languor and phantasies of all kinds. The sea strengthens the whole constitution, for it brings riches and enjoyment, comfort and good cheer within the reach of the mass of the people. Sea-going nations laugh at economists who cling to dry land and preach systems of penury and starvation, for they know well that the sea has an inexhaustible store of good things for those who have courage and strength to take them."

The moral List drew was the urgent need for strengthening the Zollverein by the accession of the Hanse Towns, in spite of the English leanings shown by Hamburg.

Though the tariff question overshadowed all others, he worked with untiring vigour for other means of advancing national unity—for a German postal system, for railway extension, and above all for Parliamentary government in place of the narrow bureaucracy which hampered all the states. He pointed his advocacy by a reference to the great man who was already coming to the front in English politics.

"William Ewart Gladstone, Vice-President of the Board of Trade and Master of the Mint, is still full young, so young that according to the laws of many German states he could not marry without special leave. Yet he is Peel's right hand and will be Chancellor of the Exchequer before long. . . . Undoubtedly his great name is not factitious but real. This is proved by his work on 'Church and State' which was the beginning of his reputation, and by his labours over the tariff. This year and last the whole burden of reform rested on him and Sir Robert Peel, and though Sir Robert Peel is admittedly far his superior in readiness and dexterity of debate, yet every one knows that Gladstone provided the Premier with the main part of his materials. We cannot refrain in this connection from considering what Gladstone would have become if Fate had made him first see the light in a bureaucratic country. Probably only a practising lawyer or referendary of the third or fourth class, if he were not still immersed in preparing for his examination. Perhaps in ten or twenty years' time he would reach secretarial rank, and at the end of his life become a Councillor of Chancery, always provided that he had not through rash speeches or writings incurred the displeasure of the heads of his department. The striking difference between bureaucratic and parliamentary government is, that in the latter young talent can easily make its way, while in the former it can only reach its fitting sphere through chance or routine. Stall feeding marks a great advance in farming, but among sheep we find that the best leaders of the flock are reared in open pasture."

In September, 1844, some despatches of Lord Westmoreland (British Ambassador at Berlin) to the home Government were published. In them it was explained that the Prussian Government, with its free trade sympathies, was opposed to any further advance in the duties levied by the Zollverein, and hoped "to resist the more extensively menaced injury to the commerce of England." List seized upon the phrase and made it the text of a series of attacks upon English commercial selfishness. The Ambassador in one letter referred to him personally as "a very able writer in the employ of the German manufacturers;" to which List bitterly replied that "unfortunately it was not true, for the manufacturers did not take sufficient interest in the matter to require a paid

agent." Since his return to Germany in 1840 he
had received about three thousand florins in payment for his book, one thousand three hundred
and twenty-five florins from the manufacturers in
the Zollverein towards the publication of the
Zollvereinsblatt, and a gift of three hundred and
sixty florins from some Bohemian manufacturers.
This total of four thousand six hundred and eighty-
five florins gave him in the eight years (from 1837
to 1845) during which most of his time was devoted
to the movement, an average annual income of
about five hundred and eighty-five florins (or
£58 5s.). "I must add that the contribution from
the manufacturers (mainly those of Württemberg)
reached me the year after that (1842) in which Lord
Westmoreland wrote the despatch in question."
It is, indeed, entirely obvious that throughout his
life List was seldom actuated by motives of self-
interest. Only in the railway disputes at Leipsic do
there seem to have been monetary considerations to
embitter the quarrel. He was ever ready to predict that each fresh venture would give him riches,
but when the riches proved visionary, he made
little complaint. During 1844 he was actively
interested in negotiations between Belgium and
the Zollverein, which ended in a commercial treaty,
and he visited Brussels in pursuit of that end.
On his journey home he travelled up the Rhine
to recruit his health, which had been affected by

his exertions. Approaching Mainz, he found that
the question of a railway from the city along the left
bank of the river was just then hotly disputed, and
he composed on board the boat a sparkling dialogue
between an old colonel and a Government official.
Its aim, of course, was to help the supporters of
the railway. "When God created Germany," says
the colonel, "it was a shapeless, worthless mass
of sand and mud. Then He put the Rhine behind
it, and Germany stood up strong and straight. If
only I could find a metaphor apt enough to show
you what the Rhineland is to us. Ah, I have it!
The Rhineland, gentlemen, is the backbone of the
German ox!" The dialogue was published under
the title, "The German Railway System" in the
Allgemeine Zeitung, to which, in spite of his occupation with the *Zollvereinsblatt*, he still sent contributions. Two of the most noteworthy were on "The
Land Question, Small Holdings, and Emigration"
(1842), and "On the Relation of Agriculture to
Industry and Trade" (1844). These expanded and
emphasized the teaching of the "National System."

In the autumn of 1844 List visited Austria and
Hungary as a missionary of protection to native
industry. In both countries he was well received ;
German though he was, Kossuth, Apponyi, and
other Hungarian leaders treated him with great
cordiality, and his ideas found ready acceptance.
Indeed, before his death he declared that protection

in Hungary was being carried too far. At a complimentary banquet in Vienna he explained the
political designs that so often appear in his writings,
and referred to his visit to the city twenty-five years
earlier on behalf of the embryo Zollverein. "Born
and partly brought up under the benignant rule of
the Germanic Emperor, from my youth I have
always cherished in my heart the name of Austria.
But it was not sentiment alone which at that time
turned our steps to this capital. It was the conviction that the Empire state must lead all our
great national movements, if they are to reach
their goal." It was not until just before his death
that he came reluctantly to realize that Prussia
rather than Austria must be the leader of national
union.

During his long absence (until July, 1845) the
Zollvereinsblatt was edited by Dr. Tögel, and this
gave rise to rumours among his enemies that he
had left Germany for ever. He refuted them by
returning and taking up his work with undi-
minished vigour. Tributes of welcome poured
in upon him from all parts of Germany, but he
was in bad health and full of gloomy foreboding
for the future of his family. What would become
of them in the event of his death?

Physical and mental troubles made him feel
more acutely than of old a new series of bitter
journalistic attacks which just at this time were

directed against him. His family watched these fits of depression with anxiety, but a short visit to Bad Rippoldsau—that charming spot in the Black Forest—acted for the time as a restorative. He was able during the winter to contribute two important series of articles to the *Zollvereinsblatt* on "English Commercial Policy" and "On the Political and Economic Unity of the Germans."

The course of events in England naturally absorbed List's attention. In the "National System" (chapter xv.) and in earlier writings, he had expressed the opinion that England would soon adopt free trade, irrespective of the policy of other nations, in order to get raw material on the most advantageous terms, and to maintain the high quality of her manufactures. During the repeal agitation he had declared (*Zollvereinsblatt*, November 20, 1843) that what England understood by free trade was only the free admission of corn and tropical products; but now that Peel's policy of free imports was unmistakable, he still maintained that it would bring no benefit to Germany. The repeal of the Corn Laws (he said in a "New Year's Sermon," January 6, 1846) would ruin many of the English landed aristocracy, and those who remained would be forced to give greater freedom of tenure to their farmers. Hence the political influence of the landed interest would be greatly weakened, and the commercial and manufacturing

H

interests proportionately strengthened. Gladstone had said, "We became rich under protection, we shall become richer under free trade." But the main effect of the substitution of a revenue system would be to benefit the colonies, for the landed interest had done its best to hamper colonial agriculture. The Turkish Empire, too, was tottering, and must soon fall, when England would get into her power Egypt, the east coast of Africa, Syria, and all the country round the Euphrates, the Tigris, and the Persian Gulf. Under any tolerable form of government these regions would be able to support twenty millions of the English race. Until they and the colonies attained full development Russia and North America could supply England with corn, and these large imports would entail a correspondingly heavy export of manufactures. This in its turn would create in England an active demand for such produce as could not be imported to any great extent: among which List included cattle, meat, and butter. The cheapness of the necessaries of life would greatly increase population and general prosperity. Buildings and gardens would raise the value of land far above the agricultural level, and at the end of the nineteenth century the inhabitants of the United Kingdom would number sixty or seventy millions. Germany meanwhile would only be able to export pipes and pickles, bone phosphate and brooms.

It is curious to contrast this blend of prophecy and fancy, intuition and error, with the plain sensible letter in which Cobden six years earlier set forth the mutual benefits that might be expected from the German Zollverein on the one hand and English free trade on the other.[1] But the prospect of success in England encouraged German free traders to renewed efforts. Cobden's speeches were eagerly read; addresses of congratulation were presented to Peel; and in the "Zoll Congress" of 1845 sharp differences arose between free traders and protectionists. List, on his part, thought that a railway from Ostend to Hamburg would be the best means of counteracting the evil effects he dreaded from the new English policy. This connecting link would help on his favourite scheme of over-land transport between England and India, from which the German railways at all events would gain some advantage. As the year advanced he determined to visit England, partly to see for himself how affairs stood, partly to find more efficient correspondents for the *Zollvereinsblatt*. The paper, which he left again in Tögel's charge, had just passed into his own financial control, and he employed for his journey a subscription to the

[1] A letter on the "Prussian Commercial Union," written from Frankfort, October 22, 1840, was published in the *Anti-Corn Law Circular*, and reprinted in "Free Trade and other Fundamental Doctrines of the Manchester School," 1903.

journal of a thousand gulden sent by a union of protectionist manufacturers.   In June, 1846, he reached London.   Frequent contributions to the *Zollvereinsblatt* show the close interest with which he watched the political situation, although at times his view was curiously warped.   An article on July 15, 1846, reported on the recently published tariff that "free imports of raw material and food, and moderate protection to industry is the principle of the new policy," which would enable England to compete with foreign nations on yet more favourable terms.   The effect of Peel's measures would be in the highest degree injurious to the Continent.   List evidently thought that what benefits one country must injure another.   "Nothing will better prove the falsity or truth of the National System.   In the course of the next two or three years the civilized world will be able to judge both systems by their fruits.   We for our part await this decision with confidence." A meeting with Cobden did not shake his opinion that the new policy was adopted with intent to injure continental industry, although he could not resist the charm of the great free trader's personality.

"Last night," so runs a letter of June 26, "I witnessed two noteworthy events.   In the Upper House I saw the Corn Law expire amid their Lordships' cheers, and a few hours later, in the Lower House, I saw Peel's Ministry receive its death-blow. The very place where I sat in the Commons yesterday afforded abundant material for observation. On the bench in front of me sat the Egyptian Ibrahim with his staff, and from time to time leading politicians, among them Lord John Russell, would come to exchange a few words with him. The accomplished Lord Monteagle (Spring Rice), who was most friendly and polite, pointed out to me not only the peers and literary men who sat near us, but also the chief members of the House. Of the speeches I heard, the most eloquent were those of Mr. Shiel and Mr. Buller. In the House of Lords, Dr. Bowring said to me, 'That old gentleman in the blue frock coat with his head sunk on his breast is the Iron Duke. . . . May I introduce Mr. McGregor to you?' A friendly man with a most intelligent face shook my hand. 'Mr. Cobden wishes to make your acquaintance,' I heard from the other side, and a man still young, his eyes bright with intellect, held out his hand. 'Have you really come over to be converted?' he said. 'Of course,' I answered, 'and to seek absolution for my sins from this reverend gentleman' (Mr. McGregor). So I stood jesting for a quarter of an hour amongst my strongest political opponents. What a splendid thing political life is here! You can see history in growth."

A new scheme which also had impelled him to this English visit, was the hope of a commercial alliance between Great Britain and Germany. His admiration for English character and enterprise had always been great, in spite of his frequently professed belief that the main energies of British statesmen were devoted to crushing out German industry. Above all, the English constitution had been the object of his warmest praise. He had begun also to realize that the South German members of the Zollverein could do little to withstand the influence of Prussia, which at this time was politically friendly to England. During 1845, side by side with his most bitter attacks upon Peel, appeared other articles pointing out that Germany and England were by nature meant for friendship, and now he appeared, of course without official credentials, to ask a hearing for his scheme. List's biographers have remarked that it was the attempt of a desperate man, perhaps the first sign of the mental trouble which later overwhelmed him. How could a notorious writer against England hope unsupported to make an impression upon English diplomats? Nevertheless, he worked feverishly at his memorial, "On the Importance and the Necessary Conditions of an Alliance between Great Britain and Germany,"[1] and sent copies to Prince

[1] "Ueber den Wert und die Bedingungen einer Allianz zwischen Grossbritannien und Deutschland," published in the *Allgemeine Zeitung* after List's death, and reprinted in Häusser's "Gesammelte Schriften."

Albert, Peel, Clarendon (then Foreign Minister), and the King of Prussia. The three first copies were no doubt the English version, a draft of which lies among the Reutlingen papers.

The memorial first predicts an English war with France which will drive the latter country into the arms of Russia. The future development of the world will be in the hands of three races, the Germanic led by England, the Latin led by France, and the Slavonic by Russia. The first, mainly represented by England and Germany, will be strong enough to resist a combination of the other two, if England allows Germany to develop, and if Prussia takes her place as the leader of German political and commercial life. But England can only maintain her supremacy over the United States by extending her empire over Asia, Africa, and Oceana; for the States will absorb Canada and Texas. Thus England's main hope will be a railway from Germany down the Adriatic coast, along the Euphrates and by the left shore of the Persian Gulf to Bombay. List presses this favourite project with great earnestness. Egypt and Asia Minor are the natural link between England and her possessions in the East. Russia and France will, no doubt, put all possible hindrances in her way, but with Germany's support she can ignore them, for "the strength of Germany is the strength of England." And German strength can only be

obtained by a policy of temporary protection.   Its
advocates do not reject the theory of universal free
trade, but they argue that England herself has only
just reached the stage of development at which free
trade is beneficial.   German trade and industry
would be utterly crushed if they permitted the
competition of so wealthy and powerful a rival.
The birth of German nationality can only come
by the help of Prussia. The foundation of the
Zollverein is mainly due to that state, and the
Zollverein is the first and most important step
towards nationality.   Only let Prussia look not
to her own immediate benefit, but to the future
good of Germany, and let England refrain from
trying to influence the policy of the Zollverein for
her own ends.

The modest, conciliatory, and almost dejected
tone of the paper is curiously unlike List's ordinary
style, and seems to reflect the depression of his
mood.   He met with kindness and, by his own
account, encouragement from the Chevalier de
Bunsen, then Prussian Ambassador to England,
who held out some hopes of a diplomatic post.
But though Peel and Clarendon sent him courteous
answers, the Prime Minister said that his sympathy
with the object of the memorial could not make
him agree with the means proposed.   He dis-
believed in the benefits of a protective tariff for
Germany, and thought that prosperity could be

attained more surely by approaches to free trade. The copy sent to the King, with a letter in which List defended himself against the charge of hostility to Prussia, received a mere acknowledgment.

He returned to Germany in autumn, broken in health and spirits. His literary work remained as brilliant as ever, but he told a friend in England, "I feel as if a mortal disease were in my frame and I must soon die. If I am to lie sick, die, and be buried, I wish to do it in my own country." The failure of his self-appointed mission to England made him regard the future in the darkest colours, and he even thought that the *Zollvereinsblatt* would soon fail. The Society of Manufacturers sent him a gift of six thousand gulden. He left it untouched at his banker's, and a few months later it was handed over to his family.

Their friendly meeting in London did not prevent List from making some personal attacks upon Cobden for the speeches he had been delivering in France. He reproached the great free trader, perversely enough, for not first persuading his countrymen to change the "relatively high protective taxes" on French commodities, such as silk and brandy, into revenue duties. This, of course, was one of Cobden's chief endeavours, and was consummated fourteen years later by his negotiation of the French Commercial Treaty.

Friends in Augsburg found List much altered;

his old irritability had left him, and with it his old energy. He suffered from sleeplessness and constant pains in the head, and although he still worked at new projects he left them half finished. The chief interest remaining to him was the foundation of a Society of Trade and Industry for Bavaria. In November he went to Munich to arrange this, and his family took leave of him in the hope that the journey, as often before, would restore his health and spirits. A few days later came a note from Tegernsee in the Tyrol; he was on his way to Meran to try the effects of a milder climate. This was the last news they received.

Bad weather turned him aside from his proposed route, he went instead to the little Tyrolese town of Kufstein and took up his quarters at an inn. The landlord allotted him a comfortable room; but List, though he was well supplied with money, refused, saying, "I am too poor, give me the worst room in the house." He ate little, so the landlord said afterwards, and spent much of his time in bed; for he was in great pain, and the weather continued to be wretched. On the morning of November 30 he left the inn. Night came and he did not return. A letter found by the landlord in his room disclosed the visitor's identity. Its contents alarmed him, and search parties were sent out. After some hours the body of List was found close to the town covered with newly fallen

snow. He had shot himself. The letter to Kolb
—a half-coherent and scarcely legible scrawl
with many erasures and corrections—revealed the
unhappy man's state :—

" DEAR KOLB,

"I have made several attempts to write to my
family, to my precious wife, to my splendid children, but
brain, hand, and pen refuse their service. May Heaven give
them strength.! I hoped that exercise and a short stay in a
warmer country would fit me again for work, but each day of
my journey the pains in head and body increased. And then
the frightful weather ! I turned back to Schwatz but only
reached Kufstein, where I remained and still remain, lying in
deep dejection. The blood rushes to my head and all is confusion, especially in the morning. And the future,—if I can
gain nothing by my pen I shall be forced to live on my wife's
resources (I have none), and these are not sufficient to provide
for the children and herself, except with the barest necessaries.
I am on the brink of despair. God have mercy on those
belonging to me. Each night of the past four, and to-night
for the fifth time, I have determined to go to Augsburg, and
each morning my heart fails me. God will reward you and
my other friends for all you do for my wife and children.
Farewell.

"FR. LIST."

By the kindly offices of strangers he was buried
in this secluded corner of the greater Germany on
behalf of which he had so long and so fervently
preached the gospel of national unity and commercial enterprise. When the tragic story of his
death was known it aroused universal pity, not

unmingled with remorse.   Practical sympathy was
not lacking, and it placed his wife and children
beyond fear of want.   In 1848 the Württemberg
Legislature, which had driven him out in his
impetuous youth, passed a unanimous resolution
in his honour.   Sixty years after his death a
stately memorial was raised at Kufstein by contributions from all parts of Germany and Austria;
the base of the statue now bears a simple inscrip-
tion, which happily touches on two of List's outstanding characteristics, a patriotism uncorrupted
by self-interest and a gift of prophetic foresight—

> " Ein Anwalt ohne Sold bemüht fürs Vaterland,
>   Ein Kämpfer, dem kein Gold den starken Willen band.
>   Ein Held, der weit hinaus sah über seine Zeit,
>   Ein Sämann, dem als Haus das Sternenwelt bereit." [1]
>
> MARTIN GREIF.

[1] "A defender of his country who toiled without reward, a
warrior over whose strong will gold cast no fetters.   A hero who
saw beyond his own age far into the future, a sower for whom the
starry world is prepared as a dwelling."

CHAPTER IV

CONCLUSION—THE ECONOMIC TEACHING OF LIST

THE economic and political situation in Germany during List's lifetime presented some obvious analogies with that of the United States during the first years of its separate existence. In both cases there were a number of distinct commercial and fiscal entities with more or less political independence. The States, however, attained both commercial and political union at an early stage by the establishment of the federal constitution; while Germany had to build up her Zollverein by slow degrees, and did not gain full political unity till 1871. But just as the Napoleonic War had given an artificial stimulus to some German industries at the cost of the German consumer, so the continental blockades, Jefferson's Embargo of 1807, the Non-Intercourse Act of 1809, and the consequent war with England greatly hampered the international trade of the United States, raised prices, and gave an impulse to home manufactures, which were also aided by the withdrawal of capital from the hazards of shipping and commerce. In

their subsequent development American manufactures progressed with the rapid growth of population as it spread over vast tracts of free land;
whereas in Germany the movement for internal
free trade long overshadowed the demand for
protection against foreign competition.   Rabbeno
points out that the older founders of the Zollverein
worked for "freedom of internal commerce and
a united customs administration, with a protective
policy as a subordinate and occasional expedient
to turn the flank of foreign rivalry." Nebenius
was himself a theoretical free trader and follower
of Adam Smith, though he considered that at the
stage of development which Germany had reached,
and in view of the customs barriers in other
countries, a temporary protective tariff might
foster her "infant" industries. List, in a passage
already quoted, acknowledged in unstinted measure
his indebtedness as an economist to observation
of American conditions; he is silent regarding the
influence of American writers, but this was no
doubt also an important factor in his mental
development. His change of view is clearly shown
in his published writings. Five years before his
visit to America he wrote two addresses to the
Federal Congress on behalf of the Handelsverein
(1819–20); his "Outlines of American Political
Economy" appeared in 1827, and in 1837, six years
after his return to Europe, he wrote the essay for

the French Academy which formed the basis of the "National System." In the addresses to the Bund he pleads for the abolition of all internal customs, and advocates import duties only as a means of retaliation against foreign countries until they shall have "adopted the principle of European free trade." But he makes an important reservation as to the universal validity of free-trade principles. They are true, he says, in theory and would be true in practice if the world were free trade; but in the case of a country like Germany, surrounded by states which bar out her products while flooding her with their own, the consequent export of precious metals must weaken her, so that it would not necessarily be an economic error to shut out the foreign product even if by so doing the price were raised to the consumer. Thus in 1820, List, although a theoretical free trader, favoured the practice of retaliation and had doubts as to the validity of free trade for his own nation.

The chief writers on economics whose works would come in his way during his residence in America were Alexander Hamilton, Thomas Cooper, Matthew Carey, and Daniel Raymond. Cooper's "Lectures on Political Economy" (1826), written with some ability in a spirit of dogmatic free trade and individualism, roused all List's antagonism, and his own "Letters" of 1827 were

intended to refute this book. He refers to it
again in the "National System," being especially
severe on Cooper's description of the word
"nation" as a mere "grammatical invention."

Daniel Raymond of Baltimore published in 1820
"Thoughts on Political Economy," which went
through four editions in the next twenty years.
Matthew Carey and other leading Protectionists
praised the book warmly, since its practical conclusions pointed towards an increased tariff. As
a matter of fact, it has little value from either a
literary or scientific standpoint, and its main
thought—the distinction between public and private
economy—is borrowed from earlier writers, Sir
James Steuart, Lauderdale, and Ganilh. But many
of Raymond's arguments bear a striking resemblance to those afterwards urged with greater
ability by List. He attacks Adam Smith on the
ground that his system is individual, not political,
economy, for the political economist must regard
the nation as an organic unity. He rejects Adam
Smith's theory of value, and his distinction between
productive and unproductive employments, and
with them his arguments for free trade, declaring
that national wealth consists not in commodities
but in "capacity," which can be best attained by
the harmonious development of agriculture and
manufactures within the nation. Hence it is the
duty of the American Government to take active

steps by means of tariffs and subventions to attain the desired end. A careful American student[1] has summed up the question in his statement that " Raymond and List hit upon the same principles as the basis of their system of political economy; that Raymond had given his principles to the public some years before List had shown evidence of having conceived similar ideas; and that List only gave his system to the world after he had had such opportunities for becoming acquainted with Raymond's work that it is difficult to believe he did not actually have a knowledge of it."

Matthew Carey, father of the more famous Henry Carey, was an Irish immigrant, who became a leading citizen of Philadelphia and founded there a great publishing house. It still survives, after various changes, as Lea Brothers and Company. Carey, who was strongly anti-English and Protectionist, became the moving spirit and President of the Pennsylvania Society for the Promotion of Manufactures and the Mechanic Arts. In this capacity (perhaps also through his friendship with Lafayette) he made the acquaintance of List, who must almost certainly have known some at least of the copious series of pamphlets and addresses

[1] *Vidè* p. 63 in "Daniel Raymond, an Early Chapter in the History of Economic Theory in the United States," by Charles Patrick Neill. Baltimore, 1897.

I

issued by him from the year 1819 onwards. Many
of them bore the imprimatur of the Pennsylvania
Society. Some of the arguments with which List
himself made most play in the "Outlines" and later
writings are reiterations and adaptations of Carey's
lively polemics. The enlightened policy by which
Russia protected her industry, the decline of Spain
and Portugal, nations which still clung to a system
of free trade, the fallacies of Adam Smith, and
the ruin entailed on countries if they followed the
system of buying in the cheapest market—all these
appear in Carey's pamphlets, and in the pages of
the *Weekly Register* published by his friend and
fellow-worker, Hezekiah Niles of Baltimore. In
passing, a curious circumstance may be noticed.
Throughout the tariff controversy of 1827–28 Niles,
anxious as he seems to have been to collect
Protectionist arguments and illustrations from all
quarters, never once alludes to List, to the "Outlines," to the Harrisburg address, or to the projected work on political economy. A short and
slightly ill-natured notice in 1831 of the Senate's
refusal to ratify his appointment at Hamburg is
the only passage in the journal where List's name
appears. The inference is that such consistent
silence was intentional, and the German exile had
not hit it off with the American editor.

Among the early American writers on economics
and finance Alexander Hamilton stands first in

chronological order and first, too, in importance. The celebrated "Report on Domestic Manufactures" (1791) had been republished in 1824 by the Philadelphia Society, with a preface by Matthew Carey. A second edition followed in November, 1827. The Report is sufficiently well known to require only a brief notice here, and must surely have been read by List, although he does not mention it either in the "Outlines" or in the "National System." In the notes to this edition of the former the chief resemblances of thought are pointed out. Both the American and the German maintain that free trade to be beneficial must be universal, that manufactures and agriculture benefit one another, for the former assures a home market to the latter, and—quoting Adam Smith—the home market is the most important of all markets for the produce of the soil. They agree that protective duties increase the productive powers of a nation, and that the high prices they cause are only temporary and will be lowered by internal competition. Both disapprove of excessive protection, while the five conditions which Hamilton requires in the case of any article to be protected are stated by List, less definitely indeed, but with practical agreement.[1] The differences are equally marked : Hamilton founds his argument on expediency, List mainly

[1] See Letter V. in the "Outlines," and the note quoting Hamilton.

on his theory of nationality. Hamilton prefers
bounties to taxes, and is willing to protect agriculture; in the "National System" List shows little
favour to bounties and distinctly refuses to admit
the claim of agriculture to protection. Professor
Eheberg ascribes the resemblances merely to the
influence of List's American experiences. "It is
obvious," he says, "that if List knew Hamilton's
'Report' he would find in it confirmation of the
accuracy of his own views; but he had no occasion
to borrow Hamilton's ideas, since he had formed
similar ones before his arrival in America. Besides, Hamilton could not influence the new theories
which List added to his old ones in these 'Letters,'
for they have no similarity to those in his
'Report.' The beneficial influence exerted on
List by his stay in America arose from practical
circumstances, not from printed books."[1] This
argument would be more convincing if the "similar
ideas" had appeared in List's writings before he left
Germany. Eighteen years later, in the preface to
the "National System," he declared that they arose
in his mind during his work for the Handelsverein;
but as the account of his American and French
experiences in the same passage contains several
obvious inaccuracies, too much weight must not be
given to this assertion. The "new theories,"
again, in the "Letters" have a striking resemblance

[1] Eheberg's introduction to the "National System," p. 149.

to those of Carey and Raymond. It is difficult to avoid the conclusion that Hamilton, Raymond, and Carey had a strong positive, and Cooper a strong negative influence upon List's later work. His practice of only mentioning other economic writers to criticise them accounts for his silence regarding the three first-named. Such a conclusion in no way affects List's leading merits. The arguments for which Raymond and Carey could only arouse a passing interest were clothed by List's eloquence with such attraction that for sixty years they have been able to sway the policy of nations. In the United States, however, tariff policy underwent too many fluctuations to show the influence of a consistent theory. The "tariff of abominations" marked the highest wave of the first protectionist period, and the protests of the South gave weight to a free trade movement. The tariff of 1832 was intended to keep the protection at a more moderate level, but it had to yield in 1833 to the "Compromise," which was largely the work of Henry Clay. The Compromise provided for a gradual reduction of duties until 1842, and a rapid decline in that year to a twenty per cent. average. The Whigs who then succeeded to office brought in a distinctly protectionist tariff, which was, however, modified in 1846. Indeed this tariff is generally considered by American historians as free trade, although Professor Taussig more reasonably describes its average of twenty-four per cent. as moderate protection. It was still further reduced in 1857, after which the United States enjoyed until 1861 the nearest approach to free trade that it has had since 1816. Tariff conditions since 1861 have been quite exceptional; Professor Taussig has shown "how the exigencies of the Civil War caused duties to be greatly increased; how these high duties were retained and even increased in an unexpected and indefensible way, and how the tariff, as it now stands, is still in the main the product of war legislation. A history of the existing tariff is simply a history of the way in which the war duties were retained, increased, and systematized, and of the half-hearted attempts at reduction which have been made from time to time."[1]

The last question which arises in connection with America is List's relation, if any, to Henry Charles Carey. Professor Gustav Schmoller, in an article on Carey,[2] assumed that the "National System" was the principal source of Carey's ideas; and Professor Marshall formerly gave some support to this view. But in the last edition of his "Principles of Economics" (1907) he says only that Carey's indebtedness to List is a disputed point.

[1] Taussig, "Tariff History," p. 155, 1889.
[2] "Zur Litteraturgeschichte der Staats- und Sozialwissen-schaften," 1888.

Mr. Carey-Baird, a grandson of Carey, has dealt with the matter in a somewhat vehement pamphlet.[1] His main arguments against the assumption may be briefly summarized. Carey's early books, from 1835, were free trade. He did not pronounce for protection until 1848 in "The Past, the Present, and the Future," but none the less his books show a harmonious development of principle. The working of the tariff of 1842 convinced him of the expediency of protection ; but he could not reconcile it to economic theory until 1847, when he evolved his well-known doctrine of land cultivation and rent. "Lying in bed one morning, picturing to himself the settlers on the sides of the hills moving down into the valleys, and approaching each other, as wealth, power, and civilization grew, he realized the vital importance of bringing the consumer to the side of the producer, and as he said to me, 'I jumped out of bed, and, dressing myself, was a protectionist from that hour.'" As to List, Carey did not know German until 1856, so that he did not read the "National System" before 1851, when Richelot published a French translation. Carey's copy of the work, now in the Library of the University of Pennsylvania, is little marked, and he apparently made small use of it. "A great admirer of Frederick List for what he had done in building up the German Empire—a work without

---

[1] "Carey and Two of his Recent Critics," 1891.

which Bismarck, Von Moltke, and William I.
would never have been heard of in history—Carey
had but a poor opinion of List's 'National System
of Political Economy,' for the very good reason that
it lacked just what he had aimed to present in his
own books . . . broad, deep, and enduring fundamental principles, interlocked and interwoven into
one grand and harmonious whole, like Carey's
own great and noble ' Principles of Social Science.'
Indeed no such voluminous writer as Carey has
ever lived and written who has paid so little heed
to the writings of other economists." Mr. Baird's
piety leads him into some exaggerations, but there
is no doubt that part of the external evidence goes
strongly against the influence of List on Carey.
On the other hand, Carey's ignorance of German
would not prevent him from reading List's English
"Outlines," and remembering the father's intimate
connection with List during the tariff controversy
of 1827–28, it seems strange that the son (who was
head of the firm from 1821 to 1835) should not know
of him until 1851. There are certainly marked
similarities of argument between Carey's later
writings and List's "Outlines" and the "National
System." The late Professor Rabbeno made
the interesting comment that many of Carey's protectionist arguments are far more suited to the
epoch between 1820 and 1830 (that is, to the period
covering List's activity in America) than to the

time at which he actually wrote. Points of resemblance (some of these, indeed, may be traced
back to Hamilton) are, the importance of the home
market and of a varied development of industry,
the beneficial influence of manufactures on agriculture, the idea that nations must pass through four
stages of economic progress, and a general belief
in the economic enmity of nations, and especially
in the oppression of America (or Germany) by
England.

There are also minor resemblances : both writers
are uncritical and unscientific in their treatment of
facts and authorities ; both are much dominated by
existing political conditions. But List stands on
firmer ground than Carey ; he founds himself on
his doctrine of nationality and productive power,
while Carey's protectionism is inextricably mingled
with his theory of value and wages, and his belief
in economic harmony and in the importance of
association for industrial progress. He went so
far as to oppose international copyright, on the
ground that producers and consumers of books
ought to live within the same country. In one
respect he is more logical than List, for he supports
the taxation of corn and raw materials. Indeed, in his
view all foreign trade is bad, and the ideal country is
isolated and self-supporting. At times he seemed
to agree with List that free trade is the ultimate
ideal, but unlike List he considered no country yet

ready for it.   Even England, he thought, had injured herself and her customers by its adoption.   As a general rule protection was to him a lasting maxim of politics, and although he declared in the preface to his "Principles of Social Science" that protection would bring about entire free trade, his conception of free trade was peculiar to himself. "Protection looks to raising the value of labour and thus promoting the annexation of individuals and the establishment of perfect free trade between ourselves and the peoples of Europe, *by inducing them to transfer themselves to our shores.*"

It is in the "National System" that the most exhaustive, though perhaps not the final, statement of List's ideas is to be found.   Soon after its publication List was accused by Brüggemann of being a mere plagiarist from the romantic reactionary Adam Müller.   They had met at Vienna in 1820.   But Müller, who seriously proposed to revert to the economic and politic system of the Middle Ages, could have had little sympathy with List's enthusiasm for manufactures and steam transport.   Knies says of the two men ("Politische Oekonomie," p. 194), "they are the forward and backward-looking faces of a Janus-bust, their opposition to Adam Smith is the line of connection between them."   On another point List had been anticipated.   Rau, in his "Studies in Economics" (1820), had distinguished four different periods of national development, which bear a general resemblance to List's four "stages."

The "National System" as it stands consists of a preface, introduction, and four books. Two more books were planned, "The Politics of the Future," and "The Influence of Political Institutions on National Wealth and National Power," but we can only guess their general tenor from the essays contributed by List to the *Allgemeine Zeitung* and the *Zollvereinsblatt* during the last four years of his life. The preface is of importance in the light it throws on the author. It professes to give the history of his opinions, but the account is not always strictly accurate. After a description of his part in the foundation of the Handelsverein, and a refutation of claims made on behalf of others to be the originators of the scheme, he says that it was during his two years' work for the society that he conceived the distinction between cosmopolitical and national economy as well as the theory of productive powers. His accounts of his American and French experiences have already been summarized. After a short apology for the imperfections of his book, which he did not wish to delay longer, and an expression of gratitude to his friends Kolb and Cotta for the opportunities they have granted him for the publication of his opinions, he proceeds to refute the common report that he is a mercantilist. He has only re-stated the truth in the mercantile theory; for he is an eclectic, and in his book the valid arguments of Smith and his school first find their proper setting.   He has no wish to attack living German economists—but this restraint is atoned for by some sharp, and indeed arrogant, criticisms of the dead.   Even his former colleague Rotteck does not escape, and Nebenius alone (who was still living) receives some qualified commendation for his work on the Zollverein.   German economists, however, List says, have this to their credit : they have grasped the fact that there is a special economy of the nation which they include under "Polizeiwissenschaft."   In a short digression he pauses to lavish unmeasured praise on a young student, Alexander von der Marwitz, who died prematurely in 1810.   On the strength of some letters in which the boy of twenty-four passed judgment on the "narrowness and tediousness of Adam Smith," List entitles him Germany's greatest political economist.   This leads to an attack on Adam Smith, who introduced a spirit of sophistry, confusion, and hypocrisy into political economy, nay, even burned his papers on his deathbed for fear lest they should betray his true opinions !   This assumption has proved too much for later German protectionists, and Dühring has put forward the counter-supposition that Adam Smith was an orderly man, and burnt his papers merely to save his executor trouble.

The main difference, List continues, between his teaching and that of the cosmopolitan school is the idea of nationality, the nation as a link between the individual and mankind. In his exposition he has had one aim before all others, that of making the subject popular. "If the theory of political economy is to help national interests it must forsake the studies of learned men, the lecture-rooms of professors, the cabinets of statesmen, and resort to the offices of manufacturers, merchants, and shipowners, the bureaux of public servants, the homes of agriculturists, and most of all, to the chambers of the legislature. In a word, it must become the common property of all educated men." With this end in view, he had cultivated a simple style, and was shocked when a friend, after reading part of the manuscript, remarked that it had some "fine passages." "I did not want to write fine passages. A fine style does not suit national economy. It is no improvement, but a mistake, for it has often been misused to hide unsound or weak logic and to give sophistical arguments the force of deep principles." Nor has he quoted many authors, although he has read widely. He ends with an appeal to the German nobility to take to heart the example of England, and help in the creation of a Germany founded on freedom and national unity.

The Introduction, which is translated in this

volume, gives a summary of List's economic belief and teaching. Book One, "The History," is based upon the essay for the French Academy, and deals with the economic development of Italy, the Hanse towns, the Netherlands, England, Spain and Portugal, France, Germany, and North America. The conclusion is (p. 108)—

"History teaches us how nations which Nature has endowed with all resources necessary to attain the highest grade of wealth and power, may and must—without abandoning the end in view—modify their systems according to the measure of their own progress: in the first stage adopting free trade with more advanced nations as a means of raising themselves from a state of barbarism, and of making progress in agriculture; in the second stage fostering the growth of manufactures, fisheries, shipping, and foreign trade by means of commercial restrictions; and in the last stage, when they have reached the highest level of wealth and power, gradually reverting to the principle of free trade and unrestricted competition in both home and foreign markets, so that their agriculturists, manufacturers, and merchants may be kept from indolence and stimulated to retain the supremacy they have won. In the first stage, we see Spain, Portugal, and the Kingdom of Naples; in the second, Germany and the United States; France seems to be very near the last stage; but Great Britain is the only country which has actually reached it."

In the seventeen chapters of the Second Book, "The Theory," List labours with much repetition to establish a distinction between cosmopolitical and political economy, and his theory of productive powers is expounded in its relation to the activities of the nation. Here occurs the famous attack on Adam Smith's definition (carefully limited and explained by its author) of "productive labour" (p. 128)—

"The man who rears pigs is thus a productive, the man who teaches men is an unproductive, member of society. He who prepares bagpipes or jews-harps for sale is a producer, the greatest virtuosos are non-productive, because the harmonies they evoke cannot be brought to market. The physician who saves the lives of his patients does not belong to the class of producers, but the chemist's boy does, although the exchange-values (the pills) which he produces may only exist for a few minutes before they become valueless. A Newton, a Watt, or a Kepler is less productive than an ass, a horse, or a plough-ox (labourers who have lately been included by Mr. McCulloch among the ranks of the productive members of society)."

Book Three, "The Systems," criticizes first the Italian economists, represented by Macchiavelli, Serra, and Beccaria, then the industrial (List's name for the mercantile) system, that of the Physiocrats, and the system of "values of exchange" formulated (according to List) by Adam Smith, J. B. Say, and "the School." Book Four, "The Politics," deals with the malignant influence of England's "insular supremacy" on the manufactures of the Continent and North America, and with the future commercial policy of the Zollverein.

List's main arguments are, in brief, as follows:
The nation is a separate entity whose interests
are not necessarily the same as those of individuals,
but to whom individual interests must yield.
National wealth consists not in the quantity of
"exchange values" or commodities that a nation
possesses, but in the development of its productive
powers.   The highest national well-being demands
the equal and harmonious development of agriculture, manufactures, and commerce, which can
only take place in a state possessing political
freedom, popular education, and effective means
of transport.   But only the countries of the
temperate zone are suited to this development,
while the tropics have a natural monopoly of certain
products.   Hence they become two non-competing
groups between which exchange can take place.
Temperate countries, again, all pass through four
stages of development: pastoral; agricultural;
agricultural and manufacturing; agricultural, commercial, and manufacturing.   The same economic
system is not suited to all the stages.   In the
early development of a nation free-trade is beneficial; the exchange of raw materials for manufactures stimulates agriculture and arouses higher
wants.   When the country has begun to manufacture
for itself the State must provide a suitable system
of protection under which, shielded from the
competition of stronger rivals, the industries can

develop. When they have gained sufficient strength the protection must be withdrawn, to admit the healthy influence of competition. The moral for Germany was the need of economic union for all German states, the extension of her boundaries to the sea by way of Belgium, Hamburg, and Austria, the establishment of a national marine and national railway system, and the furtherance of industry by a moderate and temporary protective tariff.

Neither in form nor in substance is the book scientific. List was neither accurate nor consistent, and in reading his remarks on England or on early commercial history it is difficult not to feel that his mind was warped, and that he was apt to make history to fit and illustrate his theories. His account of the results of the Eden Treaty, for example, almost reverses the facts; and he is always more ready to quote the compilations of party writers than to consult the actual statistics of trade and commerce. The argument *post hoc, ergo propter hoc* occurs only too often in his pages, while his account of English commercial policy is curiously perverse. It has been well said by a recent writer,[1] "The theory is that 'England' in the eighteenth century was skilfully building up equally each of her great national industries by vigilant protection. In reality there was not in existence any such political organization as List

[1] Mr. J. M. Robertson, "Trade and Tariffs," pp. 49 and 70.

K

imagines.   There was merely a chronic clamour
of self-seeking classes in Parliament. . . ."   And
though we can hardly join in the censure of List
as a deliberate distorter of history, it is impossible
not to agree that it was a "vain chimera" that
his mind created when he saw England as "an
entity with one continuous will and one high
conception of national interest, conscious of destiny
and sagaciously preparing for freedom by con-
straint."

Professor Eheberg, in his learned introduction
to the seventh German edition, made some moderate
and valuable criticisms of the chief flaws and limitations in List's arguments.   Professor Nicholson, in
his Preface to Mr. Lloyd's translation, has met
most of the attacks upon Adam Smith ; and immediately upon the appearance of the book, John
Austin dealt trenchantly with its superficial contradictions.   His answer to List's charge of English
hypocrisy is still worth quotation.   "The enlightened minority which has contended for a
liberal policy, and the majority which has stuck
steadily to the wisdom of our ancestors are,
according to him, one party : and out of the one
party formed by the confusion of two contending
parties, he makes a fictitious personage whom he
calls England.   Accordingly England is playing
the part of a double dealer.   She preaches the
principles of free trade to the other nations of

the world and would fain persuade them to take her manufactures, but she still means to stick to her own restrictive policy, and has not the smallest wish for their raw products."[1] Even from this brief account it is plain that List's protection is not an end, or final state, but a means. It would not be necessary but for the conflict of national interests and the danger of war. Inverting a popular free trade argument, he says that a condition of perpetual peace would necessarily bring with it universal free trade. Wars have a double influence in favour of protection. They call into existence home industries, which on the restoration of peace require the support of a tariff (an obvious allusion to the long Napoleonic war and the condition of Germany in 1815), while the constant danger of war makes it necessary for each nation to be able to provide itself with the means of support. It is hardly consistent with this last argument to find that List rejects the idea of protection to agriculture. He certainly underestimated the development of transport, believing that many agricultural products (among them butter and meat) enjoyed a strong natural protection. But the chief arguments in chapter seventeen in favour of free imports of food and raw materials are, notwithstanding his disclaimers, just as applicable to the benefits of free exchange

[1] *Edinburgh Review*, July, 1842, vol. 75.

in general. He disapproves of retaliation, "a principle which would lead to the most absurd and ruinous measures," except in so far as it can be used as a means of establishing manufactures— that is, as protection, not as retaliation proper.

The most curious example of inconsistency is List's view of the proper scale for customs duties. In one passage he endorses the general opinion that there is a difference between "the case of a nation which contemplates passing from a policy of free competition to one of protection, and that of a nation which proposes to exchange a policy of prohibition for one of moderate protection: in the former case the duties at first must be low, and be gradually increased; in the latter they must be high at first, and be gradually diminished." But within a few pages he asserts that "where any technical industry cannot be established by means of an original protection of forty to sixty per cent., and cannot succeed in maintaining itself under a continued protection of twenty to thirty per cent., the fundamental conditions of manufacturing power are lacking."

With all its faults of temper, inaccuracy, wordiness, and repetition, the book has a singular charm. The freshness of style and the enthusiasm of the writer combine to emphasize its truths, while they cast a glamour over its errors. Roscher declared that List was not merely the prince of

journalists, but a great prophet, even if he sometimes laboured under a false inspiration. As a
prophet he helped to call into life the German
railway system and the German Zollverein, and to
arouse the spirit of national unity which thirty
years after the publication of the " National System "
led to the foundation of the Empire.

This chapter may conclude with a few sentences
from the eloquent eulogy which Professor Eheberg
uttered at the unveiling of the Kufstein memorial
in 1906. " List was fitted as few have been to read
in the book of the world. He went through life
with his eyes open for all political and economic
phenomena, and each impulse he received he
passed on to others. His intercourse with statesmen, scholars, merchants, and manufacturers of
all nations gave breadth, depth, and diversity to his
knowledge, and continuously influenced by and
active in the daily affairs of life, he grew to be a
great economist, a far-sighted politician, a most
effective and brilliant writer. . . . An important
society of German merchants informed us that it
could not subscribe to the statue because, in view
of the present protectionist tendencies in the
Empire, the time was inopportune to do honour to
the champion of protection. One hardly knows
whether to smile or sigh over such want of understanding. Many circles in Germany and Austria
connect List's name almost exclusively with the

struggle for free trade or protection, and rightly in so far as List was the first and most important advocate of protection. Under his influence, consciously or unconsciously, Prince Bismarck broke with free trade in 1879, and his utterances are still the most incisive weapons in the protectionist camp. Rightly too, in so far as List realized that Germany could receive no economic impulse, make no economic progress, until she became a united commercial territory, and her crushing internal tolls were exchanged for the uniform customs boundary. No sensible man can blame him for wishing to foster the budding German industries, crushed as they were by the overwhelming English output. But those entirely misunderstand List who look on him as a mere protectionist. He was never a man of cast-iron views. 'If I had been an Englishman,' he said himself, 'I should have been a free trader.' He always had before him as the goal of his endeavours universal free trade."

PETITION TO THE FEDERAL ASSEMBLY
OUTLINES OF AMERICAN POLITICAL ECONOMY

AND

INTRODUCTION TO THE NATIONAL SYSTEM

INTRODUCTORY NOTE

THE Letters on American Political Economy were originally published during the month of July, 1827, in the *Philadelphia National Journal*, from which they were copied by papers throughout the States. They were reprinted at the instance of the Pennsylvania Society for the Promotion of Manufactures, in two pamphlets, the "Outlines of American Political Economy," containing Letters I. to VIII. (40 pages), and the "Appendix to the Outlines," containing Letters IX. to XI. (13 pages). The letters of Jefferson and Madison added by the publisher to the first pamphlet deal with the general question of the tariff and State rights, but have no obvious connection with List's work.

His speech is contained in a third pamphlet, "Account of the Dinner given to Professor List." All three are so scarce as almost to have attained the rank of bibliographical curiosities. Two petitions to the Federal Assembly are reprinted in Häusser's selection from List's writings ("Gesammelte Schriften"). One (translated here) is the firstfruits of his work for the Handelsverein, written at Frankfurt in April, 1819; the other, a part of his unwearied activity at Vienna from January to May, 1820.

The introduction to the "National System" (published 1841) is the nearest approach List ever made to a co-ordinated and complete exposition of his theory of economics.

PETITION ON BEHALF OF THE HANDELS-VEREIN TO THE FEDERAL ASSEMBLY, APRIL, 1819

THE humble petition of the German merchants and manufacturers, met together at Frankfort-on-Main for the Easter Fair of 1819, for the removal of all custom-duties and tolls in the interior of Germany, and the establishment of a universal German system founded on the principle of retaliation against foreign states. Presented by Professor List of Tübingen as agent for the petitioners.

Worshipful Federal Assembly. (1) We, the undersigned German merchants and manufacturers met together at the Fair in Frankfort, approach with deep respect this the highest representative assembly of the German nation in order to set forth the causes of our suffering and to beg for help. In a country where it is common knowledge that the majority of manufacturers are either entirely ruined or drag on a precarious and burdensome existence, where the fairs and markets are filled with foreign wares, where merchants have almost lost their occupation, there is little need of detailed proof to show the intensity of the evil. The ruinous condition of German trade and manufactures must be due either to individuals or to the conditions of society. But who can reproach the German with lack of talent or industry? Is he not proverbial for these qualities among all the nations of Europe? Who can deny his enterprise? Did not those towns which now serve as the instruments of foreign competition once conduct the trade of the world? (2) It is only in the faults of the social organization that we can find the cause of the evil.

Rational freedom is the first condition of all human development, whether physical or mental. As the individual mind is hampered by restrictions on the exchange of ideas, so the prosperity of nations is impaired by the fetters which are placed on the production and exchange of material goods. Not until universal, free, and unrestricted commercial intercourse is established among the nations of the world will they reach the highest degree of material well-being. If, on the other hand, they wish to become irrecoverably weak, then let each not only impede, but entirely destroy the import, export, and transport of goods by means of prohibitions, duties, and embargoes. A certain opinion has become a dogma among statesmen, although all experienced merchants and manufacturers are convinced of its error. It is that internal industry can be created by taxes and dues.

Such imports, on the one hand, act as premiums for the smuggler who can simultaneously defeat the main and the secondary aim of the statesman—the advancement of home industry and the raising of revenue. On the other hand, they recoil on the home industry, because the taxed country can lay similar restrictions on the products of the taxing country. Of course, when the other state does not retaliate, but suffers itself to be stripped and ruined by prohibitions or high duties, then the policy may be advantageous. This is the case among our neighbours; encircled by the custom barriers of England, France, and Holland, Germany can do nothing effective to help the cause of universal free trade, by means of which alone Europe can reach the highest stage of civilization. But the German people impose still narrower restrictions upon themselves. Thirty-eight customs boundaries cripple inland trade, and produce much the same effect as ligatures which prevent the free circulation of the blood. The merchant trading between Hamburg and Austria, or Berlin and Switzerland must traverse ten states, must learn ten customs-tariffs, must pay ten successive transit dues. Any one who is so unfortunate as to live on the boundary-line between three or four states spends his days among hostile tax-gatherers and custom-house officials; he is a man without a country.

This is a miserable condition of things for men of business and merchants. They cast envious glances across the Rhine where, from the Channel to the Mediterranean, from the Rhine to the Pyrenees, from the Dutch to the Italian borders, a great nation carries on its trade over free rivers and free roads without ever meeting a custom-house official. Customs and tolls, like war, can only be justified as a means of defence. But the smaller the country which imposes a duty, the greater is the loss, the more harmful the effect on national enterprise, the heavier the cost of collection; for small countries are all boundary. Hence our thirty-eight customs boundaries are incomparably more injurious than a line of custom-houses on the external boundary of Germany, even if in the latter case the imposts were three times as heavy. And so the power of the very nation which in the time of the Hansards carried on the world's trade under the protection of its own fleet, is now ruined by the thirty-eight lines of customs.

We think that we have brought forward sufficient reasons [to prove to your august assembly that only the remission of the internal customs, and the erection of a general tariff for the whole Federation, can restore national trade and industry or help the working classes.

The chief objection generally made to such a measure is the expected loss to the revenues of the individual states. But this objection is easily met.

(1) Up to the present no Government has openly affirmed that it imposes dues and customs with the single aim of raising money : rather, the preambles of most tariffs declare that the duties are levied for the promotion of native industry. But if we can prove that they are the cause of its ruin, then the secondary consideration that they are a source of revenue can be no reason for their continuance.

(2) Much of the loss will be covered by the revenue from the Federal tariff. The rest could— much to the advantage of the states as well as of the manufacturing and trading interests—be raised through direct taxes. The Governments will thus be saved from a harassing branch of administration, and the citizens will gain the considerable amount that is now absorbed in cost of collection.

(3) Looking at the matter from a higher standpoint than that of the financier, the advantages of removing internal customs appear far more important. It is generally recognized that the evasion of customs is no longer considered culpable even by men of high character. The individual is forced into an attitude of war against the tariff, and fights it with the weapons of deceit. But nothing is more prejudicial to national character than for Governments to force their subjects,

particularly their educated subjects, to break accepted moral laws. Nothing is more derogatory to the power of the State than to force a part of the civil service (the customs officials) into a position of hostility towards the public.

(4) Finally, the nature of the German Federation calls for such action as we have proposed. The aim of the Federation is to unite the forces and interests of all the German peoples for defence against enemies from abroad and the promotion of national well-being at home, in so far as these objects cannot be attained by the separate Governments. But it is not only foreign armies which endanger national interests—foreign tariffs are the canker worms which devour German prosperity. In our view federal obligations include defence not merely through armies but through a tariff. A federation of states, like any other society of citizens, will remain a mere name if it does not found itself upon a community of individual interests. Hence we consider the internal dues of Germany (which fall as heavily on other German states as on the foreigner) to be fetters, and as long as they remain they will prevent all national prosperity or national patriotism.

In addition we venture to allude to the cause of our humble remonstrance, viz. the new Prussian tariff. (3) This tariff, we admit, at first sight filled us and all Germany with the greatest consternation, for it seemed directed not so much against French and English as against German trade. The duties are imposed according to weight. But since the trade of foreign lands with Prussia is mainly in fine goods, while the adjoining states, whose manufactures have been already stunted by English competition, sell to Prussia mainly coarse goods of considerable weight, it follows that the duty paid by foreign countries amounts on the average to 6 per cent., while her German neighbours generally pay 25 per cent. to 30 per cent., nay, even 50 per cent., which is as effective as an express prohibition. The transit duties, too, fall as heavily on our traders. However, we recovered from our consternation when we reflected that by the strict maintenance of this tariff law German industry would be absolutely ruined, and that it is sharply opposed to the spirit of the German federation. The Prussian Government, from the geographical position of its country, is forced beyond all other states to wish for perfect freedom of trade in Germany, so we cannot but conclude that the tariff aims at compelling the rest of the country to adopt this measure. The suspicion becomes certainty when we observe that Prussia is prepared to make separate commercial treaties with her neighbours.

Your petitioners recognize in this an important signal to call their attention to the necessities of the situation, and they therefore venture most humbly to request the Federal Assembly that (1) the inland duties and tolls should be remitted, but (2) a tariff system should be established based on the principle of retaliation against foreign nations, until such time as they too recognize the principle of European free trade. Your humble petitioners realize that the injurious effects of the inland customs on individual states, towns, and branches of trade and industry should be explained in greater detail. They will, on their return to their several homes, undertake this exposition with the aid of the general body of merchants and manufacturers, and will publish it in due course as a supplement.

We remain, with expressions of the greatest loyalty to your honourable assembly.

[Here follow the signatures of seventy German merchants and manufacturers from Saxony, Bavaria, Württemberg, Electoral Hesse, Baden, Hesse-Darmstadt and Nassau.] A large number (4) of signatures of merchants and manufacturers in full accord with this petition are not yet to hand. The pressing need of the occasion forbids us to wait for them, and they will be presented later.

Frankfort, April 14, 1819.

NOTES.

Page 137. (1) *Federal Assembly*. It consisted of delegates from the Governments of the various states belonging to the German Confederation (founded 1814), under the Presidency of Austria. It soon became a mere tool in the hands of the reactionary rulers.

Page 138. (2) *These towns*, *i.e.* the Hanse towns.

Page 142. (3) *The new Prussian tariff* introduced May 26, 1818, which abolished internal taxes and established a uniform customs boundary. Huskisson said of it (House of Commons, May 7, 1827), "We are told of the Prussian prohibitions against, and high duties on, British merchandise. What are the facts? First, the transit duties in Prussia are very moderate, not exceeding one-half per cent.; secondly, the duties on the internal consumption of British goods are what we should consider very low—upon most articles fluctuating from five to ten per cent.—upon no one article, I believe, exceeding fifteen per cent.; and thirdly, there is not, in the whole Prussian tariff, a single prohibition. I trust that the time will come when we shall be able to say as much for the tariff in this country."

Professor Eheberg, in his introduction to List's "National System" (pp. 72, 73), gives a description of the tariff. In the "National System," chapter vii., List himself gives it high praise for its effect upon Prussian industry.

Page 144. (4) *A large number*. List's petition was followed on July 1, 1819, by one presented on the part of E. W. Arnoldi of Gotha, signed by more than 5000 merchants and manufacturers.

OUTLINES

OF

AMERICAN POLITICAL ECONOMY

IN A

SERIES OF LETTERS

ADDRESSED BY

FREDERICK LIST Esq.

LATE PROFESSOR OF POLITICAL ECONOMY AT THE UNIVERSITY OF TUBINGEN, IN GERMANY

TO

CHARLES J. INGERSOLL Esq.

VICE-PRESIDENT OF THE PENNSYLVANIA SOCIETY FOR THE PROMOTION OF MANUFACTURES AND THE MECHANIC ARTS

TO WHICH IS ADDED

THE CELEBRATED LETTERS

OF Mr. JEFFERSON TO BENJAMIN AUSTIN, AND OF Mr. MADISON TO THE EDITORS

OF THE

LYNCHBURG VIRGINIAN

PHILADELPHIA

PRINTED BY SAMUEL PARKER, No. 48, MARKET STREET

1827

LETTER I

Dear Sir,

Feeling myself honoured by your requisition, I would not have hesitated a moment to comply with it, had I not been prevented by a temporary illness. After having recovered, I hasten to communicate to you the results of my reflections on political economy, produced not only by a study of many years, but also by long practical exertions in my capacity as a counsellor of the Society of German Manufactures, for the purpose of obtaining a system of German National Economy.

After having perused the different addresses of the Philadelphia Society (1) for the Promotion of National Industry, the different speeches delivered in Congress on that subject, *Niles' Register*, (2) etc. etc., it would be but arrogance for me to attempt a supply of practical matters, so ingenuously and shrewdly illustrated by the first politicians of the nation ; I confine my exertions, therefore, solely to the refutation of the theory of Adam Smith and

Co., the fundamental errors of which have not yet been understood so clearly as they ought to be.

It is this theory, sir, which furnishes to the opponents of the American System the intellectual means of their opposition. It is the combination of the *soi-disant* theorists with those who believe themselves interested in the *soi-disant* free commerce, which gives so much seeming strength to the opposite party. Boasting of their imaginary superiority in science and knowledge, these disciples of Smith and Say are treating every defender of common sense like an empiric whose mental power and literary acquirements are not strong enough to conceive the sublime doctrine of their masters. Unfortunately, the founders of this dangerous doctrine were men of great minds, whose talents enabled them to give their castles in the air the appearance of strong, well-founded buildings. The important truths they brought to light were the unhappy cause which gave to their whole system the credit of a doctrine too elevated to be questioned by future generations. This doctrine, sir, was embraced by the greater part of those who made politics their particular study, and after having admired a doctrine for ten or twenty years, found it difficult to divest themselves of it. It requires a mind of perfect independence to acknowledge that for so long a time we gave full credit to an erroneous system, particularly if that system is advocated by private interests.

In consequence of this exposition, I believe it to be a duty of the General Convention at Harrisburg, not only to support the interests of the wool growers and wool manufacturers, but to lay the axe to the root of the tree, by declaring the system of Adam Smith and Co. to be erroneous—by declaring war against it on the part of the American System—by inviting literary men to uncover its errors, and to write popular lectures on the American System—and, lastly, by requesting the Governments of the different states, as well as the general Government, to support the study of the American System in the different colleges, universities, and literary institutions under their auspices.

The last work of Dr. Cooper (3) shows pretty clearly the necessity of such measures on the part of the supporters of the American System. According to this work (a mere compilation), you and I, and all the gentlemen of the convention, and all the supporters of the American System, are nothing else than idiots; for it is "*ignorance* to support an industry by duties when the commodities may be procured cheaper by foreign commerce,"—"ignorance if a Government guards and protects the industry of individuals," etc., etc.

(See p. 195, where you find *eleven ignorances* recorded which you make applicable to yourself by going to Harrisburg.) This, sir, is now the only elementary work from which our youth and people may learn the principle of what is styled political economy. What fruit can be expected from such seed? And if the supporters of the American System are convinced of the superiority of their doctrine, is it not their duty to go on theoretically as well as practically? Ought they not to procure for the people, and especially for the youth of their country, elementary works and professional teachers, explaining the principles of political economy according to their own system, (4) which must ultimately prevail in proportion as the national legislature becomes convinced of its propriety?

I remember an anecdote of a physician, who, finding his patient consulting a medical work about his disease, admonished him to take care not to die of an error in print. So, sir, I would admonish the people of these United States who rely on the celebrated systems of Smith, to take care not to die of a *beau ideal*. Indeed, sir, it would sound almost like sarcasm if, in after ages, an historian should commemorate the decline of this country in the following terms :—

"They were a great people; they were in every respect in the way to become the first people of our earth ; but they became weak and died, trusting in the infallibility of two books imported into the country, one from Scotland, the other from France—books, the general failure of which was shortly afterwards acknowledged by every individual."

As the idea of denouncing in the name of an enlightened community that theory of political economy would be useless if this denunciation cannot be supported by sufficient evidence of its failure, I feel it my duty to submit to the examination of your superior mind the following views. The short space of time and room allowed for my communications permit me only to touch on the topics of the science.

In consequence of my researches, I found the component parts of political economy to be (1) individual economy; (2) national economy; (3) economy of mankind. Adam Smith treats of individual economy and economy of mankind. He teaches how an individual creates, increases, and consumes wealth in society with other individuals, and how the industry and wealth of mankind influence the industry and wealth of the individual. He has entirely forgotten what the title of his book, "Wealth of Nations," promised to treat. Not taking into consideration (5) the different state of power, constitution, wants and culture of the different nations, his book is a mere treatise on the question : how the economy of the individuals and of mankind would stand if the human race were not separated into nations, but united by a general law and by an equal culture of mind. This question he treats quite logically ; and in this supposition his book contains great truths. If the whole globe (6) were united by a union like the twenty-four States of North America, free trade would indeed be quite as natural and beneficial as it is now in the union. There would be no reason for separating the interests of a certain space of land, and of a certain number of human beings, from the interests of the whole globe and of the whole race. There would be no national interest, no national law contrary to the freedom of the whole race, no restrictions, no wars. All would flow in its natural current. English capital and skill, if in superabundance in that island, would overflow to the borders of the Seine and Elbe, of the Rhine and Tagus ; they would have fertilized the woods of Bohemia and Poland long before they would flow to the borders of the Ganges and of the St. Lawrence, and everywhere carry along with them freedom and law. An Englishman would as readily emigrate to Gallicia and Hungary as now a New-Jerseyman emigrates to Missouri and Arkansas. No nation would have to fear for their independence, power and wealth from the measures of other nations.

This state of things may be very desirable; it
may do honour to the heart of a philosopher to
wish for it; it may even lie in the great plan of
Providence to accomplish it for after ages. But,
sir, it is not the state of the actual world. Adam
Smith's system, in the world's present condition,
goes therefore along with the good Abbé St.
Pierre's (7) dream of eternal peace, and with the
systems of those who fancy laws of nations. I
myself believe it indeed to be a postulate of reason,
that nations should settle their differences by law
as now the United States do among themselves.
War is nothing but a duel between nations, and
restrictions of free trade are nothing but a war
between the powers of industry of different nations.
But what would you think, sir, of a Secretary of
War, who, embracing the doctrine of the Friends,
should refuse to build fortresses and men-of-war,
and to supply military academies, because mankind
would be happier if there were no war on earth?
And yet, sir, the conduct of this Secretary of War
would be just as wise as the conduct of those who,
embracing the system of Adam Smith in its present imperfection, leave their national interests to
the direction of foreign nations and foreign laws,
because in a more perfect but entirely imaginary
state of the human race, free trade would be
beneficial to mankind. (8) I am yet by no means
of opinion, sir, that Adam Smith's system, in a

scientific view, is without its merits. I believe, on the contrary, that the fundamental principles of the science could only be discovered by his researches in the economy of individuals and of mankind. His error consists in not adding to those general principles the modifications caused by the fraction of the human race into national bodies, and in not adding to the rules the exceptions, or to the extremities the medium member. Economy of individuals and economy of mankind, as treated by Adam Smith, teach by what means an individual creates, increases, and consumes wealth in society with other individuals, and how the industry and wealth of mankind influence the industry and wealth of individuals. *National economy* teaches by what means a certain nation, in her particular situation, may direct and regulate the economy of individuals, and restrict the economy of mankind, (9) either to prevent foreign restrictions and foreign power, or to increase the productive powers within herself; or, in other words, how to create, in absence of a lawful state, within the whole globe of the earth, a world in itself, in order to grow in power and wealth to be one of the most powerful, wealthy, and perfect nations of the earth, without restricting the economy of individuals and the economy of mankind more than the welfare of the people permits.

In my next letter I shall dwell more upon this subject. For the present remains but space enough to request your indulgence on account of my inability to express myself correctly and eloquently in the language of this country.

Very respectfully your most humble servant,

FR. LIST.

NOTES TO LETTER I

Title-page 147. *Charles Jared Ingersoll* (1782–1862) was a leading citizen of Pennsylvania. From 1815 to 1829 he was United States District Attorney for the State. He took an active part in politics, and was appointed Secretary of Legation to Prussia in 1837. From 1841 to 1847 he was a member of Congress, and in 1847 was appointed United States Minister to France, but the appointment was not ratified by the Senate.

Page 148. (1) *Addresses of the Philadelphia Society*. Amongst these the Society published in 1824, Alexander Hamilton's "Report," edited, with a preface, by Matthew Carey. This reached a second edition in 1827.

Page 148. (2) *Niles' Register*. Hezekiah Niles (1777–1839) founded *Niles' Register*—a Baltimore weekly—of which he remained editor till 1836. "*Niles' Register*, which had said little about the tariff before 1819, thereafter became a tireless and effective advocate of protection" (Taussig, "Tariff History of the United States," p. 70, note).

Page 150. (3) *Dr. Cooper*. Thomas Cooper, M.D., LL.D., a well-known Republican and man of science ; b. London, 1759 ; d. South Carolina, 1839. He was educated at Oxford, studying law and medicine. At the time of the Revolution he was sent with James Watt by the democratic clubs of England to greet those of France. He sided with the Girondists, and his Republican sympathies brought him into conflict with Burke. A friend of Priestley, he emigrated to America in 1795, and landed in Philadelphia, afterwards becoming Professor of Chemistry and Political Economy in Columbia College, South Carolina. He wrote works on law politics, and political economy. In politics he supported Jefferson, Madison, and Monroe, and was an ardent advocate of the claims of the South and of "State rights." A speech made by him at Charlestown attacking the tariff proposals of 1827–28 attracted much attention. The "last work" was "Lectures on the Elements of Political Economy" (1826), of which McCulloch said in his "Literature of Political Economy," "This work, though not written in a very philosophical spirit, is the best of the American works on political economy that we have ever met with."

Page 151. (4) *Their own system.* List himself acted on these principles, both as Professor in Tübingen (1819), and in his contributions to the *Staatslexicon* (1833).

Page 152. (5) *Not taking into consideration.* This statement is far from correct. "The Wealth of Nations" abounds in comparisons and contrasts of different nations, and their different conditions. See, for example, Book I. chaps. i., v., viii., ix., etc.

Page 153. (6) *If the whole globe.* Cp. Hamilton's "Report on Manufactures," p. 26 (ed. of 1825). "If the system of perfect liberty to industry and commerce were the prevailing system of nations, the arguments which dissuade a country, in the predicament of the United States, from the zealous pursuit of manufactures would doubtless have great force. . . . A free exchange, mutually beneficial, of the commodities which each was able to supply on the best terms might be carried on between them, supporting in full vigour the industry of each."

Page 154. (7) *The Abbé St. Pierre.* Charles Rénée Castel, Abbé de St. Pierre (1658–1743), man of science, philosopher, and philanthropist, published 1712–1716 a "Projet de Paix Perpetuelle." It was praised by Leibnitz and Rousseau, the latter writing a critical exposition of the scheme in his edition of the Abbé's works.

Page 154. (8) *Beneficial to mankind.* This, of course, overlooks the view that it may be beneficial to single nations. Cobden said, "It is our policy to receive from every country, and if foreign countries exclude us, it is only a stronger reason why we should throw open our ports more widely to them" (Dundee, January 16, 1844). Again, "I remember at the last stage of the Corn Law agitation, our opponents were driven to this position, ' Free Trade is a very good thing for us, but you cannot have it until other countries have it too ; ' and I used to say, ' If Free Trade be a good thing for us, we will have it. Let others take it if it be a good thing ; if not, let them do without it ' " (January 10, 1849).

Page 155. (9) *Restrict the economy of mankind.* Cp. " Congressional Debates," May 28, 1834, McDuffie. " This idea of a conflict between domestic and foreign industry is the lurking fallacy which lies at the very foundation of the American system."

LETTER II

Reading, July 12, 1827.

Dear Sir,

As soon as the three component parts of political economy are revealed, the science is brought to light, and the errors of the old theory are clear. The object of individual economy is merely to obtain the necessities and comforts of life. The object of economy of mankind, or to express it more properly of *cosmopolitical economy*, is to secure to the whole human race the greatest quantity of the necessities and comforts of life. An individual living in Pennsylvania, considered solely as a part of mankind, has no particular interest that wealth and productive powers should be increased rather in Vermont, or Maine, than in England. If this individual happens to be the agent of a foreign manufactory, he may even be injured in his livelihood by the growing industry of his next neighbours. Nor is mankind interested which spot of the earth, or which people excels in industry; it is benefited by every increase of industry, and restrictions are as obnoxious to mankind at large, as restrictions of the free intercourse between the twenty-four United States would be injurious to the wealth and productive powers of this nation. The idea of *power* is neither applicable to an individual, nor to the whole human race. If the whole globe were to be united by a general law, it would not be of any consequence to a particular people, as regards its freedom and its independence, whether it is strong or weak in population, power and wealth ; as it is now, it is of no consequence for the State of Delaware, as regards her freedom and independence, that her wealth, population and territory are ten times surpassed by her next neighbours, the State of Pennsylvania.

This, sir, is the theory of Adam Smith and of his disciple, Dr. Cooper. Regarding only the two extremities of the science they are right. But their theory provides neither for peace nor for war, (1) neither for particular countries nor for particular people ; they do not at all recognize the fracture of the human race into nations. In this sense Mr. Say (2) censures the Government of his country for having employed French ships in carrying French military stores from Russia to France, whilst the Hollanders would have done it fifteen francs per ton cheaper.

The benefit arising from these shipments for our navy, he adds, regards not *economy*, it regards *politics !* And as disciples are commonly in the

habit of surpassing their masters in hardy assertions, some of our members of Congress asserted
quite seriously that it would be better to import
gunpowder from England, if it could be bought
cheaper there than manufactured here. I wonder
why they did not propose to burn our men-of-war,
because it would be better economy to hire, in
time of war, ships and sailors in England. In the
same sense our American champion of the old
theory, Mr. Cooper, drops, in his lecture on political economy, the notable sentence: "Politics, it
must be remembered, are not essentially a part
of political economy" (see p. 15). What would
Dr. Cooper, the chemist, think if I should venture
to say that "Chemistry, it must be remembered, is
not essentially a part of chemical technology."

Indeed, so wrong are these adherents of the
Scot's theory, that in spite of the very name they
chose to give their science, they will make us
believe that there is nothing of politics in political
economy. If their science is properly called *political economy*, (3) there must be just as much *politics*
in it as *economy*, and if there is no *politics* in it, the
science has not got the proper name; it is then
nothing else than *economy*. The truth is that the
name is right, expressing the very thing these
gentlemen mean to treat, but the thing they treat
is not consonant to the name, they do not treat
political economy, but *cosmopolitical* economy.

M

To complete the science we must add the principles of national economy. The idea of national economy arises with the idea of nations. A nation is the medium between individuals and mankind, a separate society of individuals, who, possessing common government, common laws, rights, institutions, interests, common history, and glory, common defence and security of their rights, riches, and lives, constitute one body, free and independent, following only the dictates of its interests, as regards other independent bodies, and possessing power to regulate the interests of the individuals, constituting (p. 15) that body, in order to create the greatest quantity of common welfare in the interior and the greatest quantity of security as regards other nations. The object of the economy of this body is not only wealth and individual and cosmopolitical economy, but power and wealth, (4) because national wealth is increased and secured by national power, as national power is increased and secured by national wealth. Its leading principles are therefore not only economical, but political (5) too. The individuals may be very wealthy; but if the nation possesses no power to protect them, they may lose in one day the wealth they gathered during ages, and their rights, freedom, and independence too. On a mere economical view, it may be quite indifferent to a Pennsylvanian whether the manufacturer who gives him cloth in exchange for wheat lives in Old England or in New England; but in time of war and of restriction, he can neither send wheat to England nor import cloth from there, whilst the exchange with New England would for ever be undisturbed. If the manufacturer grows wealthy by this exchange, the inhabitant of Old England increases the power of his enemy in time of war, whilst the manufacturer of New England increases the defence of his nation. In time of peace the farmer of Pennsylvania may do well in buying English guns and gunpowder to shoot game; but in time of war the Englishman will not furnish him with the means to be shot.

As power secures wealth and wealth increases power, so are power and wealth, in equal parts, benefited by a harmonious (6) state of agriculture, commerce and manufactures within the limits of the country. In the absence of this harmony, a nation is never powerful and wealthy. (7) A merely agricultural state is dependent for its market as well as for its supply on foreign laws, on foreign good-will or enmity. Manufactures, moreover, are the nurses of arts, sciences, and skill, the sources of power and wealth. A merely agricultural people remain always poor (says Say himself); and a poor people having not much to sell, and less with which to buy, can never possess a flourishing commerce, because commerce consists in buying and selling.

Nobody can deny these truths. But it is questioned, sir, whether Government has a right to restrict individual industry in order to bring to harmony the three component parts of national industry; and, secondly, it is questioned whether Government does well or has it in its power to produce this harmony by laws and restrictions.

Government, sir, has not only the right, but it is its duty, to promote everything which may increase the wealth and power of the nation, if this object cannot be effected by individuals. So it is its duty to guard commerce by a navy, because the merchants cannot protect themselves; so it is its duty to protect the carrying trade by navigation laws, because carrying trade supports naval power, as naval power protects carrying trade; so the shipping interest and commerce must be supported by breakwaters; agriculture and every other industry by turnpikes, bridges, canals, and railroads; (8) new inventions by patent laws; so manufactures must be raised by protecting duties, if foreign capital and skill prevent individuals from undertaking them.

In regard to the expediency of protecting measures, I observe that it depends entirely on the condition of a nation whether they are efficacious or not. Nations are as different (9) in their conditions as individuals are. There are giants and dwarfs, youths and old men, cripples and well-made persons; some are superstitious, dull, indolent, uninstructed, barbarous; others are enlightened, active, enterprising, and civilized; some are slaves, and others are half-slaves, others free and self-governed; some are predominant over other nations, some independent, and some live more or less in a state of dependency. How wise men can apply general rules to these different bodies, I cannot conceive. I consider so doing no wiser than for physicians to prescribe alike to a child and a giant; to the old and young in all cases the same diet and the same medicine.

Protecting duties in Spain (10) would deprive the Spanish nation of the trifling industry she yet retains. Having no navy, how could she support such measures? A dull, indolent, and superstitious people can never derive any advantage from them, and no foreigner of a sound mind would submit his capital and his life to a brutal absolute power. Such a Government can do nothing better than translate Dr. Cooper's work in order to convince the people that *laissez faire* and *laissez passer* is the wisest policy on earth. Mexico and the southern republics would act with equal folly by embracing in their present situation the manufacturing system; a free exchange of their raw materials and of the precious metals for foreign manufactures is the best policy to raise the industry and minds of those people, and to grow wealthy. Surely everybody would laugh, if either should advise the Switzer to make navigation laws, the Turks to make patent laws, the Hanse towns to create a navy, and the Hottentot or Indians to make railroads. Even the United States, after having just converted themselves from a colony to an independent nation, did well to remain for a while in economical vassalage. But after having acquired the strength of a man it would be absurd to act as a child, as the Scripture says: "When I was a child, I acted as a child, but when I became a man I acted as a man."

The condition of this nation cannot be compared with the condition of any other nation. The same kind of government and same structure of society were never seen before; nor such general and equal distribution of property, of instruction, of industry, of power and wealth; nor similar accomplishments in the gifts of nature, bestowing upon this people natural riches and advantages of the north, of the south, and of the temperate climates, all the advantages of vast seashores and of an immense unsettled continent, and all the activity and vigour of youth and freedom. There is no people, nor was there ever a people, doubling their number every twenty-five years, doubling the number of their states in fifty years, excelling in such a degree of industry, skill, and power, creating a navy in a few years, and completing in a short time public improvements which, in former times, would alone have distinguished a nation for ever.

As the condition of this nation is unexampled, the effects of her efforts to raise manufactures will be without example ; while minor states must submit to the English naval ascendency, the Americans can raise their heads and look it full in the face. If poor, uninstructed, indolent and depressed people cannot rise by their own efforts, this free, enterprising, instructed, industrious, and wealthy people may. If other people must restrict their ambition to live in a tolerable dependence and economical vassalage, this nation would do injustice to the call of nature if it should not look up to full independence, (11) if it should not aspire to an unexampled degree of power to preserve its unexampled degree of freedom and happiness. But a high degree of power and wealth, a full independence, is never to be acquired, if the manufactured industry is not brought into harmony with agricultural and commercial industry. Government would therefore not only do well in supporting this industry, but wrong in not doing it.

American national economy, according to the different conditions of the nations, is quite different from English national economy. English national economy has for its object to manufacture for the whole world, to monopolize all manufacturing power, even at the expense of the lives of her citizens, to keep the world, and especially her own colonies, in a state of infancy and vassalage by political management as well as by the superiority of her capital, her skill, and her navy. American economy has for its object to bring into harmony the three branches of industry without which no national industry can attain perfection. It has for its object to supply its own wants by its own materials and its own industry; to people an unsettled country; to attract foreign population for capital and skill; to increase its power and its means of defence in order to secure the independence and the future growth of the nation. It has for its object, lastly, to be free and independent (12) and powerful, and to let every one else enjoy freedom, power, and wealth as he pleases. English national economy is *predominant;* American national economy aspires only to become *independent.* As there is no similarity in the two systems, there is no similarity in the consequences of it. The country will not be overstocked with worthless goods any more than it is now overstocked with cabinet ware; the manufactories will not produce vice, because every labourer can earn enough to support his family honestly; nobody will suffer or starve from want of labour; therefore if the labourer cannot earn enough to support his family otherwise, he can cultivate the earth. There is yet room

enough for hundreds of millions to become independent farmers.

After having explained the fundamental error
of Smith and Say in confounding *cosmopolitical*
economy with *political* economy, I shall attempt to
demonstrate in my next letter by what errors both
of these celebrated authors have been induced to
assert that a nation's wealth and industry cannot
be increased by restriction.

Very respectfully, your most humble and
obedient servant,

FR. LIST.

NOTES TO LETTER II

Page 160. (1) *Neither for peace nor for war.* The whole
argument of this letter rests upon the assumption of the necessity
of war.

Page 160. (2) *Mr. Say.* In his "Principes d'Économie politique,"
I. chap. ix., he takes the instance of hemp, and does not call it a
military store. He adds, "It is hardly necessary to caution the
reader that I have throughout been considering maritime industry
solely in its relation to national wealth. Its influence upon national
security is another thing."

Page 160. (3) *If their science is properly called political
economy.* The modern tendency is to call it rather *economics*.
"From whatever point of view we look at it, political economy is
best described as a *social* science; and if a distinction is drawn
between social and political science, it must, notwithstanding its
name, be regarded as belonging to the former, and not to the latter
category" (Keyne's "Scope and Methods of Political Economy,"
p. 91).

Page 162. (4) *Power and wealth.* "National System," Book II. chap. xii. "The power of producing wealth is infinitely more important than wealth itself," and many other passages.

Page 162. (5) *Political.* Hamilton, "Report," p. 20. "The substitution of foreign for domestic manufactures is a transfer to foreign nations of the advantages accruing from the use of machinery in the modes in which it is capable of being employed with most utility, and to the greatest extent.

Page 163. (6) *Harmonious.* This idea is developed in the "National System," Book II. chaps. xiii., xvii., xx. "The agricultural power of production is so much greater the more intimately a manufacturing power, developed in all its branches, is united locally, commercially and politically with agriculture. . . . We call this relation the balance or harmony of the productive powers" (chap. xiii.).

Page 163. (7) Hamilton "Report," p. 20. "The mere separation of the occupation of the cultivator from that of the artificer, has the effect of augmenting the productive powers of labour, and with them the total mass of the produce or revenue of a country.

Page 164. (8) List does not consider whether any of these results can be attained by voluntary effort.

Page 164. (9) *Nations are as different.* Cp. "National System," II. chap. xv. "An infinite difference exists in the conditions and circumstances of the various nations: we observe among them giants and dwarfs, well-formed bodies and cripples, half-civilized and barbarous peoples : but in all of them, as in the individual human being, exists the impulse of self-preservation, the striving for improvement which is implanted by nature. It is the task of politics to civilize the barbarous nationalities, to make the small and weak ones great and strong, but above all to secure to them existence and continuance. It is the task of national economy to accomplish the economical development of the nation, and to prepare it for admission into the universal society of the future."

Page 165. (10) *Spain.* Yet in the "National System," I. chap. v. List maintains that the protective system in vogue in Spain during the eighteenth century under Bourbon rule greatly promoted the development of Spanish manufactures.

Page 167. (11) *Independence.* Cp. Hamilton, "Report," p. 46. "Not only the wealth, but the independence and security of a country appear to be materially connected with the prosperity of manufactures. Every nation with a view to these great objects ought to endeavour to possess within itself all the essentials of a national supply. These comprise the means of subsistence, habitation, clothing, and defence.

Page 168. (12) *Independent.* On this theory, List would now advocate free trade for America.

LETTER III

Reading, July 15, 1827.

DEAR SIR,

The system of Adam Smith has assumed
so great an authority that those who venture to
oppose it, or even to question its infallibility,
expose themselves to be called idiots. Mr. Say,
throughout his whole work, is in the habit of
calling all objections to his sublime theory the
opinion of the rabble, vulgar views, etc., etc.
Mr. Cooper on his part, probably finding it not
quite proper to speak in this country as much as
the Parisian about rabble population, etc., uses the
term "ignorance." He regrets very much that both
the Pitts, as well as Mr. Fox, were such block-
heads as not to conceive even the fundamental
principle of the sublime theory. These infallible
theorists assure us, as gravely as modestly, that
minds like those of Edward III., Elizabeth, Col-
bert, Turgot, Frederick II., Joseph II., Pitt, (1)
Fox, Napoleon Bonaparte, Washington, Jefferson,
Hamilton, a chart of the minds of the most
enlightened men of all ages, were not enlightened

enough to comprehend the true principles of political economy. Though, therefore, an opponent of Mr. Say finds himself in tolerable good company amongst the ignorant, yet I consider it necessary to state that, during many years I was not only a very faithful disciple of Smith and Say, but a very zealous teacher of the infallible doctrine ; that I not only studied the works of the masters, but also those of their ablest disciples in England, Germany, and France, with some assiduity and perseverance, and that I did not become a convert till arrived at the age of maturity. I saw then in my native country the admirable effects of what is called the continental system and the destroying effects of the return of what they call trade after the downfall of Napoleon. German industry, though fostered but partially by the continental system, because enjoying protection only against English competition and remaining exposed to French competition, whilst the borders of France were closed to it, made admirable progress during that time, not only in the different branches of manufactured industry, but in all branches of agriculture, which, though labouring under all the disadvantages of the wars and of French despotic measures, were flourishing. All kinds of produce were in demand and bore high prices, and wages, rents, interest of capital, prices of land, and of every description of property were consequently enhanced. But after the downfall of the continental system, after having acquired the enjoyment of English goods a great deal cheaper than the nation could manufacture them, the manufactures languished. The agriculturists and noble land proprietors were at first much pleased to purchase at so low a price, particularly the wool growers who sold their wool to England at very high prices. The principles of Smith and Say were highly talked of. But the English, after having acquired the German market for their manufactures, did not hesitate to foster their landed interests too by corn and woollen bills; the price of wool and grain, and in consequence rents, wages, and property in Germany sunk more and more, and the most ruinous effects followed. At the present day agricultural produce is three or four times cheaper there than under the continental system, and property has scarcely any price at all. The wool grower and agriculturist, as well as the manufacturers, are ruined, and under present circumstance they are not able to procure a third part of the quantity of cheap English goods that they enjoyed formerly of the higher priced domestic manufactures. The contemplation of these effects induced me first to doubt of the infallibility of the old theory. My eyes being not sharp enough to discover at a glance the errors of a system so ingeniously built up and supported by so many valuable truths, I judged the tree by its fruit. I conceived that, as a theory in medicine, however ingeniously invented, and however supported by brilliant truths, must be fundamentally erroneous if it destroys the life of its followers, so a system of political economy must be wrong if it effects just the contrary of that which every man of common sense must be supposed to expect from it. In consequence of this conviction I came out openly against the followers of this theory, and so popular was this opposition that in a few weeks a society of many thousands of first-rate manufacturers, merchants, etc., dispersed throughout the whole ancient German Empire, was founded, for the purpose of establishing a system of German national economy. Elected their counsellor I visited, accompanied by deputies of the society, the different courts of Germany (and the Congress of German Ministers held at Vienna in 1820) in order to induce the several Governments of the necessity of such a system. All people, in the interior, were convinced at last of this necessity, agriculturists, wool growers, proprietors of estates, as well as manufacturers. No opposition was heard anywhere, except in the Hanse towns and in the city of Leipzig, and even there none but the agents of English firms and the bankers, whose momentary interests were at stake, took part in this opposition. These adversaries of the common welfare were headed and supported by a few learned disciples of Smith and Say, who, either offended in their literary pride by the opposition against a theory, the development and illustration of which formed their literary renown, or bound by personal interests and by their situation, still rode on the old hobby-horse of free trade, and harped upon its beneficial effects, whilst free intercourse was checked in every possible way by foreign restrictions. The most enlightened theorists of the interior, on the contrary, gave way to the principles of the society, and many of them (particularly Count Soden, (2) the most celebrated German author in political economy) contributed much valuable matter for a weekly journal (3) I edited at that time in order to prepare the public mind for a national system. All the German Governments of the second and third rank (except Hanover and the Hanse towns) were at last convinced of its necessity, and a preliminary treaty adapted to the interests of the nation was concluded in 1820 at Vienna. If this treaty is not carried into effect even now, it is only to be ascribed to the difficulties of executing such a treaty amongst different states, each independent of the other and not enjoying the advantages of a general legislature for their common interests. But if rumour speaks truth, the present King of Bavaria, a ruler who excels as much by his enlightened views and strength of character as by his liberal sentiments towards the welfare of the whole German nation, will soon overcome those difficulties. Being in duty bound during several years (4) to contend every day against the disciples of Smith and Say, all parts of the old theory were at last revealed by these exertions, and that perseverance and circumstances effected what humble talents never would have performed.

I trouble you, sir, by this long apology in order to excuse myself for having undertaken with such humble means so great a task as the refutation of the literary productions of the most celebrated men in political economy. I travelled in the same way which the patriots of the United States did, and in which even Say found a powerful opponent in his countryman, the Count Chaptal, (5) a chemist and statesman, who by his researches in chemistry as well as by his political exertions did more for the promotion of the industry of France than even one man did in any other country. Read, I request, Chapter XV. (vol. i.) of his celebrated work, "de l'Industrie Française" (1819), and you will find there a most practical and material refutation of Say's theory, though he appears not to oppose him directly.

I hope the authority of men like Chaptal will, even in the minds of those who are in the habit of giving more credit to names than to argument,

N

be some excuse to me for having undertaken this task, and perhaps some inducement to others to enter into an impartial investigation of these arguments. For those who are in the habit of alleging the late wonderful conversion of the English Ministry to the system of Smith and Say, in order to prove its all-conquering and irresistible power, I only state here the results of my reflections, reserving to myself to treat in another letter upon that interesting subject, and upon the English national economy generally. These results are: that the seeming adherence of Messrs. Canning and Huskisson (6) to Messrs. Say and Smith's theory, is one of the most extraordinary of first-rate political manœuvres that have ever been played upon the credulity of the world. These gentlemen, with cosmopolitical principles on their lips, design to persuade all other Powers to cede their political power in order to render England's productive and political power omnipotent. Mr. Canning went to Paris (7) with Mr. Say's treatise in his hands, showing to M. de Villele (8) the chapters according to which it would be most beneficial to mankind if he, Mr. Villele, would place the whole French manufactural interests at his, Mr. Canning's, mercy, for the benefit of importing wines and spirits into the British Empire. Now, sir, what would have been the consequence, or what will be the consequence, if the French minister were complaisant enough to become a second time the dupe of Mr. Canning? The French manufactories, and with them the French manufacturing skill and power, would undoubtedly be destroyed in a few years. It is true the French would sell, and therefore produce and manufacture, a great deal more of wines and spirits than they did before. But, sir, will it not afterwards lie in the power of Mr. Canning, or of any other succeeding Premier of England, to destroy this wine market in one hour? And if destroyed, either by a restrictive law or by an open war, can the French then take up their manufactural power in the same hour in which the English are destroying their wine-markets? No, sir; it would take ages and hundreds of millions to build it up again. Would, in consequence of this, France, from the day of the agreement of the treaty, not feel herself as dependent upon England, as Portugal feels since the day of the celebrated treaty of Mr. Methuen, in 1703, with the agreement of which she converted her condition as an independent state into the condition of being the vineyard and province of England? It is even very likely Mr. Villele would learn after a short time from the *Courier* of London, that Mr. Canning had made a speech in Parliament, containing a boast that Mr. Villele had been duped by him in so vital a question, as was the case last year respecting his political course in regard to the occupation of Spain by French troops. These two cases are, indeed, admirably parallel. When Spain was about to be invaded by French troops, Mr. Canning, adverting to the law of nation, said, it was against those laws for England to interfere in this affair; but last year, in a fit of self-praise, asserted freely in open Parliament, (9) that he had played a trick upon the French Government, by engaging it in Spain, charging it with the occupation of that country, and by weakening and paralyzing thereby its power, by that trick enabling himself to call the Republics of South America into existence, and to open an immense market to the English manufactories. Well done, Mr. Canning, but after having revealed the true motives of your respect for the law of nation, will not every man of common sense, and, I hope, Mr. Villele too, divine the true motives of your respect for the principles of cosmopolitical economy? It is not very cunning, indeed, to boast publicly of having duped those whom we wish to dupe again, as the only profit a man can derive from having been duped is to learn not to be duped a second time; and I would consider this, on the part of Mr. Villele, by far a better plan than to request Mr. Canning to alter his speech, and to make it different from what it was in its delivery.

I hope to have said enough on the subject to prevent every American citizen from participating in the enthusiasm of President Cooper, when alluding to the wonderful conversion of Messrs. Canning and Huskisson.   Indeed, there is no event which could do more essential injury to the glory of Mr. Say and of his system than the carrying of the same into practice by the cunning of Mr. Canning.   I am sure the history of his country would not transmit his name as a public benefactor, convinced as I am that free trade with England, in the present state of things, would do more injury to the independence of France than the two invasions of the Holy Alliance.

Before I enter again into the matter itself, I must make some further observations to show how it was possible that this theory could assume such a degree of authority over the learned men of all nations.   Mr. Smith brought many a valuable truth to light, never before acknowledged, and his work contains many beauties on detached matters, which are written with superior talent, sagacity, and experience.   These merits were the more creditable to his system as it was the only substitute for the system of the economists, the failure and weakness of which was acknowledged by mankind.   The literary world wanted a system of political economy, and Mr. Smith's was the best extant.   Dictated by a spirit of cosmopolitism, it was laid hold of by the age of cosmopolitism, in which it made its appearance.   Freedom throughout the whole globe, eternal peace, rights of nature, union of the whole human family, etc., were the favourite subjects of the philosophers and philanthropists. Freedom of trade throughout the whole globe was in full harmony with those doctrines. Hence the success of Smith's theory. It moreover afforded a fine consolation to the weaker nations. Not having power enough to support a national system, they made an appeal to the beloved system of free trade, as they appealed to Grotius and Vattel, to Puffendorff and Martens, if they had not strength to defend themselves by the argument of the bayonet. It was, lastly, a very easy task to enter into its mysteries; they could be delineated in some few phrases: "Remove the restrictions from industry—make it free —let it alone." After these precepts were given, it required neither great talents nor great exertions, nor much practice, to act the part of a very wise statesman. You had nothing else to do but to let everything go as it pleased—to let everything alone—for being numbered amongst the most wise and most learned men upon earth. That is an easy task indeed. For such a system of passive regulations the great men of England could have no taste, as Mr. Fox confessed in Parliament; being unwilling to let things go as they would, and to let everything alone: those men intended to raise their country in wealth and power, by their political measures, beyond all reach of competition by other nations.

And if in our days the great men of England affect to embrace the system of Adam Smith (by parliamentary speeches (10) only, not by facts), they do nothing else than Napoleon would have done if he, in the midst of his glory and of his power, should have proposed to the nations of the earth the disbanding of their armies and the dismantling of their fleets, in order to live in general peace together as brothers and friends, who could have no interest in slaying and murdering each other, and in injuring the general welfare by keeping up, at heavy expense, the means of war.

But the world has advanced wonderfully in experience and intelligence since the time of Adam Smith. Between him and us lie the American and French revolutions—the English omnipotence on the sea and the French omnipotence on the European continent, the restoration of the old Government in France, the Holy Alliance, and the emancipation of the South American republics. A new people, with a new form of government and new ideas of general welfare and freedom, has arisen. This people has learned by a general and free discussion of every political matter, to distinguish the true from the false, visionary system from clear perceptions, cosmopolitical from political principles, sayings from doings. This people cannot be accused of selfishness if it intends to rise by its own exertions to the highest degree of power and wealth without injuring other nations, but likewise without taking upon themselves the charge of promoting the welfare of mankind, because if it should not pursue that policy its standing amongst the powerful nations of the earth, and its whole system of society, would be lost. Napoleon would have been very willing to charge himself with the trouble of uniting the whole surface of the earth, and to procure to the human race the blessings of a general free intercourse, but the English, it seems, did not like the prospects of such a general happiness. So the Americans, I suppose, would never like to exchange their national independence and power for a general law of nations founded upon English power—they would not like the prospect.

It seems, therefore, cosmopolitical institutions, like those of free trade, are not yet ripe for being introduced into practice. First, it must be decided whether the social system of Napoleon, or that of England, or that of the United States will prevail on earth. Several centuries may yet elapse before this decision is effected, and those who act seriously as if it were really effected may be very honest, very high-minded men, but they are short-sighted politicians. Desiring to serve the cause of humanity they ruin their country. History will censure them for having separated national economical views from national political views, as it censures Poland for having sold her independence and power for the benefit of selling wine, as it laughs at Esau for having sold his primogenitive birthright for a mess of pottage rather than to rely on his own power for procuring the means of existence.

After this long digression I shall re-enter into the matter itself in my next letter.

I am most respectfully,

Your obedient servant,

Fr. List.

NOTES TO LETTER III

Page 172. (1) *Turgot and Pitt.* The one a friend, the other (as he called himself) a "scholar" of Adam Smith, appear oddly enough in this catalogue.

Page 176. (2) *Soden.* Friedrich Julius Heinrich, Reichsgraf von Soden (1754-1831). A Prussian official till 1796, when he retired owing to a disagreement with the Government. He took up the study of Political Economy at the desire of Karl Friedrich of Baden. His "National-Oekonomie," 9 vols., 1805-1824, arose out of a review of the "Wealth of Nations." In the main he accepts Smith's theories, but he does not always state them correctly. Though he condemns mercantilism, prohibition, and high duties, he is not an unconditional free trader. He disparages the form of the "Wealth of Nations," and considers Smith "narrow and insular."

Page 176. (3) *A weekly journal. Organ für den deutschen Handels- und Gewerbesstand.*

Page 177. (4) *Several years.* But List's activity as Consulent lasted only from April, 1819, to July, 1820.

Page 177. (5) *Count Chaptal.* Jean-Antoine, comte de Chanteloup (1756–1832). A famous French chemist and follower of Lavoisier. During the Revolution he was a Girondist, but became Minister of the Interior under the First Consul.

Page 178. (6) *Messrs. Canning and Huskisson.* The charge is amplified in the " National System," I. chap. vi., note, and IV. chap. xxxiii.

Page 178. (7) *Paris.* His second visit in 1827 is meant here.

Page 178. (8) *Villele.* Comte de (1773–1854). The leader of the French Ministry, 1821.

Page 180. (9) *In open Parliament.* An allusion to the famous speech of December 12, 1826, in which Canning exclaimed, " I called the New World into existence to redress the balance of the Old." It is curious that List's version is much closer to the misquotations of Lord Grey in the House of Lords Debate, May 6, 1827, than to Canning's actual speech. Canning said, " The House knows—the country knows—that when the French army was on the point of entering Spain, His Majesty's Government did all in their power to prevent it ; that we resisted by all means short of war. . . . If France occupied Spain, was it necessary in order to avoid the consequences of that occupation that we should blockade Cadiz ?" Earl Grey said, he " found in the speech published by Mr. Canning that he had connived at the invasion of Spain by France," and quoted it as, " If I allowed France to occupy Spain, was it necessary that we should blockade Cadiz ?" (" Political Life of Canning," by Stapleton, vol. iii. pp. 401–8).

Page 183. (10) *Parliamentary speeches.* Canning, in his Budget Speech, June 1, 1827, after pledging himself to reform, quoted a speech of Pitt in 1792, " in which that great man speaks of Adam Smith as an author whose writings from his extensive knowledge of detail, and depth of philosophical research, furnished the best solution to every question connected with the history of commerce. Sir, we hear often nowadays that the application of philosophy to the affairs of trade is an innovation. I, however, am content to go back to the year 1792, and to take the words that I have now quoted into my mouth, words which were then used by Mr. Pitt, which I have treasured up in my mind, and to adopt them as the guide and pole-star of my own policy."

LETTER IV

Reading, July 18, 1827.

DEAR SIR,

In re-entering into the matter itself, I am disposed to assail at first the main pillars of the system of Messrs. Smith and Say, leaving the task of attacking less essential points to those who feel indisposed to overthrow the whole building.

As these theorists confounded cosmopolitical principles with political principles, so they entirely misapprehended the object of political economy. This object is not to *gain matter in exchanging matter for matter* as it is in individual and cosmopolitical economy, and particularly in the trade of a merchant.   But it is to gain *productive and political power* by means of exchange with other nations, or to prevent the depression of productive and political power, by restricting that exchange.   They treat, therefore, principally of the effects of *the exchange of matter* instead of *treating of productive power*.   And as they made not the productive power, and the causes of its rise and fall in a nation, the principal object of their inquiry, they

neither appreciated the true effect of the different
component parts of productive power nor the true
effect of the exchange of matter, nor of the consumption of it. They called the existing stock of
matter produced by human industry by the general
name of capital, and ascribed to the different component parts of this stock not only a *common and
equal*, but an *omnipotent* effect. The industry of a
people is, according to them, restricted to the
amount of capital, or stock of produced matter;
they did not consider that the productiveness of
this capital depends upon the means afforded by
nature, and upon the intelligence and social conditions of a nation. It will be shown hereafter
that if the science required for the existing stock
of produced matter the general term of capital, it
is equally necessary to create for the existing
stock of natural means, as well as for the existing
state of social and intellectual conditions, a general
term : in other words, there are a *capital of nature*,
a *capital of mind*, and a *capital of productive matter*,
and the productive powers of a nation depend not
only upon the latter, but also and principally upon
the two former.

I cannot expect that any man will be able to
comprehend, by this short exposition, the principles
of the new system, or the failure of the old theory.
They require a scientific development. But as
these letters are principally destined to elucidate

a practical question, I will attempt first to show the correctness of my ideas in applying them to the subject of the woollen and cotton trade between the United States and Great Britain.

Suppose, sir, the United States sell raw cotton, etc., to the amount of twelve millions, to Great Britain, and take in exchange for it twelve millions of woollen and cotton goods. Mr. Say says this commerce is profitable to both nations; it is better to raise cotton and to exchange it for English cloth if there is a better opportunity to plant cotton than to manufacture cloth and cotton goods, and if we can purchase manufactured goods cheaper than we can make them at home. He only contemplates the gain in matter for matter, as a merchant does; he judges after the principles of individual economy. But as a citizen of the United States, or as a political economist, he ought to reason thus: A nation is independent and powerful in the degree as its industry is independent and its productive powers are developed. This exchange makes us dependent, in our market as well as in our supply, upon England, the most powerful and industrial nation on earth, and in purchasing cotton and woollen goods from England, an immense productive power is lost. If our merchants gain some millions of money, and our cotton planters the advantage of clothing themselves in fine woollen and cotton goods, let us see what the nation in general loses by being depressed in its manufacturing power. It is a fact that a population of seventeen millions in Great Britain, by the completion of its productive powers, is enabled to consume and to sell for fifty-five millions of pounds, or 235 millions of dollars, of woollen and cotton manufacture.

The population (2) of these United States will amount after thirty years to at least thirty millions, and if we complete our productive powers in that time so as to make them equal to those of England, in proportion to the population, the value ; of woollen and cotton manufacture will amount to the enormous sum of 415 millions a year, which will be produced totally by our own labour, possessing land and pasture enough to raise cotton and wool as much as we want. But suppose you realize not more than the fourth part of the English manufacturing power—*i.e.* one hundred millions—in what a proportion stands this power of creating every year and for an infinite time, such an immense mass of productions, with those beggarly twelve millions, exchange of matter, if only compared in the amount of money! Take further into consideration what an increase of population and of capital, of mind as well as of matter, and in consequence what an increase of material strength, must be effected by this completion of our productive power, and you cannot fail to perceive that Messrs. Smith and Say's system, in only taking the exchange of matter for matter into consideration, must be fundamentally wrong.   Mr. Say says, this completion of productive powers can only be effected by the trade in increasing your capital; by political measures you cannot increase the capital; you only can give it another direction (3) than industry would give to it unaided, because if it would be more profitable to manufacture broad cloth and cotton goods than to raise wheat and raw cotton, the individual would prefer the former kind of industry, and complete the productive power without your aid.

This reasoning, partly correct in individual and cosmopolitical economy, is quite incorrect in political economy.

I. *In the first place*, population, capital, and productive skill have by their nature the tendency to extend themselves over the whole globe without the aid and interposition of political power and national interests; to overflow from those countries where they are in superabundance to those where they are scarce.   Hundreds of millions applied to raise and maintain an English naval power, armies, and fortresses would have gone to increase industry elsewhere; English capital would not be contented at home by an interest of two or three per cent. on account of its superabundance; English skill and experience in the manufacturing arts would rather have gone elsewhere to increase foreign industry than remain to perish at home. English capital of mind and matter is, therefore, formed by English political power and separate national interest into one mass—effecting the elevation of that island above the whole globe, and changing its natural tendency into the suppression of the manufacturing power of all other nations. This pernicious change of effect cannot be prevented by the skill and industry of the individuals of other nations; a single individual is as unable to overcome the united force of the capital and skill of a whole nation by his individual strength, as an American merchant would be unable to defend his single ship by his own strength against the aggressions of the English navy, without the aid of an American navy.

II. It is not true that the productive power of a nation is restricted by its capital of matter. Say and Smith having only in view the exchange of matter for matter, to gain matter, ascribe to the matter an omnipotent effect which it has not. Greater part of the productive power consists in the intellectual and social conditions of the individuals, which I call capital of mind.

Suppose ten single woollen weavers in the country possess a thousand dollars capital each; they spin the wool by the wheel, they possess very inferior tools, they are not skilled in the art of dyeing, each of them manufactures for himself, must do everything himself, and therefore each produces not more than a thousand dollars of cloth a year. Suppose now the ten manufacturers unite their capital and their labour, they invent (4) a spinning machine, a more perfect weaving machine, they are instructed in the art of dyeing, they divide the labour amongst them, and in this way they are enabled to manufacture and to sell every month ten thousand dollars' worth of broad cloth. The same capital of matter (5) amounting to $10,000 produced formerly only $10,000 worth of broad cloth a year, produces now by the improved social and intellectual conditions, or by the acquired capital of mind, $100,000 worth of broad cloth. So can a nation with the same existing matter improve its productive power tenfold in improving its social and intellectual conditions.

III. The question is only whether this nation is enabled :

1. By its natural means to increase its productive power, by fostering cotton and woollen manufactories ? (capital of matter).

2. Whether by its present industry, instruction, enterprising spirit, perseverance, armies, naval power, government (capital of mind), it is reasonably to be expected that it can acquire the necessary skill to complete in a short time its productive

o

power by these manufactories, and whether it can protect them by political power if acquired.

And lastly :

3. Whether there exists so much super-abundance of food, utensils, materials, raw stuff, etc. (capital of matter), as to go on fairly by using the capital of nature and employing the capital of mind.

I. There is pasture enough to raise a hundred million of sheep, and land enough to raise cotton for the whole world, besides all other materials and provisions. If it would be sheer folly for the Swedish Government to establish those manu-factories, because it possesses neither opportunity to raise a sufficient quantity of wool and cotton, nor the necessary naval power to secure its supply from abroad, or a foreign market for its manufacture, would it not be equal folly for these United States not to establish and foster them ?

II. There exists in the United States a degree of industry, of instruction, of emulation, of enter-prising spirit, of perseverance, of unrestricted intercourse in the interior, an absence of all hin-drances of industry, a security of property, a market and consumption of necessaries and comforts of life, and a freedom, such as are not to be found in any other country. If the Government of Spain could not by any arrangements whatever raise in a hundred years ten prosperous manufacturing establishments, and if raised could never protect them, this country can raise in a few years a hundred, and give them every kind of protection.

III. There exists in these United States an immense quantity, a superabundance of all kinds of necessaries of life; and of labour, to nourish double the present number of inhabitants, to build them houses and shops and mills, to procure them materials and tools. What else is necessary to establish manufactories, and what branch of industry may not be carried on by such means upon the largest scale? Look at the coarse cotton manufactories, and tell me whether the capital used in this branch has been derived from any other branch of industry where it was more profitably employed. The manufacturers built houses and constructed machinery—they wanted materials: timber, iron, bricks — did agriculture therefore lose hands for labour (which it acquired), or one log, or one pound of iron? No, sir, these things existed all in superabundance. The manufacturers wanted raw cotton, but did the material not exist in superabundance within our own limits? Could it not be brought from New Orleans, converted into coarse cotton, and carried back to New Orleans for payment of the raw material in half the time in which it was formerly carried to Liverpool, to lie there until sold and converted into manufactures, and brought back to our own country? They wanted provisions for those men who made their buildings and their machinery, and they want them every day for those who make their goods; but did agriculture in Pennsylvania miss one bushel of wheat after having sold six hundred thousand barrels of flour to New England? Money was spent by the enterprising, but this money was not taken from agriculture; it was given to agriculture, it served to raise agriculture. From this example, sir, you may learn how far wrong Smith and Say are in asserting that capital of matter increases but slowly. (6) This was true in former times when industry was checked in every way, when the new followers of chemistry, of mechanics, etc., were not yet in existence: it was true in old settled countries, where nearly all natural means were already used; but it is not true in a new country, where not the one-tenth part of the *capital of nature* is in use, where new inventions do wonders, where industry is delivered of all hindrances, where, in short, a new state of society has a *capital of mind* never experienced. If population increases in such a country in a degree never experienced, the increase of *capital of matter* will outstrip even the increase of population, if the community be wise enough to employ its capital of mind in order to develop and use the capital of nature with which it is blessed.

IV. If the disciples of the old theory assert it would not be economical to sacrifice a certain profit of a nation, derived from exchanges of matter for matter, in order to acquire a future productive power, I will refute them by a striking example. Suppose a farmer is convinced he could improve his condition twofold if he would establish a Fulling Mill, possessing water power, timber, wool, everything necessary except skill and experience to erect the establishment and carry it on. He sends his son or another of his family to the city to acquire the necessary skill. This farmer, sir, not only loses the labour of his son, and all the wheat and grain it would produce, but he loses, moreover, the sum actually expended in the instruction of his son. He sacrifices a great deal of his capital of matter, and the balance of his account would appear to his disadvantage, so that a fool who sees no deeper than the surface would censure him. But the sum he lost in this capital of matter he made up ten times over by the increase of his productive power. This farmer, sir, is brother Jonathan. It is true some men will for the first year enrich themselves by political measures to the loss of individuals; but this is the expense incident to the completion of the productive power of the nation, and this first expense will after some years be ten times compensated by the benefit arising from a more perfect national economy. On giving patents for new inventions you are directed by the same views.   It will encourage new inventions by securing to the inventors the first advantages of them. The community pays for these advantages, but not more than the value of the new inventions and of securing them to the whole community. Without these privileges many of the most valuable inventions would die with the inventor, as in former times.

If people repeat the assertion of Smith and Say, that duties upon imports produce a monopoly to the home manufactures, they consider not the advanced state of society. In former times, when capital and manufacturing skill were scarce and rare, when the greater part of chemical technology and of mechanics was a secret, a monopoly may have been produced by protecting duties. But in our times and in this country another state of things has taken place. Every one knows, or may learn from books, how white lead, sulphuric acid, and everything else can be manufactured. There is in every part of the country capital and enterprising spirit enough to enter into any lucrative branch of industry, and experience shows that every manufacture promising an extraordinary profit is soon brought to a level by a competition, a brilliant example of which was given by the American coarse cotton manufactories, which now sell their goods one hundred per cent. cheaper than the English did.

V. Even if there were not capital and skill enough in the country they would be drawn from abroad by political measures. Under No. I. I mentioned that capital and knowledge have the tendency to extend themselves over the whole globe, and that they go from those parts where they are in superabundance to those where they are scarce. (To my knowledge the theorists (7) neither observed this tendency, nor did they justice to it.) As this tendency is checked by the policy, etc., of other nations, so it can be restored by counteracting that policy. On securing to foreign capital and skill a premium in this country, you will attract them from abroad. The United States have this more in their power than any other nation, because they possess more capital of nature (not yet taken into possession) and more capital of mind than any other nation. Here an immense mass of natural riches have not yet got a proprietor. Here an Englishman finds his language, his laws, his manner of living; the only thing he does not find are the immense taxes and the other evils of his own country. On coming here, any man, from whatever country he comes, if possessing capital,

industry and useful knowledge, improves his condition. I know of no other country which enjoys
such opportunities and means of attracting foreign
capital and skill. (8) Whilst the United States, by
protecting duties, would attract foreign capital and
skill, they would prevent in the interior a very
disadvantageous extension of population and capital
over an immense continent. I am not, sir, one of
those who estimate the power and wealth of this
union by the number of states. As the Roman
military power was weakened by the extension of
their territory, so, I fear, the power, the progress
of civilization, the national strength of this union
would be checked by an additional accession of
states. Fifty millions of Americans in one hundred
states scattered over the whole continent, what
would they do ? Clear land—raise wheat—and eat
it. The whole American history of the next
hundred years shall be contained in these three
words, if you do not what Jefferson said—place
the manufacturer by the side of the farmer. This
is the only means of preventing population and
capital from withdrawing to the west. Ohio will
soon be as popular as Pennsylvania, Indiana as
Ohio, Illinois as Indiana; they will pass over the
Mississippi, next the Rocky Mountains, and at last
turn their faces to China instead of to England.
Pennsylvania and all the eastern and middle states
can increase in population, in arts and science,

civilization and wealth, and the union can grow powerful only by fostering the manufacturing interest. This, sir, I think the true *American political economy*.

Respectfully your most humble and obedient servant,

FR. LIST.

NOTES TO LETTER IV

Page 187. (1) The whole argument of this letter is expanded in the "National System," especially chap. xiii. ("The National Division of Commercial Operations") and chaps. xxxi., xxxii. ("The System of Values of Exchange").

Page 190. (2) *Population.* In 1860 the population of United States was, in fact, 31 millions.

Page 191. (3) *Another direction.* So List himself in Letter VIII. "If such a branch is raised to an uncommon height, the business draws capital, labour, and skill from others."

Page 193. (4) *They invent.* This is not a necessary consequence of their union.

Page 193. (5) *The same capital of matter.* But this has, *ex hypothesi*, been increased by the new machines.

Page 196. (6) *Capital of matter. . . slowly.* Smith, "Wealth of Nations," II. chap. iii. "The progress is frequently so gradual that, at near periods, the improvement is not only not sensible, but . . . there frequently arises a suspicion that the riches and industry of the whole are decaying." Also Say, " Principes," I. chap. ii. "The increase of capital is naturally slow of progress ; for it can never take place without actual production of value, and the creation of value is the work of time and labour besides other ingredients.

Page 199. (7) *The theorists.* Adam Smith deals with the point at some length, " Wealth of Nations," II. chap. v. " On the Different Employments of Capitals."

Page 200. (8) Hamilton " Report," p. 21. " The powerful invitation of a better price for their fabrics or their labour ; of greater cheapness of provisions and raw materials ; of an exemption from the chief part of the taxes, burdens, and restraints which they endure in the old world ; of greater personal independence and consequence under the operation of more equal government ; and of what is far more precious than religious toleration, a perfect equality of religious privileges."   And p. 35, " When the manufacturing capitalist of Europe shall advert to the many important advantages which have been intimated in the course of this report, he cannot but perceive very powerful inducements to a transfer of himself and his capital to the United States."

LETTER V

Reading, July 19, 1827.

DEAR SIR,

In national economy, the effect of measures and of events, of the condition and of the arts of individuals, is as different as the circumstances are, in which the different nations are existing; and all that in general can be said is this, that if they are promoting the productive power of the nation, they are beneficial; if not —not. Every nation (1) must follow its own course in developing its productive powers; or, in other words, *every nation has its particular political economy*.

Further: conditions, events, etc., may be profitable in individual economy for some persons, and injurious to the community; or, on the contrary, they may be injurious to individuals, and prove highly beneficial to the community: *individual economy is not political economy*.

So measures, principles can be beneficial to mankind, if followed by all nations, and yet prove injurious to some particular countries, and *vice versâ*. *Political economy is not cosmopolitical economy*.

I. *Every nation has its particular economy.*

Does an increase of population promote the object of national economy? For the United States it does; in China and Hindostan it does not. The emigration of men from those countries where food is scarce and labour in superabundance, is a public blessing; on the contrary, it is a lamentable sight to see citizens of the United States emigrate to Canada, while the exportation of black people, though diminishing our numbers, may be considered as beneficial; it is an exportation of weakness and not of power.

Does labour promote that object? It does in countries where it is properly divided, otherwise it is partly lost. Here agricultural countries, not possessing outlets for their surplus produce, not being able to change this surplus for other necessaries and comforts, produce nothing by that surplus but an increase of population. The people prefer to spend part of their time to idleness, rather than to produce nothing by labour. Foreign prohibitions destroy therefore a part of our labour, which is only to be revised by counteracting that policy in calling another productive power into life, which consumes that surplus and gives its produce in exchange.

Can this be said of all countries merely agricultural? No. In new settled countries, the surplus of labour and produce is for a long time advantageously employed in clearing and improving land, in erecting houses and barns, in increasing the stock of cattle. We see, consequently, the western states fast developing their productive power by agriculture, while the eastern states remain stagnant. After having developed their natural means to a certain degree, they will become stagnant too, and with their surplus produce, the more it grows, the more depress the agriculture of the eastern states, if they raise not manufactories.

Restrictions, are they in all countries equally effective and advisable? No. Mexico and the Southern Republics would act unwisely in not importing foreign merchandise in exchange for their precious metals and raw produce; their people, being yet uninstructed, indolent, and not accustomed to many enjoyments, must first be led by a desire of enjoyment to laborious habits, and to improvements of their intellectual and social conditions. Russia will never succeed in raising a manufacturing power, unless the emperors of that vast empire grant free charters to their cities like the emperors of Germany, whose creations grew, in a few centuries, from barbarism to a wonderful degree of wealth and civilization. Spain must first get rid of her superstition, her absolute power, and her cloisters. There must exist first a certain stock of freedom, of security, of instruction, etc., to foster manufactories, a stock wherewith the United States are amply provided.

Would the United States act reasonably if they should foster all kinds of manufactories (2) with equal care? By no means. Every improvement must be advanced by steps. A new country like this increases its productive powers by only fostering those manufactories which employ a number of labourers, and consume great quantities of agricultural produce and raw materials; which can be supported by machinery and by a great internal consumption (like chemical produce, woollen, cotton, hardware, iron, earthenware, etc., manufactories), and which are not easy to be smuggled. In fostering finer articles with equal care they would injure the development of the productive powers. Those articles of comfort and luxury, if imported cheaper than we can manufacture them, get in use among all labouring classes, and act as a stimulus in exciting the productive powers of the nation. Its consumption becomes by-and-by more important, and by-and-by the time will arrive when these articles, with a moderate encouragement, will be manufactured too within our limits. (3)

Are canals and railroads (4) beneficial to a country? Under conditions. In bringing people and produce nearer each other, they support the exchange and promote labour if labour is properly divided. If not, they may injure certain parts of the country to the advantage of other parts, by increasing competition in the surplus of agricultural produce. So I firmly believe that the eastern parts of Pennsylvania can only derive advantage from those improvements by raising a manufacturing industry, and exchanging the surplus of their manufactures for the agricultural produce of the western.

Machinery and new inventions? For thickly settled countries possessing no commerce, little industry, and a superabundance of labourers, they may be a public calamity; whilst every such improvement in the United States is to be considered a public blessing. In time I hope the slaves of this country will be made of iron and brass, and set in movement by stone coal instead of whips.

Consumption? (5) If reproductive, says Say, it increases wealth. But the question is whether it increases productive powers? In a nation of idlers hundreds of millions may be consumed without effect, but in a nation of industrious men like this I hardly imagine an honest and innocent consumption which would not be a stimulus to productive powers if labour would be properly divided (except whisky manufacturing, which is a production of weakness, not of power). Consumption and enjoyment go hand in hand. The desire to enjoy—repeatedly—more—in indefinite time—to procure even our posterity enjoyment, begets labour and production, and production facilitates consumption. Consumption begets therefore production, as much as production begets consumption.

Parsimony? (6) If exercised in the old countries by men who are in possession of immense estates by birthright, would certainly not be a public blessing ; it only would increase the inequality of property at the expense of the lower classes. The parsimony of a farmer living in a new settlement sparing all his income and bestowing all his time and labour to improve his land, increase his stock, walking barefoot and wearing self-prepared skins, increases productive powers, because the land would not be improved without it. The same degree of parsimony in a settled country would diminish the productive powers ; there is no hatter, no shoemaker to eat bread, where no farmer is to wear hats and shoes.

Lawyers, physicians, preachers, judges, lawgivers, (7) *administrators, literary men, writers, instructors, musicians, players, do they increase the productive powers ?* In Spain for the most part they do not : lawgivers, judges, lawyers, keep down the people ; the priesthood consumes the fat of the land and nourishes vicious indolence ; instructors instruct only those burdensome classes to become more burdensome ; musicians, players, serve only to make idleness to the idler more agreeable. Even sciences are pernicious there, because they serve not to improve the condition of the people but to make it worse. All this is different in the United States, where the exertions of those men have a tendency to increase mightily the productive powers : lawyers, lawgivers, administrators, judges, improve the public condition; preachers, instructors, writers, printers, improve the mind and morality of the people; and even those men who only procure honest pleasures to the people, are beneficial in begetting enjoyment and recreation for those who need to acquire new strength for new exertions.

Money: does the importation of it increase productive powers? In Spain it did the contrary. The manner in which it was acquired and consumed, the condition of the people and the Government, rendered the same precious matter poisonous to the people and the Government which would give immense power and strength to the United States, if imported into this country in exchange for its produce. A country may have a superabundance of precious metals, as Mexico, and the exportation of it is beneficial to the productive powers. It may have too little, in comparison with its industry, and in that case the importation of it is beneficial.

It must be remembered that I intended here not to exhaust those matters, but only to allege as much of them as was necessary to prove *that every nation must follow its particular course in developing its productive powers.*

I am, very respectfully,

Your most humble, obedient servant,

Fr. List.

NOTES TO LETTER V

Page 203. (1) *Every nation.* This sentence is the keynote of the "National System;" chaps. x and xv. are especially emphatic expansions of it.

Page 206. (2) *All kinds of manufactories.* Chap. xxvi. of the "National System," "Customs Duties as a chief means of establishing and protecting the internal national power," is an expansion of this thesis.

Page 206. (3) *Limits.* Hamilton "Report," p. 61. "In the selection of objects (*i.e.* in the tariffs) five circumstances seem entitled to particular attention; the capacity for the country to furnish the raw material; the degree in which the nature of the manufacture admits of a substitute for manual labour in machinery; the fertility of execution; the extensiveness of the uses to which the article can be applied; its subserviency to other interests, particularly the great one of national defence." List adopts these tests of suitability in the "National System," chap. xv., "Nationality and the Economy of the Nation."

Page 206. (4) *Canals and railroads.* It is curious to contrast this qualified approval with List's warm advocacy of railroads some eighteen months later. In the "National System," chap. xvii., he takes the view (which, as regards Western Europe is no doubt the truer one), that improved transport is called into existence by "the manufacturing power."

Page 207. (5) *Consumption.* Cp. "National System," chap. xxv., "The Manufacturing Power and the Inducement to Production and Consumption."

Page 208. (6) *Parsimony*.   Cp. "National System," chap. xix., "Where every one saves and economizes as much as he can, no motive can exist for production."

Page 208. (7) *Lawgivers*.   This argument is dealt with at length in the "National System," chap. xii.

LETTER VI

Reading, July 20, 1827.

II. *Individual Economy* (1) *is not Political Economy.*
An individual only provides for his personal
and family purpose, he rarely cares for others or
for posterity, his means and views are restricted,
rarely transgressing the circle of his private business; his industry is confined by the state of
society in which he lives. A nation provides for
the social wants of the majority of its members, so
far as the individuals cannot satisfy these wants
by their private exertions; provides not only for
the present, but for future generations; not only
for peace but for war; its views are extended not
only over the whole space of land it possesses, but
over the whole globe. An individual, in promoting
his own interest, may injure the public interest;
a nation, in promoting the general welfare, may
check the interest of a part of its members. But
the general welfare must restrict and regulate the
exertions of the individuals, as the individuals must
derive a supply of their strength from social power.
Individuals without the regulations of a community

are savages; and the principle of letting every individual alone is most flourishing among the Indians. Here, too, the truth lies in the middle. It is bad policy to regulate everything and to promote everything by employing social powers, where things may better regulate themselves and can be better promoted by private exertions; but it is no less bad policy to let those things alone which can only be promoted by interfering social power.

Look around, and you see everywhere the exertions and acts of individuals restricted, regulated, and promoted on the principle of the common welfare. The commonplace of *laissez faire et laissez passer*, invented by a merchant,[1] can therefore only be alleged sincerely by these merchants.

This principle would be only true if individuals and national interest were never in opposition. But this is not the case. A country may possess many extremely rich men, but the country is the poorer, because there is no equal distribution of property. Slavery may be a public calamity for a country, nevertheless some people may do very well in carrying on the slave trade and in holding slaves. Notwithstanding an absence of liberal institutions may be extremely injurious to a full development

---

[1] This commonplace was invented by M. de Gourney, a French importer.

of the productive powers of a nation, some classes may find their reckoning in this bad state of things. The nations may suffer from an absence of manufacturing industry, but some people may flourish in selling foreign manufactures. Canals and railroads may do great good to a nation, but all waggoners will complain of this improvement. Every new invention has some inconvenience for a number of individuals, and is nevertheless a public blessing. A Fulton may consume his whole fortune in his experiments, but the nation may derive immense productive power from his exertions. An individual may grow rich by extreme parsimony, but if a whole nation would follow his example, there would be no consumption and, in consequence, no support of industry. The more the individuals of the Southern States endeavour to supply the low price of cotton in England by planting greater quantities, the less will cotton bring in England; the less will the nation derive income from that branch of industry. Individuals may become rich by hazardous bank schemes, but the public may lose by them.

Without interference of national power there is no security, no faith in coined money, in measures and weights, no security for the health of seaports, no security for the commerce at sea by the aid of a navy, no interference for the citizens in foreign seaports and countries by Consuls and Ministers, no titles to land, no patents, no copyright, no canals and railroads, no national road. Industry entirely left to itself, would soon fall to ruin, and a nation letting everything alone would commit suicide.

The adherents of the old theory feel this very well—wonderful to say—not to be obliged to fall by the consequences, they desperately deny the proposition. Mr. Cooper, feeling very well that an acknowledgment of the true character of a nation (as I defined it), and all the consequences of the division of the human race into nations (as I traced them in my former letters), would overthrow the whole old system, negatived this character entirely, saying in his book on political economy, " Hence the moral entity, the *grammatical being*, called a nation, has been clothed in attributes that have no real existence, except in the imagination of those who metamorphose a word into a thing, and convert a *mere grammatical contrivance* into an existing and intelligent being. It is of great importance that we should be aware of the mistake, to avoid limitation, description and periphrasis— grammatical contrivances and no more; just as we use the signs and letters of Algebra to reason with, instead of the more complex numbers they represent." (See p. 19.) (2)

The more I am convinced of the superior talents and of the great learning of President Cooper, the more I am astonished to see him build up on such false ground, a system of political economy, by which he intends to enlighten a whole nation about its interest and to prepare the youth of that nation for political life; a system which would lead this nation to ruin, to suicide. A few words are sufficient to expose the gross error in which Mr. Cooper fell in this fundamental phrase, blinded by his zeal for keeping up the old theory. Mr. Cooper confounded *a grammatical being with a moral being*, or what the civilians call *a moral person* (a chartered society, a plurality of men, possessing common rights and obligations, common interests and institutions). A grammatical being is a mere name, signifying different things or persons, being only united in the use of language, in order (as Mr. Cooper says) to avoid limitations, descriptions, etc. The names bar, yeomanry, mob are such grammatical beings; the persons denoted by this name possess neither social rights nor social obligations; they cannot prosecute a law suit under this name before a court, nor can they be accused. But the American nation can, as Mr. Cooper may learn from the title of many indictments. A being which elects presidents and representatives, which possesses a navy, land, and debts; which makes war and concludes peace; which has separate interests respecting other nations, and rights as well as obligations respecting its members, is not a mere *grammatical contrivance ;* it is not a *mere grammatical being ;* it has all the qualities of a *rational being* and real existence.   It has body and real possessions ; it has intelligence, and expresses its resolutions to the members by laws, and speaks with its enemy—not the language of individuals, but at the mouth of cannon.

With this false foundation the whole system of Mr. Cooper falls to pieces.   In vain are his ingenious reflections and parallels, in vain all his learned allegations ;   common sense rejects his reasoning, as emanating from a false principle.   It is a very instructing contemplation, to see a man of such superior talents build up a system of political economy on a ground which, as a lawyer and philosopher, and as a learned politician, he must condemn.   What would Mr. Cooper, as Attorney-General, have said, if the counsel of a defendant had opposed to one of his indictments, that the American nation is a mere grammatical being, a mere man ; which only by the contrivance of man is converted into an existing and intelligent being, and which therefore cannot prosecute a lawyer before a court ?

Very respectfully, your most humble, obedient servant,

FR. LIST.

NOTES TO LETTER VI

Page 212. (1) *Individual economy.* In the " National System," chap. xiv., " Private Economy and National Economy." List, after quoting Adam Smith, " What is prudence in the conduct of every private family, can scarcely be folly in that of a great kingdom," answers, " No ; that may be wisdom in national economy which would be folly in private economy, and *vice versâ.*"

Page 215. (2) List combats this phrase of Cooper again in the " National System," chap. xi.

LETTER VII

Reading, July 22, 1827.

I proceed to develop the third proposition in my fifth letter.

III. *Political Economy* (1) *is not Cosmopolitical Economy.*

It seems to be in the plan of Providence to improve the conditions of the human race, and to raise their powers and faculties by an eternal contest—moral and physical—between opinion and opinion, interest and interest, nation and nation. History seems to confirm this reflection. The Italian and German cities, founded by an absence of security in the open country, grew powerful and wealthy by the contest against the robbers of the age by which they were forced to unite their individual strength. Philip's hangmen created the union of the Netherlands, and the wars of the new republic against Spain elevated her to a degree of wealth and power which was never thought of before. So events which seemed at first destructive to individuals, and had, indeed, destructive effects for the present generation, became a cause of happiness for posterity. So what seemed to weaken the human race served to elevate its powers. Look at the histories of England and France, and every page will confirm this truth. And your own history, sir, affords more than any other bright examples of it. Suppose England had emancipated these United States by her own accord, would they have made such astonishing advances towards power and wealth, without the excitement of a revolutionary war? Did not the last war create a navy and lay the corner-stone of a manufacturing industry? Though, therefore, philosophers may imagine that an eternal peace, a union of the whole human family under a common law, would produce the highest degree of human happiness, it is nevertheless true that the contests between nation and nation, often pernicious and destructive to civilization, were as often causes of its promotion, as a people was struggling for its freedom and independence, against despotism and depression; and that as often as this happened, it produced an elevation of all its faculties, and thereby an advancement of the whole human race towards greater perfection.

The same may be said of the industrial contest between nations. Though we may imagine free trade would be beneficial to mankind, it is yet to be questioned whether a free and uninterrupted

intercourse under a common law would promote
the development of the productive powers like the
existing contests. (2)

But be that as it may, that stage of things
under which free unrestricted trade possibly
might exist is not the actual state of the world,
and as long as the division of the human race into
independent nations exists, political economy will
as often be at variance with cosmopolitical principles, as individual economy is at variance with
political economy.   In this present state of things,
a nation would act unwisely to endeavour to promote the welfare of the whole human race at the
expense of its particular strength, welfare, and
independence. It is a dictate of the law of self-
preservation to make its particular advancement
in power and strength the first principles of its
policy, and the more it is advanced in freedom,
civilization, and industry, in comparison with other
nations, the more has it to fear by the loss of its
independence, the stronger are its inducements to
make all possible efforts to increase its political
power by increasing its productive powers, and
vice versâ.

Mr. Cooper is not of this opinion. After having
denied entirely the character of nations, he reasons
quite logically as follows :—

" No branch of commerce, no manufacture, is worth a war.
I incline to think that when a merchant leaves the shores of

his own country and trades everywhere, he ought to do this at his own risk, and ought not to be permitted to jeopardise the peace of the nation and induce a national quarrel to be carried on at the expense of the peaceable consumers at home. His occupation is not worth the protection it demands" (p. 120). (3)

Our great shipping merchants may learn from this extract that they, too, would not escape the national suicide intended by the cosmopolitical system. Mr. Cooper places their ships at the mercy of the Bey of Tunis and of the Dey of Algiers, as he places the manufactures at the mercy of English competition, and thinks they both are not worth protection by national power. Mr. Cooper believes not in a national commerce, or a national manufacturing power; he sees nothing but individual and indirect gain. What then would be the consequence of such a policy? The first ship taken in a foreign sea with impunity, would be the signal to hunt after the property of all American merchants; our tonnage would in a short time be reduced to nothing; we could not trade with foreign countries but in foreign ships, and depending upon foreign regulations and interests; we would be placed at the mercy of the English navy; in short, our whole indepen- dence would be lost. It requires some self- government not to break out with suitable epithets against such a system of national suicide.

As the commerce of a nation wants protection against foreign aggressions, even at the great expense of the country, and even at the risk of a war, so the manufacturing and agricultural interest must be promoted and protected even by sacrifices of the majority of the individuals, if it can be proved that the nation would never acquire the necessary perfection, or could never secure to itself an acquired perfection without such protective measures. This can be proved, and I will prove it, and if the masters and disciples of the cosmopolitical theory are not convinced of this necessity that is no argument that it does not exist, but proves only that they do not understand the true nature of political economy.

A manufacturing power, (4) like a maritime power (under which name I comprehend not only the navy, but the whole shipping of a country), is only to be acquired by long exertions. It takes a long time until the labourers are experienced in the different workmanship and accustomed to it; and until the necessary number for every business is at all times to be had. The more knowledge, experience, and skill are wanted for a particular business, the less individuals will be willing to devote themselves to it, if they have not a full assurance of their being able to make a living by it for their whole lifetime. Every new business is connected with great losses by want of experience and skill for a considerable time. The advancement of every kind of manufactories, depends upon the advancement of many other kinds, upon the proper construction of houses and works, of instruments and machinery. All this makes the commencement of a new industry extremely difficult, whilst the undertakers have to contend with a want of labourers of skill and experience; the first cost of starting a business is the heaviest of all, and the wages of the unskilled labourers in countries which commence manufactories, are higher than the wages of the skilled ones in old manufacturing countries. All cost double prices, and every fault in starting the business causes heavy losses, and sometimes the failure of the whole undertaking. The undertakers possess moreover, in most cases, not a sufficient knowledge of the ways and means to get the first materials profitably, and whilst they are struggling against all these difficulties they have great exertions to make to get customers, and often to contend with the prejudices of their countrymen, who, not willing to leave their old ways in doing business, are in most cases in favour of the foreign manufactories. Often they may be right. New establishments are seldom able to procure such finished articles in the first and second year as they would in the third and fourth, if supported, and nevertheless their articles must be sold higher. It cannot be expected that the consumers as individuals, by their own accord, should support a manufactory, by purchasing less accomplished articles at higher prices, even if convinced that, in purchasing them, they would encourage the manufactories to improve their products, and to procure them after a while cheaper than foreign manufactures.

All these circumstances are the cause why so many new establishments fail if let alone. Every failure breaks a man, because the greater part of their expenditure in building machinery, in procuring labourers from abroad, etc., is lost. One example of such a failure effects a discouragement of all other new undertakings, and the most advantageous business cannot find afterwards a support from capitalists.

In old manufacturing countries we observe quite the contrary. There are plenty of skilled labourers for every kind of business, at moderate terms, to be had. All buildings, machinery, implements, are in the best condition; the expenditure for them is for the greater part reimbursed by gains already made. On the basis of the already acquired experience and skill, the manufacturer can improve daily his buildings and instruments at moderate expense; he can save expenditure and perfect his manufactures. The manufacturer himself is possessor of skill, undertaking capital, and he cannot be exposed to embarrassments by the

Q

withdrawal of one of these essential parts, as in the case with new undertakings, where often the undertaker and the performer and the possessor of capital are different men, and the whole business can be stopped by the withdrawal of one of them. Credit and confidence of the old manufactures are established; it is therefore as easy for the possessor to get new support from capitalists as it is difficult for a new undertaker. The credit of his manufactures and his market is established; he can produce finished articles at moderate prices, and yet afford his customers a liberal credit.

Such are the natural differences between an old manufacturing country and a new country just entering into business. The old country, as long as it preserves its freedom, its vigour, its political power, will in a free intercourse ever keep down a rising manufacturing power. The Netherlands (5) would never have been deprived of their superior manufacturing power by the English without the regulations of Edward, Elizabeth, and the following Governments, and without the follies of the kings of France and Spain. A new country is, moreover, the less able to contend against the manufacturing power of the old country, the more the interior market of this old country is protected by duties, and the more its competition in the new country is supported by drawbacks and by an absence of duties in the foreign markets. The effects which these artificial means are producing I shall treat in my next letter.

Very respectfully yours,

FR. LIST.

NOTES TO LETTER VII

Page 219. (1) *Political economy.* This paragraph is expanded in the "National System," into chap. xi., "Political and Cosmopolitical Economy."

Page 221. (2) *Existing contests.* But tariff wars stand on a very different footing from trade competition. The essential aim of protection is to check foreign competition.

Page 222. (3) This passage is quoted in an abbreviated form in the "National System," chap. xiv., "Private Economy and National Economy."

Page 223. (4) *A manufacturing power.* This argument for the support of "infant" industries is used in a somewhat condensed and less effective form in chap. xxiv. of the "National System," "The Manufacturing Power and the Principle of Stability and Continuity of Work." Hamilton puts forward a long and closely reasoned plea to the same effect, "Report," pp. 28–30. He gives as reasons against the natural tendency of industry to seek the most profitable course, "The strong influence of habit and the spirit of imitation; the fear of want of success in untried enterprises ; the intrinsic difficulties incident to first essays towards a competition with those who have previously attained perfection in the business to be attempted; the bounties, premiums, and other artificial encouragements with which foreign nations second the exertions of their own citizens. . . . Whatever room there may be for an expectation that the industry of a people, under the direction of private interest, will upon equal terms find out the most beneficial employment for itself, there is none for a reliance that it will struggle against the force of unequal terms, or will of itself surmount all the adventitious barriers to a successful competition, which may have been enacted either by the advantages naturally acquired from practice and previous ·possession of the ground, or by those which may have sprung from positive regulation and artificial policy."

Page 226. (5) *The Netherlanders.* This argument is expanded in the " National System," into chap. iii., " The Netherlanders."

LETTER VIII

Reading, July 27, 1827.

III. *Political Economy is not Cosmopolitical Economy—(continuation).*

The advantages procured by a judicial tariff system (1) are the political.

1. By securing the interior market to our national industry, the manufacturing power is secured against all events, fluctuations of prices, and against all changes in the political and economical conditions of other nations. Events may happen whereby a foreign nation would be enabled to sell manufactures for a time cheaper than the interior manufacturers could make them. This state of things, though transitory, may nevertheless affect the manufacturing power of the nation, because a stagnation of a few years in manufacturing business may effect the ruin of the establishments: the buildings would fall to ruin, or would be put to other purposes; the machinery would get out of order, or be sold for old iron or firewood; the labourers would either leave the country or apply themselves to another branch of

industry; the capital would go abroad or find other employments; the customers would be lost, together with the confidence of the capitalists. A single new invention made in a foreign country, and not imitated immediately because yet kept secret, would destroy, in a free country, a whole branch of the manufacturing industry in a short time, whilst a protective system would preserve it until the secrecy is revealed, and our productive power increased by it.

2. By securing the home market (2) to home manufactures, not only the manufacturing power for the supply of our own wants is for all times secured against foreign changes and events, but an ascendency is thereby given to our manufacturing powers in competition with others, who do not enjoy this advantage in their own country. It is the same advantage that a people enjoys in being defended by natural and artificial fortifications against a neighbouring people living in an open country. All contests will be disastrous to such an unprotected people; it will even be ruined by its victories; it will never enjoy the fruits of perfect security; the enemy, driven to-day with a loss from their borders, may repeat his aggressions to-morrow, and in all cases the country will be laid waste. This is exactly the case in a country protected by a wise tariff system, and another following the principle of free trade.

Every man acquainted with manufacturing business knows that the existence of an undertaking depends upon a sufficient and speedy sale of such quantities of manufacturing goods as will cover the interest of the capital, the costs of the production, and a reasonable gain for the undertaker. As long as a manufactory has not reached that point, the business can only be carried on in the hope of attaining it, and if this expectation is not fulfilled after a longer or shorter time, the undertaking will go to nothing. Everybody knows, moreover, that the cost of production in manufacturing business depends a great deal on the quantity that is manufactured. A manufacturer may manufacture a thousand yards of broad cloth a year, and sell a yard for six dollars, and he may lose money; but he may manufacture twenty thousand yards of the same quality, and get no more than four dollars a yard, and he may make money. This circumstance has a mighty influence in the rise and fall of manufacturing power. If the large supply of the home market is secured to an English manufactory, a steady sale of that quantity which is necessary to sustain his establishment is secured to him thereby. He is, for instance, sure to sell ten thousand yards of broad cloth a year in his own country for six dollars a yard to cover thereby the expenses of his establishment, and to clear besides a sufficient sum of money for himself. By this home market he is enabled to manufacture yet other ten thousand yards of broad cloth for the foreign market, and to accommodate his prices to the existing circumstances abroad. The expenses of his establishment being already covered by the sales at home, the costs of producing other ten thousand yards for the market abroad comes by far less high, and he may still profit by selling them for three or four dollars a yard; he may even profit in future if he gains nothing at present. Seeing the manufacturers of a foreign country lying in distress, he may sell for some years without any profit in the hope to get seven or eight dollars a year, and to clear twenty thousand dollars or thirty thousand dollars a year for a long time after the foreign manufactories are dead and buried. He carries this contest on with perfect tranquillity; he loses nothing, and the hope of future gain is certain to him, whilst the manufacturer of the open country is struggling against a daily loss, nourishing a vain hope, leading him at last to a certain, inevitable, and radical ruin. This unhappy man is in quite a different situation from that of his projected competitor. He struggles, as we mentioned before, with all the difficulties of establishing a new business, which all conspire so that he cannot sell even for such a price as after some years would render him a fair profit; he struggles against the prejudices of his own countrymen; his credit is shocked; the little he sells makes his produce dearer and his losses larger. He is forced to enhance his prices for the first years, whilst his competitor is enabled to diminish them. There must be in the commencement, particularly in broad cloth, a difference of from fifty to eighty per cent. This contest cannot last long without national interference. His business is going to nothing, and affords a warning example to all his fellow-citizens—not to have enterprising spirit in a country where the national interests are not understood; rather to do nothing at all, to let everything alone, just as would be the case with the shipping merchants if their industry were not protected by navigation laws, by the expense of a navy, or by his running the risk of a foreign war, in case of foreign aggressions, if their ships (as Mr. Cooper advises) should be placed at the mercy of the Dey of Algiers. They might then do better to dig the grounds in the backwoods, and convert their anchors into ploughshares.

Hence we learn that duties, drawbacks, navigation laws, by Mr. Smith and Say, are improperly called monopolies. They are only monopolies in a cosmopolitical sense in giving to *a whole nation a privilege* of certain branches of industry. But on the ground of political economy they lose this name, because they can procure to every individual of the nation an equal right of taking a share in the benefits of the national privilege. And the privilege given to the English nation by the English Government of supplying the interior market, is so long an injury to the American nation as its Government procures not the same privilege to its own citizens.

3. How another old commonplace of the cosmopolitan theory, "*to buy from abroad if we can buy cheaper than manufacture*," may stand against such an exposition I cannot conceive. We buy cheaper from foreign countries only for a few years, but for ages we buy dearer; we buy cheap for the time of peace, but we buy dear for the time of war; we buy cheaper apparently if we estimate the prices in their present amount of money, but we buy incomparably dearer if we estimate the means wherewith we can buy in future. From our own countrymen we could buy our cloth in exchange for our wheat and cattle; from foreign countries we cannot. Our consumption of cloth is consequently restricted by our means which foreign nations take for payment, which are diminishing every day: our consumption of home-made cloth would increase with the increase of our production of provisions and raw materials, which are almost inexhaustible, and with our population which doubles itself every twenty years.

Into such gross errors fall wise and learned men,

if their theory has a wrong basis, if they take cosmopolitical for political principles, if they treat of the effects of exchange of matter instead of treating the cause of the rise and fall of productive powers. Smith and Say advise us to buy cheaper than we can manufacture ourselves, in contemplating only the gain of matter in exchanging matter for matter. But weigh the grain of matter with the loss of power, and how stands the balance? Let us see.

Smith and Say themselves estimate the amount of internal industry a great deal higher than foreign commerce; they do not venture on exact calculation, they say in all countries external commerce is of small consequence in comparison with internal industry. (Say Bk. I. chap. ix.) But other French writers estimate internal industry to exceed foreign commerce from twenty to thirty times. Mr. Cooper estimates it from ten to twelve times higher. We would not be far out of the way if we should take the modicum between the two extremities (twenty times), but to be quite moderate we will follow Mr. Cooper. If we have now proved, under No. 2, beyond all doubt that foreign industry aided by a productive system destroys the whole cloth manufacturing power of our own country, will the benefit of buying eight millions of broad cloth, about two or three millions cheaper from England than we could manufacture it ourselves in the first two or three years, not be acquired at the sacrifice of a manufacturing power which, if brought up by the aid of a national system, would produce for ever twelve times more cloth than we import, *i.e.* 72 millions of broad cloth, or after having doubled our population and our consumption (after twenty years) 144 millions? To justify this view we have only to divide the amount of the imported broad cloth, (on an average of the last three years 8,000,000) amongst the inhabitants of our country, which gives, for *three-quarters of a dollar*, broad cloth and woollen goods in general to every individual. If manufactures were properly protected and labour properly divided, every individual in these United States might be as well clothed as he is now nourished, and were this the case, every individual would at least consume for six dollars of woollens a year, which makes a manufacturing power of 72 millions a year or of 144 millions after twenty years. The present gain in exchanging matter for matter is about two or three millions a year. Such is the difference between reasoning according to cosmopolitical principles and reasoning according to true sound political principles.

4. There is a general rule applicable to all undertakings which has been entirely overlooked by the founders and disciples of the cosmopolitical

theory, though, upon its being put in practice, in the most cases a fortunate success of individual as well as national industry is depending. This rule is steadiness (3) in *prosecuting a certain branch of industry once thought necessary and found practicable.* Every new undertaking is connected with great expenses, with mistakes and want of experience and of knowledge of a thousand little things in manufacturing, in buying and in selling. The longer a business is carried on, the more it becomes profitable, the more manipulation is improved, the more the manufactured articles are accomplished, the more and cheaper can be sold. This is the reason why we see prosper so many men following exactly the line they once entered, and why we see so many running aground when in the habit of changing often. The same consequences are to be perceived in national economy. There is nothing more pernicious to the industry of a nation than events and circumstances which affect the productive powers unsteadily, at one time raising a certain branch of industry to an uncommon height, at another stopping it entirely.

If such a branch is raised to an uncommon height, the business draws capital, (4) labour, and skill from others; the uncommon profit raises property to an uncommon price; it raises wages, it increases consumption and the wants of the working people, as well of the undertakers and capitalists; and such a period of uncommon prosperity, if merely momentary and occasional, and followed by a period of uncommon decline, effectuates exactly the opposite extreme ; property falls not only, but has no price at all; the labourers earn by their habitual business not even the necessities of life; capital has no employment, houses and machinery fall to ruin; in short, bankruptcy and distress are to be seen everywhere, and what first seemed to be public prosperity, turns out to have been only the first step to public calamity.

One of the first views a nation has to take in its economy is, therefore, to effectuate *steadiness* by political measures, in order to prevent as much as possible every retrograding step, and the principal means of attaining the end is a judicious tariff. As the more a nation effectuates by this means steadiness in market and supply, in prices, wages and profits, in consumption and wants, in labour and enterprise (even promoting the step forward, even preventing the fall backwards), the more this nation will effectuate the development of its productive powers.

Mr. Smith, in ascribing the economical prosperity of England (5) to her constitution, to the enterprising spirit and laborious as well as parsimonious habits of her people, and in denying the salutary effects of the English tariff laws, was entirely destitute of correct views respecting this cause of national prosperity. Since the time of Elizabeth, no English cloth manufactory was destroyed, either by a foreign war on English ground, or by foreign competition. Every succeeding generation could make use of what the preceding generation built, and could employ its means and powers in improving and enlarging those buildings. Look at the contrast in Germany; how far was she advanced in those ancient times, and how trifling is her progress in comparison with that state of things; events and competition from abroad destroyed, often twice in one century, the creation of the former generations, and every generation had to begin again from the commencement.

Contemplate, sir, in this respect the fate of your own country. How often was the manufacturing interest, and even the agricultural interest, raised by events, and how often depressed again by foreign competition to the utmost calamity of the country. Contemplate only the period from the last war till now. The war made the establishment of manufactures and the wool-growing business necessary and profitable: the peace destroyed manufactories and sheep. The war encouraged agriculture, and increased prices of produce, wages, and property to an uncommon height: the peace and foreign policy reduced all this to such a degree that the farmers, who, during the preceding period, had accommodated their consumption to their revenue, who made improvements according to the presumed value of their land, etc., were ruined. Now are the manufactories again restored to a little animation, but English competition is at this moment about to prostrate them again. A war, if in the course of time we should have one, would undoubtedly enliven them again, but peace would destroy them again. And in that manner we will go through centuries in building up at one time what was destroyed in another, and will be destroyed again if we erect not by judicious laws, forbearance for securing our productive powers (as we erect them for securing our territory) against foreign aggressions, foreign events, foreign laws and regulations, foreign capital, industry, and policy.

Steadiness alone in protecting the manufactories of this country would raise our productive powers beyond the conception of the most sanguine.

A nation exposing its industry to the slightest storm from abroad, how can it compete with a nation which protects its establishments for all futurity?

Very respectfully, your most humble, obedient servant,

FR. LIST.

NOTES TO LETTER VIII

Page 229. (1) *Tariff system.* Cp. the arguments in chaps. xxvi., xxvii. of the " National System."

Page 230. (2) *The home market.* The same arguments are used in the " National System," chap. xv., "Nationality and the Economy of the Nation."

Page 237. (3) *Steadiness.* So the " National System," in chap. xxiv., " The Manufacturing Power and the Principle of Stability and Continuity of Work."

Page 237. (4) *Draws capital.* Contrast Letter IV., p. 191.

Page 238. (5) *England.* Compare the arguments in the " National System," chap. iv., on the sources of English prosperity.

APPENDIX

TO

THE OUTLINES

OF

AMERICAN POLITICAL ECONOMY

IN

THREE ADDITIONAL LETTERS

ADDRESSED BY

PROFESSOR FREDERICK LIST

OF THE UNIVERSITY OF TUBINGEN IN GERMANY

TO

CHARLES J. INGERSOLL Esq.

VICE-PRESIDENT OF THE PENNSYLVANIA SOCIETY FOR THE PROMOTION OF
MANUFACTURES AND THE MECHANIC ARTS

PHILADELPHIA

PRINTED BY SAMUEL PARKER, No. 48 MARKET STREET

1827

APPENDIX

LETTER IX

Political Economy is not Cosmopolitical Economy—
(continuation)

Reading, July 26, 1827.

DEAR SIR,

After having read the foregoing letters, can you believe that Mr. Canning and Mr. Huskisson became convinced of the truth of Mr. Smith's and Mr. Say's cosmopolitical theory? No, sir, Mr. Canning was as far from being convinced of this truth as Pitt was, though the latter (as the disciples of Smith assure us triumphantly) was in the habit of carrying everywhere along with him a volume of Adam Smith's. Mr. Pitt certainly carried that volume in his pocket for no other purpose than to act quite contrary to the advice of the author; and Mr. Canning, it seems, has learned these volumes by heart, in order to allege the opinions of Adam Smith as often as he intends to act contrary to them. This new manner of alleging an authority has certainly not been invented for home use but for export, as a lively man of this country (1) wittily observed.

The more English policy, in this moment, seems to be contradictory to itself, and the more the mysticalness with which it is covered may become injurious to this country ; and on the contrary, the more it is necessary for this country to understand it plainly as it is, the more I hope to be excused if I should fail in my undertaking to unveil it.

It is indeed strange to see at the same time the present Ministry of England hated by the ultras of France and Spain, etc., and supported by the King of England, beloved by the British people, and nevertheless profess a common theory, which, if carried into effect, would deprive the English nation of the monopoly hitherto enjoyed, and yet jealously watch to prevent every progress of other rival nations, particularly of the United States. There must be—everybody feels it—some difference between sayings and doings. That Mr. Canning is a noble, feeling, liberal man who would venture to doubt? But nevertheless we know, from his own acknowledgment, (2) that he suffered the Spanish nation to be given up to three monsters, despotism, anarchy, and foreign invasion and occupation, in order to call the South American Republics into existence. And this deed certainly did not originate in disinterested love of freedom and humanity, but a desire, as he confessed himself, to open for England immense markets. It is a very liberal act, indeed, to provide Portugal with a free constitution (for that the Emperor of Brazil would have given this constitution from his own accord nobody can believe), and to hasten with an army, on twenty-four hours' notice, to Portugal in order to defend this new constitution against the aggressions of the fanatics of Spain ; but even if we acknowledge the duty of England to support her ally's constitution, we see this expedition executed with so much haste and zeal, that nobody can doubt there must have been a good deal of self-interest in it. In this movement is Mr. Canning treating for the evacuation of Spain ? For what purpose ? If the monster Occupation should leave that country, it will be exposed to the monster Anarchy.

Mr. Canning may give different reasons in Europe to the different people for his different political measures as it may suit his interest. But in this country we are at liberty to judge a man's intention by his conduct, not according to the pretexts he may invent to mask the true motives of his actions. We are in the habit of finding out at first a man's aim : sometimes we consult history, from which we learn that nations, during ages and centuries, like individuals, are prosecuting some one principal aim. Inquiring after the aim of England, we find that it consists in raising her manufacture, commerce, and naval power beyond the competition of all other nations. For reaching this aim we see her support at home liberal principles; play the conqueror in Asia, and use and support their despotic powers; whilst contenting herself in the West Indian islands and Canada with a paternal Government, mixed and sweetened with some rights and some free institutions. We see her give the republic of Genoa, her former ally, to a monarch, and restore the Hanse Towns to their former independence (in order to possess staple places in Germany for her manufactures): we see her hire armies against the French Republic, and manufacture a free constitution for Sicily: we see her subsidize the armies of the European monarchies to conquer France, and convert the republic of Holland into a kingdom: we see her suffer the destruction of a free constitution in Spain, call a number of republics into existence in South America, project a free constitution for Portugal, defend it against the aggressions of the fanatics, and treat with France for the evacuation of Spain. When we judge this conduct by principles, there is nothing but contradiction; but when we look at the aim of the country, there is nothing but conformity. Her aim was always and ever to raise her manufactories and commerce, and thereby her navy and political power, beyond all competition of other nations, and always she accomplishes her conduct to circumstances—using at one time and in one place liberal principles, at another, power or money—either to raise freedom or to depress it, as it suited her. Even her measures against the slave trade (3) are said to have originated from her interest, and gave her a pretext to prevent other nations' colonies from supplying themselves, whilst her own possessed already the necessary quantity. Can any man of sound mind believe this aim of England was changed by Mr. Canning, or could be changed, even if he had the intention to sacrifice national views and national interests for promoting cosmo-political views and interests? No; Mr. Canning has only changed the means of reaching this national aim according to present circumstances. If it suited the interests of England, fifteen or twenty years ago, to subsidize half Europe in order to destroy the continental system of Napoleon, and to send armies there, the same Powers who aided to overthrow the empire of Napoleon having now partially revived a continental system them-selves, stand at present in the light of her aim, threatening not only to destroy the influence of English power upon the Continent, but even to take their share in the trade with South America. There is, consequently, no more use for the principles of Lord Castlereagh for England; on the contrary, there is now use for such means and prices as are calculated to raise the influence of England upon the Continent and counteract the policy of the continental Powers. Mr. Canning gives this pretty clearly to be understood in his celebrated speech, in alluding very expressly to the gigantic power which England possesses in having liberal ideas on the Continent for an ally. To give his threatenings the necessary stress, he seems to have previously provided Portugal with a liberal constitution, in order to gain ground on the western extremity of the European continent for his new allies, the liberal ideas ; his predecessor, Lord Castlereagh, first took ground in that country with his bayonets and his money, in the contest against Napoleon's continental system. Whether Mr. Canning has the intention to force the continental Powers, by his threatenings, to enter into disadvantageous commercial treaties, or whether he has the intention to prepare the public mind for a contest between absolute power and liberal ideas, nobody can tell who is not intimately acquainted with the mysteries of cabinets ; but so much is certain, that he intends to attain his aim either one way or the other. His speech bears distinct marks of dissatisfaction with the French Ministry, from which we conclude that he must have been disappointed by that ministry in a darling plan. He was a short time before on a visit (4) at the French Court, and it transpired that

a treaty of commerce was about to be concluded.
We have some reasons to draw such a conclusion
from the behaviour of the English newspapers,
which were at that time uncommonly busy to
praise the great advantage which the cosmopolitical system of Smith and Say, if put in practice,
would have for both nations, in enabling the
English to go on prosperously with their manufacturing business, and the French to increase the
vine-planting business. On uttering such feelings
of dissatisfaction, Mr. Canning acted certainly from
greater motives than a desire of taking personal
satisfaction; an English minister would never
permit himself to express feelings of personal disappointment, at the risk of affecting by this
conduct the policy of his nation. The threatenings
of Mr. Canning were not likely to be misunder-
stood in France; and the late request of evacuating
Spain from French troops shows pretty clearly
that Mr. Canning has the intention to gain pre-
liminarily the whole Peninsula for his new ally.

It is, however, not my intention to treat on European policy. I only went so far to state generally
the aim of Mr. Canning's policy, which is to
counteract the continental Powers of Europe and
to monopolize the South American market. In
respect to this country, Mr. Canning has not to
fear a present manufacturing power but a rising
one, which menaces the interest of the English

manufacturing power in a threefold way: in the first place, in depriving the English manufactures of our interior market; secondly, in sharing with them the South American market; and thirdly, in increasing our internal and external shipping immensely, which is the basis of the future ascendency of our naval power. There was no occasion, and there will perhaps not in the course of centuries reappear such an opportunity as the event of the emancipation of the South American people for raising the manufacturing power of the United States, in a few years wonderfully, and taking an equal standing in power and wealth with England by developing our internal productive powers, and extending our foreign commerce and our internal and external shipping. Let only a few years pass and England will have taken exclusive ground in the South, and will have raised her power and wealth by Mr. Canning's policy beyond all conception. There will then be no possibility for an American competition with England, neither in industry nor in political power. On the relations, sir, between two rival nations, not to grow in strength and to become weak are synonyms. If England grows twice as powerful as she is, whilst you remain stationary, you become twice as weak as England. It is quite clear that Mr. Canning had a great interest to check this country in executing a national system. But what means has he to do this? On our own continent there is no foe to raise for frightening us. Nothing is to be done but to make use of the interest of our commission merchants and of the perversity of the *soi-disant* theorists to raise the feelings of our shipping merchants and of the Southern planters, in deluding them with false demonstrations, as if the shipping and cotton-growing interest would be depressed for the purpose of promoting the individual interest of some manufacturers. We shall see hereafter with what good reason this is done, and every man of sound mind must be astonished to see such an excitement against measures which promote at last all interests.

Very respectfully yours,

FR. LIST.

NOTES TO LETTER IX

Page 246. (1) *Man of this country.* In the " National System " the epigram is attributed to Chief Justice Baldwin.

Page 246. (2) *Acknowledgment.* See note on Letter III. p. 180.

Page 249. (3) *Slave trade.* This charge is elaborated, with some qualifications, in chap. xxxv., of the " National System," " Continental Politics."

Page 250. (4) *Visit.* In October, 1826.

LETTER X.

Political Economy is not Cosmopolitical Economy—
(continuation)

Reading, July 27, 1827.

DEAR SIR,

A nation may become dependent by its exports as well as by its imports from other nations, and a great source of raw materials and provisions to foreign countries may oftener become a source of calamity and of weakness in the interior and of dependence upon foreign Powers, than of prosperity.

Mr. Canning, aware of the great interest of England, to keep down the manufacturing interest of this country and to monopolize the South American market would, I am convinced, readily open the ports of England for our wheat, could he persuade the landed interest in both Houses of Parliament of the expediency of such a measure. It is dubious whether the farmers of this country would refuse a momentary gain for a future and permanent advantage ; it is probable that Mr. Canning would gain by such a measure the landed interest of this country for his *free-trade theory*. What would be the consequence of such a measure ? The manufactories of this country, left at the mercy of free competition, would be immediately ruined. The greatest part of all capital invested in manufacturing business would be lost, and all that would be saved would be invested in farming business. Labour, skill, all productive powers engaged in manufactures would return again to farming business. The price of wheat and grain would enhance to $1\frac{1}{2}$ dollars, the price of land and wages would raise in an equal proportion, and the farmer would again accord his consumption and improvements to the increased profits he could make. The banks would increase their business in an equal proportion. In the mean time England would increase her manufacturing power immensely, and monopolize the Southern and all other markets. This would be well enough, had England not in her power to give a mortal blow in one hour to this whole industry. Any change in the mind of Mr. Canning, or in the administration, or in the Government, or in both Houses of Parliament, could produce such a destructive effect. After having improved her manufactures, she would very likely take up again the old plan of improving the condition of her land proprietors by reviving the corn laws; a war would happen between the two countries, or a hostile feeling of a minister could inspire him with the plan of weakening the wealth and power of the United States, and of disturbing their tranquillity and internal peace, by excluding again the American grains, and by giving the preference to the produce of Prussia, Poland, etc., as it was the case last year respecting the English possessions in the West Indies. Certain is this, that from the day of such an economical dependence the majority of the inhabitants of the United States would have to tremble before every new opening of the English Parliament, having more to fear and to expect from the proceedings and regulations in Westminster than from those in Washington, and that the independence of interests and feelings in the United States would be lost. For what would be the consequence of every check of exports of our grain? What you have seen the last fourteen years—a fall of wages, of profit, of capital, and of land prices, a disproportion between an habitual consumption and a diminishing income, between improvements and rent, and in consequence, bankruptcy, sheriffs' sales, broken banks, and national calamity. Would it not have been better if we had not sold a single grain of corn to England? Would it not stand at the mercy of a foreigner, of a riot, of a hostile power, to break down our national prosperity in one hour, and to throw it backwards for a whole country?

Here, sir, is the proper place to mention an intimate connection between our present banking system, and the system of our political economy, which, I believe, has heretofore been but imperfectly understood. This banking system stands, rises, and falls, with the price of land and property. Banks issue generally a great deal more notes than they possess cash. Mr. Cooper allows them a threefold amount of their cash to issue in notes, wherefrom I conclude that they at least issue that much. If only a third part of these circulating notes represent cash, what do the other two parts represent? For, being nothing more of themselves than stamped rags, nobody would take them if they would not represent anything of value. They represent a nominated quantity of money consisting in the value of property and land. But the real value of property and land depends upon the market price of land: if that price rises, the security of the paper rises; if it falls, the security falls. If no price at all can be realized, there is no possibility to convert property into cash, and the security is lost to the holders of the notes, insomuch as the bank is founded on land and property. The price of land, and the possibility of converting it into money, rises and falls with the price of the produce. If the price of wheat is high, the price

of wheat land is high too ; and if the produce will
scarcely bring so much money as to pay the
labour, nobody would be so great a fool as to
give much money for wheat-land. Every cause,
therefore, which effects a fall of the prices of the
raw products, effects likewise a fall of the land
prices and of the country bank business, and *vice
versâ*. The principal condition of a banking system
like this is, therefore, steadiness of the market of
the agricultural products, effectuated by a national
system, which prevents great fluctuation, which
can only be attained by securing the home market
to the products by a manufacturing industry.
Under this condition, a banking system works as
a productive power, whilst in an open country it
destroys from time to time the roots of industry—
CREDIT. Look fourteen years back : had the United
States Government, immediately after the last war,
protected manufacturing industry, wheat, wages,
land prices, profits would never have sunk so low ;
banks would never have been ruined; not the
tenth part of the citizens would have been expelled
from house and home. This distress of so many
land proprietors arose not chiefly from the bank
mania, as it was generally believed, but from a
revolution in the prices of produce and land caused
by the dependence on foreign markets, foreign
fluctuations of prices, foreign regulations and restrictions. It may be that swindling bank schemes

and the faults of the legislature added to the distress; but the effect—the ruin of a number of land proprietors—could not have been prevented otherwise than by preventing the chief cause by a national system, and this effect will as often return as the cause will reappear, even if there is no country at all in the United States. A rise of land prices, by an uncommon rise of grain prices, will, if there is no bank, induce land proprietors to sell their land for nominal sums; they will be contented with receiving a third or a fourth part of the purchase money in cash, and for the remainder they will readily take judgments and mortgages on the property they sold. Men without property, and in possession of some cash, will be glad to get that way in possession of land, hoping to be able to deliver it, by the aid of the high corn prices, from the mortgage; the most part of those who by the way of inheritance get in the possession of land of which they were only partially owners, will engage themselves in such a manner against their co-heirs. Others who sell not their land, will undertake improvements in proportion to the increased value of the land, and enter mortgage obligations. If such a state of things only lasts for some years, and then breaks at once, it will always break the majority of the citizens, and destroy the morals, the industry and the credit of the country, for half a century. In Germany we saw the same effects from the same causes without country banks. As long as produce, and in consequence, land prices were high, there were great sales of land; credit increased, a man with comparatively a small sum of money could buy high-valued estates, in giving mortgages for the remainder. By inheritance, sales, contracts, etc., etc., more than the moiety of the country changed proprietors, and was mortgaged under the high prices. The owner of a mortgage, trusting to the steadiness of grain prices and land prices, was not anxious to recover his money, and even if he wanted money, he asked rarely the debtor for it; he could effect this easier by selling his paper to capitalists who desired to empty their money and had confidence in the security. But with the moment of what was called the *restauration*, with the moment of free trade, by which *free trade* the English were allowed to destroy the German manufactures, by importing their manufactures, and destroy the landed interest of Germany, by prohibiting the importation of German grain and wool in their country, by corn and woollen bills, the prices of land and of property sank, the confidence in the paper was lost, as well as the possibility of recovering the money by selling the property, and the same ruin of the majority of farmers followed, like in this country. In the present moment, the value which can be recovered by selling properties there, amounts not to the sum of the mortgages.

The founders of the cosmopolitical system forgot entirely to say anything about the causes of the rise and fall of land prices, and about the consequences of it. This is the more astonishing, as the prosperity of the greater part of a nation depends upon the steadiness of the prices of land and property (which forms the greater part of the riches of a nation). The cause of this omission is, however, obvious. In those countries in which Mr. Smith composed his system, the greater part of land property, forming life estates, is not in free commerce, and therefore he only perceived alterations in rents (1) and not in land prices. Mr. Say, who lives in a country in which nearly all real estates are in free commerce, overlooks the omission by blindly following his master, as he always does, except in some matters of little consequence. In this country there is more exchange in real property than in any other, and here we can point out a particular deficiency of the celebrated theory, which, if overlooked by a nation, may at least once in twenty-five years break down the land-proprietor of a country. Indeed, the more I advance in developing the principles I expressed in my former letters, the more I am inclined to declare Mr. Say's system a total failure, calculated rather for destroying common sense in political economy and the

prosperity of those nations who contemplate its
hollow phrases as profound wisdom.

Very respectfully yours, etc., etc.,

F<small>R</small>. L<small>IST</small>.

NOTE TO LETTER X

Page 261. (1) *Mr. Smith . . . rents.* But see the passage Book
II. chap. iv., on "The Ordinary Market Price of Land." Say also
in his "Principes," Book II. chap. ix., discusses the price of land
in relation to rent and profit.

LETTER XI

Political Economy is not Cosmopolitical Economy—
(continuation)

Reading, July 29, 1827.

Dear Sir,

As a foreign grain market which may be destroyed every day by the regulations of a foreign Power is rather a source of weakness than of power, so it is with a foreign cotton market depending on a country which, like England, by its predominant political power is enabled, and by its rival feelings against this nation induced, to procure its supply after a short time from other subjected countries. The Southern orators would certainly do better to call their fellow-citizens to stand by their reason instead of by their arms, and they will certainly do it if they investigate the subject coolly and deliberately.

In the first place, let us see who is the silly boy who killed the goose laying golden eggs, whom an eminent statesman of the South toasted late so emphatically. I am obliged to refer for that purpose to what President Cooper is delighted to

style "*the annual nonsense of finance reports*,"
from which I nevertheless venture to draw something of tolerably good sense. The tables of the
Treasury give the following result :—

EXPORTS.

				Dollars.
1816.	81 millions of pounds of raw cotton brought			24,000,000
1826.	204 "	"	"	25,000,000

Two and a half pounds brought consequently in
1826 just as much as *one pound* in 1816, because
Europe could not digest the number of cotton
bales which the Southern States gave her to
swallow. Had every planter thrown the half of
his cotton crop into the Mississippi he would undoubtedly have received as much money for the
other half as he now got for the whole, and he
would besides have saved the trouble of bagging
one-half the number of bags. So true is it that
men may labour for nothing, and that a productive
power may destroy itself, and that a production
which is beneficial to mankind may be destructive
for a particular country ; so true is it that individual
economy is not political economy, and political not
cosmopolitical economy. The planter receiving in
1825 very small interest for his capital on account
of the low cotton prices, thought to make up this
loss by increasing the quantity of his crop, which
was very good individual economy. But all planters

had the same plan; the quantity of the whole cotton crop consequently increased in the same proportion, whilst the demand in the European markets had but little increased; the prices fell in consequence in the same proportion in which the quantity had increased, and the planters received not a cent. more for their increased quantity than in the preceding year. We see here in clear numbers that, if in material production twice two makes four, it may make in production of value sometimes one and a half, or something less; and I venture to predict that the cotton planters will every year produce this result, and that they will at last plant three hundred millions of pounds, and not receive more than twenty-five millions, or something less, until they perceive that every supply must correspond to the demand. According to cosmopolitical principles, it matters not, however, how much the cotton planters cleared by their industry. The riches of the world were increased, and all is well. But I incline to doubt whether the Southern planters would not prefer to lessen the comforts of mankind a little by increasing their private income.

The cause of the great disadvantage from which the Southern States now are suffering, is just the same cause which depresses the grain-growing states; these raise too much grain, those too much cotton. Both want a proper division of labour

There and here a part of the inhabitants must seek for another, for a more profitable employment. This is the whole secret for improving both countries.

But what else can the Southern States do with their slaves in a profitable manner? Some say they ought to raise silk; others to plant vines. I, for my part, believe that neither the one nor the other would yield, for the present, a sufficient profit to supply their losses, which opinion I shall qualify in another place. But why should they not be able to make coarse cotton (coarse shirtings, ginghams, etc.)? I cannot see the reason why not. After the machineries are erected, the labour of spinning and weaving coarse cotton certainly exceeds not the faculties of the slave. The Pacha of Egypt does very well in applying his slaves to this kind of work; and the ancient Greeks carried on all their manufacturing with slave labour. After having started the machineries, the inhabitants of the South would even enjoy peculiar advantages: first, they could apply their labourers from the prime of their youth to a certain branch of business, and their skill would be secured to the manufactory for their whole lifetime; secondly, for the spinning mills they could turn the labour of the females and of the children, who are now of very little use for them, to a better account; thirdly, they would have the cotton cheaper, and the South American market nearer; fourthly, they could dye with home-raised colour-plants, particularly indigo, without any preparation.[1]

Let us see what the result would be if with the fourth part of their cotton-planting slaves they would only convert the eighth part of their cotton into coarse goods.

	lbs.
They plant now	204,000,000
For employing the fourth part of their slaves in coarse cotton manufactories they will plant less raw cotton	51,000,000
Remainder	153,000,000
From this quantity they work themselves up one-eighth	20,000,000
Remainder	133,000,000

	Dollars.
For this reduced quantity they will receive, according to the quantity and price of 1820 (when they sold 127,000,000 lbs. for 22½ millions of dollars)	24,000,000
And 20,000,000 lbs., manufactured at 3½ millions, and the value six times increased	21,000,000
Total	45,000,000

Instead of twenty-five millions a year.

Thus the whole manufacturing labour would be clear gain, and though not more than the fourth

---

[1] On that important subject, how to use slave-labour in manufacturing, I will expose my opinion in a particular letter. (1)

part of the cotton-planting labour, it would yet bring nearly as much as the other three-fourths. By this the Southern planters may learn that they receive for all their slave-holding trouble, and all their land, not the twentieth part of the value that may be produced in Europe from their raw cotton. Verily, verily, the Southern planters will, as well as the French ultras, fail of their aim in resisting the wants of the present time obstinately, instead of complying with them reasonably. The good old times are not to be revived otherwise than by good new ideas, carried into effect by standing at machinery, not by aims.

Whilst the Southerns destroy the fruits of their labour by self-competition, it is quite certain that England is looking about for supply to other countries, standing more under their command than the United States. They intend to encourage Brazil and other South American states in this business. The downfall of the Turkish Empire, which in all probability if not overthrown from abroad must sink under its own weight, will moreover bring vast cotton countries under their suzerainté. In such a case they probably aim at Egypt and Minor Asia, not only in this respect, but to get the key to the Red Sea and consequently to East India. The example of the Southern States itself teaches that with the aid of slaves and of a proper soil a country may increase its cotton

immensely. Then they will more and more
exclude American cotton, and place the Southern
States with their cotton bills in the same situation
as they did the grain and wool-growing countries
with their corn and wool bills.

The calamity arising from such a measure can
only be avoided by taking precaution in due time.
In her present situation England cannot dispense
with American cotton, she must buy it. By
commencing now to raise a cotton manufacturing
industry the South will by-and-by diminish the
quantity of raw cotton and increase home manufactories.

Whilst they gain thus in a double way, they
will moreover secure their cotton market in
England. This is effected in the following manner :
if the Americans raise cotton manufactories they
will rival in foreign countries the English manufactories; should then the English exclude or
exonerate the importation of American cotton,
the prices of raw cotton would be raised in their
countries and the American cotton manufactories
could sell cheaper in foreign countries. This is
yet the greatest of all advantages which will grow
out of an American manufacturing industry for
the Southern States, that they place by this
measure England in a dilemma which cannot fail
in one case or in the other to turn out to their
advantage, whilst in following their old course

they will be lost in every way either by their own over-production, or by foreign measures.

Mr. Niles, in his excellent essay on American Agriculture, has with good reason shown that the Southern States would yet receive some millions less for their cotton in Europe, were it not for the home manufactories, which already consume the quantity of 60 millions of pounds a year. This quantity has been questioned by some opponents of domestic industry, but, I am confident, with little reason. According to the statements of the Count de St. Crique, Director of the French Customs, the consumption of France last year was not less than 30 millions of kilograms, or 64 millions of pounds, and the consumption of the preceding year was not more than 24 millions of kilograms, or 48 millions of pounds ; the consumption of France had consequently increased in one year 16 millions of pounds. This consumption makes for each inhabitant two pounds a year. But in France, where everybody wears linen for shirts, etc., cotton is not half so much in use as in the United States : we cannot, therefore, at least estimate the average consumption at four pounds per head, which would make a quantity of 48 millions without exports.

I regret very much that I am not in possession of the statistical tables of England, from which I could derive the internal consumption of that country. The total import of raw cotton was estimated last year at 200 millions, from which quantity certainly two-fifths are consumed in England. According to this example, France may increase her consumption in the course of the next ten years to 100 millions of pounds, and so may the United States, which would make nearly the double of the quantity we sell at present to England. The interior of Germany and Switzerland, which begin to supply themselves by the way of Havre de Grace, (2) will increase in an equal ratio their consumption. In the mean time, while these markets increase their demand, England cannot do without American cotton, and consequently nothing can be lost, while all may be gained. France is neither in possession of an overwhelming naval power, nor has she the aim to inundate the world with her manufactures; she will ever be a good and sure market for American cotton. There are strong reasons to believe that France would readily increase the importation of other products from the United States, particularly tobacco, ham, lard, and tallow, if the United States would take proper measures to increase their importation from France. The true policy of this country respecting England and France has certainly too long been neglected. The United States acquired their political independence by separating from England and by uniting with

France, and in that way—only in that—they can acquire their economical independence.

Very respectfully yours,

Fr. List.

NOTES TO LETTER XI

Page 267. (1) *A particular letter.* No trace of this letter remains, although List himself, in the preface to the " National System," speaks of " the *twelve* letters in which I expounded my system."

Page 271. (2) *Havre de Grace.* Whence List sailed in 1825.

EXTRACT FROM PROFESSOR LIST'S SPEECH

At a dinner given to him by the Pennsylvania Society for the Encouragement of Manufactures at the Mansion House, Philadelphia, November 3, 1827.

EXHAUSTED by persecution, the bitter fruit of a constitutional struggle for the welfare of my native country—invited by that illustrious man who has filled two hemispheres with his military glory and three ages with his civic virtues—I reached the happy shores of freedom early enough to witness the greatest spectacle the world ever saw. I was present at his triumphal entry into Albany, and into this celebrated city, when he traversed the beautiful fields of Lancaster and the magnificent Hudson, hailed by hundreds of thousands. I heard the shouts of a grateful nation in our modern Tyre on that ever-memorable celebration of American Independence. I saw the tears of grief when a free nation's first magistrate spoke that classical production of genius and exalted feeling on the day of his departure. Such was my motive for coming and such my introduction into this great country, where heroes are sages and sages rulers; where for the first time a great empire was founded on industry, on equal rights, and on the moral force of the citizen; where the Governments are mere committees of the people, and conquests made for no other purpose than a participation in freedom, civilization and happiness with the conquered. To have contributed in the least degree to a work of such greatness I estimate to be the highest praise, worthy a lifetime of exertions.

It fell to my lot, gentlemen, to cultivate the political sciences, particularly the economy of nations, and more than ten years since I began to doubt the infallibility of the dominant theory and to discover its errors. When I came here I found the common sense of the nation struggling against those scholastic errors; and perceiving an opportunity to make myself useful to your great community, I lost no time in acquiring sufficient knowledge of its commercial policy and its internal resources and wants. Diffident, however, as I was, in my ability to speak in public and to write a language I never wrote before, my plan was confined to a scientific work, which I intended to publish after having properly matured it. But the generous patronage of the gentleman in the chair, whose popularity and high standing in society is equal to his brilliant talents, and his truly American patriotism determined me to publish thus early and thus abruptly the outlines of my system. It would be a silly undertaking to assail celebrated men merely to bring an unknown name before the public, but if such men endanger by their scholastic errors a nation which is the hope of mankind, I consider it a crime against the human family to remain silent even if our talents should not answer our intentions. We intend not to detract from the merits of Adam Smith in expressing our opinion that he did not observe the fundamental distinction between political and cosmopolitical principles ; that he did not do justice to the influence of the moral and intellectual riches or material riches, and *vice versâ*, nor to the causes of the increase and diminution of the productive *powers ;* that he created a vague term under the name of capital, by the use of which he committed immeasurable errors ; that he overlooked entirely matters of the first importance in practice, such as the causes of the rise and fall of the prices of land ; that whilst he treats detached matters with great ingenuity and experience, his system, considered as a whole, is so confused and distracted, as if the principal aim of his books were not to enlighten natives, but to confuse them for the benefit of his own country ; and that, in short, his system of political economy is, in our days, just of as much practical value for this and every other nation as the printing apparatus of Faust would be for one of our printers. We intend not to blacken the merit of the great inventor of the black art if we maintain that his apparatus has only an antiquarian value. In respect to Mr. Say I have only to add that he adopts all the truths and nearly all the errors of his predecessor, and that his principal merit is to have clothed both, by a superior talent, in the brilliant garment of a fine style, and arranged them in a new order, very pleasant to those who prefer an apparently logical system to plain truth. That he intermeddled neither with facts nor with numbers we cannot contemplate as an improvement. But Mr. Say likes no facts; he is almost an enemy to facts; he banishes them to a particular literary apartment called *statistics*, not to be troubled by them, and with the few he alleges he is tolerably unfortunate.

I trust, gentlemen, America will make a system of political economy of her own, and for herself, and send the books of the founders of the pseudo-cosmopolitical system to the Westminster Abbey of the science, to take henceforth an honourable standing in its history by the side of Quesnay and his adherents, who, in their time, flourished too, brilliantly for a considerable time, but were at last dethroned by Mr. Smith and his disciples. This country is not likely to be duped out of its prosperity by empty names and barren systems. Your wise fathers, too, gentlemen, ventured, in spite of the united wisdom of Rousseau, Voltaire, and

Montesquieu, and of English philosophers of equal celebrity, who maintained that a democratic government was only practicable in a city, or in a small territory, to make a large one, yes, a whole system of republics; and behold! they succeeded admirably well, and the splendour of the book wisdom of these great philosophers has vanished before the lustre of the common sense of your fathers, and you, their sons, may now reverse the old axiom and say, a democratic government is only possible in a large country: so the fathers did, and so with the sons American common sense will build up a system of political economy in spite of all foreign book wisdom; but it will not request for that purpose the patronage of the Pharisees and scribes of the age, who are turning at all time in a circle of learned errors decorated by high-sounding names. Our business is with the people. We will speak to the people the language of the people, and the people will understand us, and we will have a verdict of the people.

For Mr. Say's popularity with the Liberals in France there are particular reasons. Opposing strongly the prodigality of government, recommending public parsimony, censuring public vices, he teaches the doctrine of the Liberals, and is considered, and *justly* considered, as one of their most prominent defenders among the theorists. In their view he has undoubtedly great merit with his Liberal countrymen. As to his "laissez-faire" theory, it is considered there is a harmless fancy sanctioned by the opinion of the great Adam Smith. . . . For, gentlemen, unanimous as are the French *theorists* in their doctrine, the French *people* and the French statesmen are fully convinced that the present protective system has raised France to that high degree of power and wealth on which she now stands, and that the free trade theory would carry France to ruin. . . . I called the dominant school the pseudo-cosmopolitical, and I believe not without good reason. The whole nature and tendency of this union being cosmopolitical, she certainly will never shrink from true cosmopolitical principles. She assuredly would be the first country in the world to form a true, upright, and well-warranted union of all nations for free, unrestricted commerce throughout the whole world. But is mankind ripe for such a union? The first condition of it should be to remove the restrictions, not merely to talk about free trade and to act quite contrary; the second, that all naval Powers, by burning their fleets, should give a pledge of their sincerity. Is it to be expected that the English ever would agree to such conditions? Never. We call, therefore, the free trade theory the *pseudo-cosmopolitical*, because it has, in the present condition (1) of the world only its existence in books and speeches, not in reality

—because those who profess it never think, and never will think, of executing it, and those who execute it must unavoidably become the sacrifice of their credulity, of their inexperience, of their ignorance. As all hopes of the true cosmopolitics rest on the success of the United States, and as the United States certainly never could succeed in following a cosmopolitical system when men and things are not yet ripe for it, their aim would be ultimately lost by such premature engagements.

Yes, gentlemen, it is my firm belief that in after ages this country will proclaim cosmopolitical principles, but true—not simulated ones. When the United States shall count a hundred millions of inhabitants in a hundred states; when our industry will have attained the greatest perfection, and all the seas will be covered with our ships; when New York will be the greatest commercial emporium, and Philadelphia the greatest manufacturing city in the world; when Albion, in industry and wealth will be nearly equal to Pennsylvania, and no earthly power can longer resist the American Stars, then our children's children will proclaim freedom of trade throughout the world, by land and sea. Who will reproach us with having thus painted a visionary futurity? Do you not possess all those means which made England the greatest country in the world in a higher degree and perfection, you Americans?

Are you not blessed with treasures of nature and with gifts of mind like those Islanders, you Pennsylvanians? And where is there within your limits a single one of those causes to be found which, in that island, with all its immense riches, moral, intellectual, and physical, produce and accumulate their masses of pauperism, of vice, and of ignorance.

I must confess, however, that the present condition of this union presents a very striking contrast with such great prospects. Often when I contemplate the present state of things, I cannot help remembering olden times, when the Spanish adventurers came to this Western world for bartering with the aborigines. It seems to me as if the nature of commerce since that time had not altered much. An English ship is below, your population run to the wharfs, they are offered fine clothing, frippery, baubles for sale; they offer bread, corn, and many useful things in exchange; but the foreigners do not like those things; they ask you for small, round, bright, yellow-looking pieces of metal; your people give all they have—but, alas! their stock ran out, their power is gone. . . . The "laissez-faire" men will reply to this splendid exposition,[1] that all these results were attained in spite and not in consequence of the protecting system. They deny the daylight in face of the sun.

[1] Of the benefits of protection in France since 1812.

But we, gentlemen, can give a double counter-evidence. What was our condition in 1814 in comparison with France? We were rich, and they were exhausted; we bought cheap manufactures from England, and they bought none; we are now exhausted and they are rich. Again, what was Germany thirty years ago, and what was France? Germany, industrious and wealthy, exported all kinds of manufactures to all parts of the world; France, without flourishing industry, received immense masses of manufactures from there. Germany bought cheap from every country, and ruined her immense productive powers, and France, exports at present masses of manufactures to Germany, a country now degraded in such a degree that her ingenious and persevering sons export nothing but inventions to seek for reward and protection in Paris and London, and books, by which other people may learn how to become rich. France, after having been conquered by the sword, conquered Germany a second time by the power-loom. England takes nothing from her in exchange for immense quantities of manufactures but rags, on which to print their cosmopolitical principles, and bones from her battlefields to manure her soil.

No, gentlemen, France attained those splendid results in aid of her protecting system, but in spite of heavy taxes, in spite of a government which depresses more and more her freedom and the rights of her people, in spite of a low state of popular instruction. This people paid nearly one *thousand millions* of francs a year, or two hundred millions of dollars, *a sum which surpasses twice the amount of all your exports and imports,* and of which, not the fifth part is spent for the common welfare, whilst your trifling taxes are applied altogether for the real wants of the community.   Mr. Dupin (2) reckons one subscriber of a newspaper for every 427 inhabitants, and that two Frenchmen amongst five can read; in this country it would be a hard task to find a white inhabitant above the first stage of infancy who cannot read, and I live in a county of about 50,000 inhabitants, where there were at the beginning of the present year six newspapers with six thousand subscribers, making eight persons for every subscription.   Mr. Dupin complains that individual rights in France are restricted to such a degree that the citizens are not even permitted to meet for deliberating on their common wants and wishes.   We in this country had not long ago the great spectacle of beholding, on motion of your high-minded and efficient society, the people of fourteen states meet in their respective counties in their states, and lastly, in a national Convention for discussing the causes and the remedies of the present depression of our national industry.   A protective system is evidently equally beneficial to all states and all parties, and that the opposition against it is either founded in false fears, false principles, or in the efforts of orators and writers who, feeling the weakness of their cause, make up by a passionate language and personalities what is wanting in reason and truth. As the language of these writers is not that of the Southern people, so their sentiments are not those of the noble-minded planters of the South. Compare, gentlemen, the Charleston memorial with Mr. Cooper's Columbia speech, and you will find the former to be an erroneous composition of cosmopolitical principles, destitute of facts and without foundation, but decent, peaceable, and respectful, whilst the language of the latter will remind you of the speeches of those violent clubs which render our recollections of the French revolution so painful. What a lamentable sight to behold men, who in former times merited well of their country, instead of resting on their laurels, or of fulfilling their duties of teaching the youth how to promote the growth and prosperity of their country, go abroad to excite the feelings of the people by inflammatory addresses, and assail from their chairs at home the worthiest statesman! I allude here to Mr. Cooper's lectures on political economy, where he represents, in the schoolmasterly tone of Mr. Say, the present Secretary of Treasury (3) as not having learned during his ambassadorship at London, from Mr. Canning and

Huskisson, cosmopolitical principles, whilst all
those who are friendly to American prosperity,
estimate the Finance Report of this gentleman
as a worthy counterpart to Hamilton's celebrated
work, and congratulate the country on having a
statesman at the head of the Treasury, who had
opportunity and talent to penetrate the mysteries
of the English commercial policy, and who sacrifices
not the welfare of his country for the vain glory
of following false book wisdom. I seize, gentleman, this occasion to express respectful feelings
towards this exalted character for the kind reception
he gave me when he was ambassador in London.
The proceedings of the convention at Harrisburg,
and its luminous reports will not fail to convince
the South of the propriety of the American
system. Virginia, high-minded Virginia, the cradle
of the great founder of this union, and of three
illustrious presidents, will give a magnanimous
example. Virginia—how can she henceforth call
on the name of her great son, if she should be
selfish enough to support a system contrary to
the future greatness of his work? How weak the
opposite cause is, she may learn from the reasons
they allege, of which the principal is a *a want of
constitutional power.*

Gentlemen, if the clear words of the constitution
are not sufficient, we will show them the proceedings of Congress in 1789, when the principal

framers of the constitution were members, when everybody acknowledged that Congress had the power and were in duty bound to protect manufacturers and nobody protested. We will read to Virginia the speeches of her illustrious Madison, when he, who may be called the father of the constitution, spoke and acted, in 1789, as you do now. We will show to South Carolina, that her inhabitants were the first who memorialized Congress for prohibiting measures; and to New York, that the second petition of that tendency came from her citizens. We will remind the Southern States in general, that they admonished, in 1789, the New England States (then in respect to the high duty on molasses, in the same spirit of opposition in which the South is now) with regard to the principle of "*general welfare*," and "*national unity*" which they now assail. *We will lastly show them the great example of the immortal Washington, who by wearing a homespun cloth on the day of his inauguration, in 1789, in that simple and expressive manner which was so peculiar to that great man, taught a never-to-be-forgotten lesson to all his successors, and to all future legislators, how to promote the prosperity of the country.*

NOTES TO PROFESSOR LIST'S SPEECH

Page 278. (1) *The present condition.* Hamilton, " Report," p. 26. " The United States are to a certain extent in the position of a country precluded from foreign commerce. They can indeed, without difficulty, obtain from abroad the manufactured supplies of which they are in want ; but they experience numerous and very injurious impediments to the emission and vent of their own commodities."

Page 282. (2) Baron Charles Dupin, a celebrated French statistician, b. 1784. He published in 1827, " Forces productive et commercielles la France."

Page 283. (3) *The present secretary.* Richard Rush.

INTRODUCTION TO THE "NATIONAL SYSTEM OF POLITICAL ECONOMY"

In no branch of political economy is there such a divergence of opinions between theorists and practical men as in regard to international commerce and commercial policy. At the same time, there is no question within the scope of this science which is of so much importance, not only for the prosperity and civilization of nations, but also for their independence, power, and continued existence. Poor, weak, and barbarous countries have become, mainly as a result of wise commercial policy, empires abounding in wealth and power, while other countries, for opposite reasons, have sunk from a high level of national importance into insignificance. Nay, in some instances nations have forfeited their independence and political existence mainly on account of a commercial policy which was unfavourable to the development and encouragement of their nationality. In our own days, more than ever before, these questions have awakened an interest far greater than that felt in any other economic problems. For the more rapid the growth of a spirit of industrial invention and improvement, of social and political reform, the wider becomes the gap between stationary and progressive nations, and the more dangerous it is to remain on the further side. If in the past centuries were required for Great Britain to succeed in monopolizing the most important manufacture of those days, the wool industry, later decades were sufficient in the case of the far more important cotton industry, and in our own time a few years' start enabled her to annex the whole linen industry of the Continent

And at no former date has the world seen a manufacturing and commercial supremacy like that which in our own day, endowed with such immense power, has followed so systematic a policy, and has striven so hard to monopolize all manufactures, all commerce, all shipping, all the chief colonies, all the ocean, and to make the rest of the world, like the Hindus, its serfs in all industrial and commercial relations.

Alarmed at the effects of this policy, nay, rather forced by the convulsions which it produced, we have lately seen a country whose civilization seemed little adapted for manufacturing, we have seen Russia seek her salvation in the system of prohibition so much abhorred by orthodox theory.   What has been the result? National prosperity.

On the other hand, North America, which was attaining a high position under protection, was attracted by the promises of the theory, and induced to open her ports again to English goods. What was the fruit of free competition? Convulsion and ruin.

Such experiences are well fitted to awake doubts whether the theory is so infallible as it pretends to be ; whether the common practice is so insane as it is depicted by the theory ; to arouse fears lest our nationality might be in danger of perishing at last from an error in the theory, like the patient who followed a printed prescription and died of a misprint ; and to produce a suspicion that this much-praised theory may be built like the old Greek horse, with vast womb and lofty sides, only to conceal men and weapons and to induce us to pull down our walls of defence with our own hands.

This much at least is certain, that although the great questions of commercial policy have been discussed by the keenest brains of all nations in books and legislative. assembles, yet the gulf between theory and practice which has existed since the time of Quesnay and Smith is not only not filled up, but gapes wider and wider each year. And of what use is a science to us, if it throws no light on the path which practice ought to follow. Is it rational to suppose that the intellect of the

U

one party is so immeasurably great that it can apprehend the nature of things perfectly in all cases, while that of the other party is so weak that it is unable to grasp the truths which its opponents have discovered and brought to light, so that through whole generations it considers manifest errors as truths? Should we not rather suppose that practical men, even if they are as a rule too much inclined to keep to the beaten track, still could not oppose the theory so long and so stubbornly if the theory were not opposed to the nature of things?

In fact, we believe that we can prove the responsibility for the divergence between the theory and practice of commercial policy to rest as much with the theorists as with the practical men. In questions of international trade, political economy must derive its teaching from experience, must adapt its measures to the needs of the present and to the particular circumstances of each nation, without neglecting the claims of the future and of mankind as a whole. Accordingly it founds itself upon philosophy, politics, and history.

Philosophy demands, in the interests of the future and of mankind, an even closer friendship among nations, avoidance of war as far as possible, the establishment and development of international law, the change of what we call the law of nations into the law of federated states, freedom of international intercourse, both in intellectual and material things; and, finally, the alliance of all nations under the rule of law—that is, a universal union.

But politics demands, in the interests of each separate nation, guarantees for its independence and continued existence, special regulations to help its progress in culture, prosperity, and power, to build its society into a perfectly complete and harmoniously developed body politic, self-contained and independent. History, for its part, speaks unmistakably in favour of the claims of the future, since it teaches how the material and moral welfare of mankind has grown at all times with the growth of their political and commercial unity. But it also supports the claims of the present and of nationality when it teaches how nations which have not kept in view primarily the furtherance of their own culture and power have gone to ruin; how unrestricted trade with more advanced nations is certainly an advantage to every nation in the early stages of its development, but how each reaches a point when it can only attain to higher development and an equality with more advanced nationalities through certain restrictions on its international trade. Thus history points out the middle course between the extreme claims of philosophy and politics.

But the practice and theory of political economy

in their present forms each takes sides with a faction, the one supporting the special claims of nationality, the other the one-sided demands of cosmopolitanism.

Practice, or, in other words, the so-called mercantile system, commits the great error of maintaining the absolute and universal advantage and necessity of restriction, because it has been advantageous and beneficial to certain nations at certain periods of their development. It does not see that restriction is only the means, and freedom is the end. Looking only at the nation, never at the individual, only at the present, never at the future, it is exclusively political and national in thought, and is devoid of philosophical outlook or cosmopolitan feeling. The ruling theory, on the contrary, founded by Adam Smith on the dreams of Quesnay, has in view only the cosmopolitan claims of the future, indeed of the most distant future. Universal union and absolute freedom of international trade, which at the present time are a cosmopolitan dream only to be realized perhaps after the lapse of centuries, can (according to the theory) be realized at the present time. It does not understand the needs of the present and the meaning of nationality—in fact, it ignores national existence, and with it the principle of national independence. In its exclusive cosmopolitanism, it considers mankind only as a whole, and the welfare of the whole race, not caring for the nation or national welfare, it shudders at (1) the teachings of politics, and condemns theory and practice as mere worthless routine. It only pays attention to history when the latter agrees with its own one-sided view, but ignores or distorts its teaching when it conflicts with the system. Indeed, it is forced even to deny the influence of the English Navigation Acts, the Methuen Treaty, and English commercial policy in general, and to maintain a view entirely contrary to truth—that England has reached wealth and power not by means, but in spite of, its commercial policy.

When we realize the one-sided nature of each system we can no longer wonder that the practice, in spite of serious errors, was unwilling and unable to be reformed by the theory. We understand why the theory did not wish to learn anything from history or experience, from politics or nationality. If this baseless theory is preached in every alley and from every house-top, and with the greatest fervour among those nations whose national existence it most endangers, the reason is to be found in the prevailing tendency of the age towards philanthropic experiments and the solution of philosophical problems.

But for nations as for individuals, there are two efficacious remedies against the illusions of ideology—experience and necessity. If we are not mistaken, all those states which have recently hoped to find their salvation in free trade with the ruling commercial and manufacturing power, are on the point of learning valuable truths by experience.

It is a sheer impossibility that the free states of North America can attain even a mediocre economic position by the maintenance of existing commercial conditions. It is absolutely necessary that they should revert to their earlier tariff. Even if the slave states resist and are supported by the party in power, the force of circumstances must be stronger than party politics. Nay, we fear that cannons will sooner or later cut the gordian knot which the legislature has been unable to untie. America will pay her debt to England in powder and shot, the effective prohibition of war will correct the errors of American tariff legislation, and the conquest of Canada will put a stop for ever to the vast system of contraband foretold by Huskisson.

May we be mistaken! But in case our prophecy should be fulfilled, we wish to lay on the free trade theory the responsibility of this war. Strange irony of Fate, that a theory based on the great idea of perpetual peace should kindle a war between two Powers which, according to the theorists, are absolutely fitted for reciprocal trade! Almost as strange as the result of the philanthropic abolition of the slave trade, in consequence of which thousands of negroes have been sunk in the depths of the sea.[1]

France, in the course of the past fifty years (or, rather, of the past twenty-five years, for the times of the Revolution and the Napoleonic War can hardly be reckoned), in spite of all mistakes, ex-crescences, and exaggerations, has made a great experiment in the restrictive system. Its success must strike every unbiassed observer. Consistency, however, demands that the theory should deny this success. Since it has already been capable of uttering the desperate assertion (and convincing the world of its truth), that England did not become rich and powerful by means, but in spite of her

---

[1] *List's Note.*—Would it not have been wiser to have induced the slave states first to make laws by which the owners of the plantations could have been obliged to allow the slaves a limited property in the soil which they cultivated, and to ensure them a limited personal freedom ; in a word, to introduce a state of mild serfdom with a view to future emancipation, and thus to prepare and fit the negroes for complete freedom ? Were the negroes any less slaves under their tyrants in Africa than in the American plantations ? Can a barbarous race ever accomplish the change from natural freedom to civilization without passing through the hard school of servitude ? Were Acts of Parliament able to transform the West Indian negroes suddenly into free and indus-trious workers ? Has not the whole human race been led to industry and freedom by this path ? Surely England was not so ignorant of the history of human civilization that she could not have answered these questions long ago. Her past and present policy in regard to abolition have manifestly quite other motives than pure philanthropy. We will explain these motives later.

commercial policy, why should it hesitate to make the less startling statement that the manufactures of France without protection would have been much more flourishing than they are now?

At all events, the assertion has been accepted by many as a piece of penetrating wisdom, and has attained wide currency, although some clear-sighted men of practical experience oppose it. Certainly the desire to obtain the blessings of freer trade with England is at present fairly general in France. And it can scarcely be denied (we shall prove this in more detail later) that mutual commerce would in many ways tend to the benefit of both countries. England's intention is obviously to exchange not merely raw materials, such as iron, but large quantities of manufactured goods in return for French agricultural produce and articles of luxury. How far the French Government and legislature will go in meeting this design is not yet clear. But if the development planned by England really takes place, the world will have a new affirmation or negation of the great question: how far under existing conditions, when one of two great manufacturing nations has a marked advantage over the other as concerns cost of production and the opening up of foreign markets, is it possible or advantageous for them to enter into free competition in their own home market, and what will be the result of such competition? In Germany these have only become vital national questions since the commercial union. Wine is the bait through which England hopes to effect the conclusion of a commercial treaty with France; but in the case of Germany corn and timber serve the same purpose. But all this is still vague hypothesis; at present it is impossible to tell whether the foolish Tories can be made reasonable enough to let the Government give such facilities for the importation of German corn and timber as would be really advantageous to the union. For even now we Germans have made sufficient progress in commercial politics to make the idea that we can be paid in moonshine and empty promises seem absurd and insulting.

Assuming that Parliament made these concessions, the most important questions of German trade would at once come under public discussion. Dr. Bowring's latest report gives us a foretaste of the tactics England will adopt in such a case. It will treat these concessions, not as an equivalent for the overwhelming and permanent advantages which its manufactures enjoy in the German markets; not as earnest-money to prevent Germany from learning gradually to spin cotton for its own needs, and so obtaining the necessary raw material direct from the tropics in return for its own manufactures; not as a means of equalizing the constant disproportion between the respective imports and exports of both countries. No!

England will regard the privilege of providing
Germany with cotton yarn as a *jus quæsitum*, and
will require for every concession a new return
amounting to nothing less than the sacrifice of
Germany's cotton and wool manufactures, and so
forth.   It will treat each concession as a mess of
pottage, and ask in return the denial of our birthright.   If Dr. Bowring did not deceive himself
during his stay in Germany; if he did not perhaps
(as we strongly suspect) take Berlin politeness for
real earnest, then those who framed the policy of
the German commercial union are wandering in
the paths of cosmopolitan theory.   That is, they
draw a distinction between the export of manufactured goods and of agricultural products, they
believe that they can advance national interests by
the increase of the latter at the expense of the
former, and they have not recognized national
industrial development as the basic principle of
the Union.   They do not hesitate to sacrifice to
foreign competition industries which, as a result
of long-continued protection, have reached such a
point that home competition has already greatly
lowered prices, although by this sacrifice they
destroy the very springs of German enterprise.
For every factory ruined by reduced protection
or any form of Government action, is like a dead
creature nailed up to scare away every living thing
of the species for a wide distance around.

As we have said, we are far from thinking that Dr. Bowring's assertions are well grounded, but it is bad enough that they can be made, and are made openly, since as a result confidence in the value of protection, and with it German industrial enterprise, has received a perceptible shock. His report also lets us realize in what form the deadly poison will be offered to German manufacturers, so that the true motive for the attempt may be hidden and it may attack more surely the very source of life.

Our specific duties will be changed to duties *ad valorem*, so that the door may be opened wide to English smuggling and defrauding of the customs. This will be particularly the case with articles of general use, small individual value, and large bulk, that is, with those which are the foundations of manufacturing industry.

We thus see of what great practical importance the question of international free trade is at present, and how necessary it is that a thorough and unbiassed inquiry should at last be undertaken to see whether and how far theory and practice are guilty of error in this matter. Thus the problem of harmonizing the two might be solved, or, at least, a serious attempt made to solve it. In very truth the author must explain (not from mock modesty, but from a real and deep-rooted mistrust of his powers) that it is only after a mental struggle of many years' standing, after he has a hundred times questioned the correctness of his views and a hundred times found them true, only after he has a hundred times tested the views and principles opposed to his own and a hundred times realized their error, that he has determined to venture the solution of this problem. This is no vain attempt to contradict ancient authorities and to found new theories. If he had been an Englishman he would scarcely have doubted the main principles of Adam Smith's system.

It was the state of his own country which more than twenty years ago roused in him the first doubts in its infallibility. It has been the state of his own country which has induced him since then, in many unsigned articles, and, finally, in longer essays under his own name, to develop views opposed to the prevailing theory. And to-day it is still mainly the interests of Germany which have emboldened him to come forward with this book, although he cannot deny that a personal consideration has also influenced him. This is, the obligation he feels to make clear through a work of some length that he is not entirely unqualified to speak a word on questions of political economy. In direct antagonism to the theory, the author first seeks the lessons of history, deduces from them his fundamental principles, develops them, subjects previous systems to a critical examination, and finally (since his aim throughout is practical) explains the present position of commercial policy. For the sake of clearness, here follows an outline of the main results of his researches and reflections.

Union of individual faculties in pursuit of a common end is the most effective means of obtaining individual happiness. Alone and apart from his fellows the individual is weak and helpless. The greater the number of those to whom he is socially united and the more complete the union, the greater and more complete is the resulting moral and physical welfare of the individual members.

The highest union of individuals realized up to the present under the rule of law is in the State and the nation. The highest imaginable is the union of all mankind. Just as in the State and nation the individual can attain his special end to a much higher extent than when he is isolated, so all nations would attain their ends to a much greater extent if they were united by the rule of law, perpetual peace, and free intercourse. Nature herself gradually urges nations to this highest union, since through varieties of climate, soil, and products she forces them to barter, and through excess of population, capital, and talent to emigrate and found colonies. International trade is one of the mightiest levers of civilization and prosperity, for by the awakening of new wants it incites men to activity and exertion and passes on new ideas, inventions, and faculties from one nation to another.

But at present the union of nations which arises from international trade is still very imperfect, since it can be shattered, or at least weakened, by war, or by the selfish action of individual nations. By war a nation can be robbed of its independence, property, freedom, laws, and constitution, its national character, and, still worse, of the culture and well-being to which it has attained. It can, in a word, be reduced to a state of servitude. By the selfish measures of foreign countries a nation can be hindered or impaired in the completeness of its economic development.

Maintenance, development, and perfecting of national spirit at present is, and must be, a chief object of national endeavour. It is no wrong and selfish aim, but a rational one, in perfect harmony with the true interests of mankind in general. It leads naturally to a final alliance of nations under the rule of law, the universal union, which can only contribute to the well-being of the human race if it is realized in the form of a confederation. A union proceeding from the overwhelming political strength and wealth of a single nation, and thus basing itself upon the subjection and dependence of all other nations, would, on the contrary, result in the destruction of all national characteristics and all international emulation; it is opposed both to the interest and sentiment of nations, since they all feel themselves destined to independence and the attainment of a high level of wealth and political importance. Such a union would only be a repetition of the former attempt by Rome, carried out indeed by means of manufactures and commerce instead of by cold steel as in former times, but none the less leading back to barbarism. The civilization, political development, and strength of nations are mainly dependent on their economic circumstances; and the converse is also true. The more its economy is developed and perfected, the more civilized and powerful is the nation; the higher the level of its civilization and power, the higher the level of its economic development.

In national economic development we must distinguish the following stages: the savage, the pastoral, the agricultural, the agricultural and manufacturing, the agricultural, manufacturing, and commercial. Obviously the nation which, possessing an extensive territory endowed with many natural resources, combines with a large population, agriculture, manufactures, shipping, and home and foreign trade, is incomparably more civilized, politically advanced and powerful than a merely agricultural state. Manufactures are the basis of internal and external trade, of shipping, of improvements in agriculture, and consequently of civilization and political power. Any nation must of necessity attain to universal dominion which succeeded in monopolizing the whole manufacturing power of the world, and in keeping other nations at such a point of economic development that they produced only food and raw materials and carried on merely the most necessary local industries.

Every nation, which attaches any value to its independence and continued existence, must strive to pass with all speed from a lower stage of culture to a higher, and to combine within its own territory agriculture, manufactures, shipping, and commerce. The transition from savagery to the pastoral state, and from the latter to the agricultural state, are best effected by free trade with civilized, that is, manufacturing and commercial nations. The transition from an agricultural community into the class of agricultural, commercial, and manufacturing nations could only take place under free trade if the same process of development occurred simultaneously in all nations destined to manufactures, if nations put no hindrance in the way of one another's economic development, if they did not check one another's progress through war and tariffs. But since individual nations, through specially favourable circumstances, gained an advantage over others in manufactures, trade, and shipping, and since they early understood the best means of getting and maintaining through these advantages political ascendency, they have accordingly invented a policy which aimed, and still aims, at obtaining a monopoly in manufactures and trade, and at checking the progress of less advanced nations. The combination of the details of this policy (prohibition of imports, import duties, restrictions on shipping, bounties on exports) is known as the tariff system.

Less advanced nations were forced by the earlier progress of other nations, by foreign tariff systems, and by war, to seek in themselves the means by which they could effect the transition from agriculture to manufactures, and to restrict the trade with more advanced countries aiming at a manufacturing monopoly (in so far as this trade was a hindrance to the transition) by the help of a customs tariff. Customs tariffs, then, are not, as is asserted, the invention of some theorist, they are the natural result of a nation's endeavours to secure its existence and well-being, or to obtain supreme power. But this endeavour is only legitimate and rational when it is not a hindrance but a help to the nation which pursues it and is not in opposition to the higher aim of mankind, the future federation of the world. Just as human society can be regarded from two points of view—the cosmopolitan, which considers mankind as a whole; and the political, which pays attention to particular national interests and conditions, so both the economy of the individual and of society can be regarded from two main aspects, as we look at the personal, social, and material forces by which wealth is produced, or the exchange value of material goods.

Hence there is a cosmopolitan and a political economy, a theory of exchange values and a theory of productive powers, two doctrines which are essentially distinct and which must be developed independently. The productive powers of a nation are not only limited by the industry, thrift, morality, and intelligence of its individual members, and by its natural resources or material capital, but also by its social, political, and municipal laws and institutions, and especially by the securities for the continued existence, independence, and power of the nationality. However industrious, thrifty, enterprising, moral, and intelligent the individuals may be, without national unity, national division of labour, and national co-operation of productive powers the nation will never reach a high level of prosperity and power, or ensure to itself the lasting possession of its intellectual, social, and material goods. The principle of division of labour has not been fully grasped up to the present. Productivity depends not only on the division of various manufacturing operations among many individuals, but still more on the moral and physical co-operation of these individuals for a common end.

Thus the principle is applicable not merely to single factories or estates, but to the whole agricultural, manufacturing, and commercial forces of a nation. Division of labour and co-operation of productive powers exist where the intellectual activity of a nation bears a proper ratio to its material production, where agriculture, industry, and trade are equally and harmoniously developed.

In a purely agricultural nation, even when it enjoys free trade with manufacturing and commercial nations, a great part of its productive powers and natural resources lies idle and unused. Its intellectual and political development and its powers of defence are hampered. It can have no shipping of importance, no extensive trade. All its prosperity, so far as it results from international trade, can be interrupted, injured, or ruined by foreign regulations or by war.

Manufacturing power, on the contrary, promotes science, art, and political development, increases the well-being of the people, the population, national revenue, and national power, provides the country with the means of extending its commerce to all quarters of the world and of founding colonies, and nourishes the fishing industry, shipping and the navy. Through it alone can home agriculture be raised to a high pitch of development.

Agriculture and manufactures in one and the same nation, united, that is, under one political authority, live in perpetual peace. Their mutual relations cannot be disturbed by war or foreign measures, consequently they ensure to the nation continued advance in well-being, civilization, and power. Nature lays down certain conditions for the existence of agriculture and manufactures, but these conditions are not always the same.

As far as natural resources are concerned the lands of the temperate zone are peculiarly fitted for the development of a manufacturing power, since a temperate climate is the natural home of physical and mental effort. Yet although the lands of the tropics are ill-suited for manufactures, they possess a natural monopoly of valuable agricultural products which are much in request by the inhabitants of temperate countries. In the exchange of the manufactures of the temperate zone for the products of the tropics ("colonial goods") we find the best example of cosmopolitan division of labour and co-operation of powers, of international trade on a large scale.

Any attempt to found a native manufacturing power would be most injurious to the tropics. Unfitted by nature for such a course, they will make far greater advances in national wealth and civilization if they continue to exchange their products for the manufactures of temperate countries.

This policy, of course, leaves the tropics in a state of dependence. But this dependence will be harmless, indeed it will disappear, when more of the nations of the temperate zone are upon an equality in manufactures, commerce, shipping, and political power; when it is both advantageous and possible for several manufacturing countries to prevent any of their number from misusing their power over the weaker nations of the tropics. Such power would only be dangerous and harmful if all manufactures, commerce, shipping, and sea-power were monopolized by one country.

Then take the case of nations in the temperate zone possessing large territories full of natural resources. They would neglect one of the richest springs of prosperity, civilization, and power if they did not, as soon as they gained the necessary economic, intellectual, and social resources, attempt to realize on a national scale division of labour and co-operation of productive powers.

By economic resources we mean a fairly advanced state of agriculture which cannot be helped appreciably by any further export of its products. By intellectual resources we mean a good system of education. By social resources we mean laws and institutions which secure to the citizen safety for his person and property and free scope for his intellectual and physical powers. We include also well-managed facilities for transport, and the absence of all institutions, such as the feudal system, which are destructive of industry, freedom, intelligence, and morality.

It is the interest of such a nation, first of all, to endeavour to provide its own market with its own manufactured goods, and then to come more and more into direct intercourse with tropical countries, so that it can export manufactured goods to them in its own ships and take from them their own products in return. In comparison with this intercourse between the manufacturing countries of the temperate zone and the agricultural countries of the tropics, all other international trade, with the exception of a few articles, such as wine, is of little importance.

For great nations of the temperate zone the production of raw materials and food stuffs is only of importance as far as their internal trade is concerned. Through the export of corn, wine, flax, hemp, or wool, a rude and poor country gets a great initial impulse towards agriculture, but a great nation has never attained riches, civilization, and power through such a course.

We may lay it down as a general principle, that a nation is rich and powerful in the proportion in which it exports manufactures, imports raw materials, and consumes tropical products.

To manufacturing nations tropical products are not merely food or the raw materials of industry, but before all things incentives to the cultivation of agriculture and manufactures. We shall always find that among the nations which consume the greatest quantity of tropical products a correspondingly large quantity of their own manufactures and raw materials is produced and consumed.

Four distinct periods can be recognized in the economic development of nations by means of international trade. In the first, home agriculture is fostered by the importation of foreign manufactured goods and the export of agricultural products and raw materials. In the second, home manufactures arise by the side of foreign imports. In the third, home manufactures supply the greater part of the home-market. In the fourth, large quantities of home-manufactured goods are exported and raw materials and agricultural products imported from abroad.

The tariff system, as a means of advancing the economic development of the nation by regulation of its foreign trade, must constantly follow the principle of national industrial *education*.

It is madness to attempt to help home agriculture by protection, since home agriculture can only be advanced on economic principles by the development of home manufactures, and the exclusion of foreign raw materials and agricultural products can only depress home manufactures.

The economic betterment of a nation which is at a low level of intelligence and culture, or in which the population is small in relation to the extent and productivity of its territory, is best accomplished through free trade with highly culti-vated, rich, and industrious nations. In the case of such a country every restriction of trade, intended to plant manufacturing industry within its borders, is premature and injurious, not only to the welfare of mankind in general, but to the progress of the nation itself. Only when the intellectual, political, and economic education of the nation has so far advanced as a result of free trade that its further progress would be checked and hindered by the import of foreign manufactures and the lack of a sufficient market for its own goods, can protective measures be justified.

The territory of some nations is not of great extent nor supplied with many natural resources, the mouths of its rivers are not within its boundaries, and it does not form a homogeneous whole. Such a nation cannot apply the protective system at all, or only with imperfect success until it has first supplied its deficiencies by conquest or treaty.

Manufacturing power embraces so many branches of science and knowledge, and pre-supposes so much experience, skill, and practice, that national industrial development can only be gradual. Any exaggeration or hastening of protection punishes itself by diminished national prosperity. The most injurious and objectionable course is the sudden and complete isolation of the country by prohibition. Yet even this can be justified if, separated from other countries by a long war, it has suffered from an involuntary prohibition of foreign manufactures, and has been forced to supply itself. In this case a gradual transition from prohibition to protection should be effected by deciding beforehand upon a system of gradually diminishing duties. But a nation which desires to pass from a non-protective policy to protection must, on the contrary, begin with low taxes, which increase gradually upon a predetermined scale. (2) Taxes pre-determined in this way must be maintained intact by statesmen. They must not lower the taxes before the time, though they may raise them if they seem insufficient.

Excessively high import duties, which entirely cut off foreign competition, injure the country which imposes them, since its manufacturers are not forced to compete with foreigners, and indolence is fostered. If home manufactures do not prosper under moderate and gradually increasing duties, this is a proof that the country has not the necessary qualifications for the development of its own manufacturing system. Duties in a branch of industry that is already protected should not fall so low, that the existence of the industry is endangered by foreign competition. Support of existing manufactures, and protection for the essentials of national industry must be unalterable principles. Foreign competition, accordingly, can be allowed only a share in the yearly increase of consumption. The duties must be raised as soon as the foreigner gains the greater part or the whole of the yearly increase.

A nation like England, whose manufacturing power has a long start of all other countries, best maintains and extends its industrial and commercial supremacy by the freest possible trade. In its case cosmopolitan and political principles are identical. This explains the preference of distinguished English statesmen for absolute free trade and the unwillingness of wise financiers in other countries to apply this principle under the existing conditions of the world. For the last quarter of a century the system of prohibition and protection has worked to the disadvantage of England and the advantage of her rivals. Most disadvantageous of all are its restrictions on the importation of foreign raw materials and food stuffs.

Commercial unions and commercial treaties are the most effective means of facilitating intercourse between different nations. But commercial treaties are only legitimate and valuable when they involve mutual benefits. They are injurious and illegitimate when the development of a manufacturing power in one country is sacrificed in order to gain concessions for the exports of its agricultural products to another country. These are "Methuentreaties," or "lion-treaties." (3) Such a "lion" treaty was that concluded between England and France in 1768. (4) All the offers which England has made since then to France and other countries are of the same character. Even if protection temporarily enhances prices, yet it ensures cheapness in the future as a result of home competition. For a perfectly developed industry can fix a much lower price for its products than the cost of transport and of trader's profits allow when raw materials and food must be exported and manufacturers imported.

The loss which a nation incurs by protection is only one of *values*, but it gains *powers* by which it is enabled to go on producing permanently inestimable amounts of value. This loss in value should be regarded merely as the price paid for the industrial education of the nation.

Protection to manufactures does not injure the agriculturists of the protected nation. Through the growth of a home manufacturing power, wealth, population, and with them the demand for agricultural products will vastly increase. Consequently there will be a considerable rise in the rents and selling prices of landed property, while as time goes by the manufactured products required by agriculturists will fall in price. These gains will outweigh the losses sustained by the agriculturists through the temporary rise in the prices of manufactured goods.

Similarly, both home and foreign trade gain from protection, since both are of importance only in the case of countries which can supply their own markets with manufactures, consume their own agricultural products, and exchange their own manufacturing surplus for foreign raw materials and food stuffs. Merely agricultural nations of the temperate zone have an insignificant home and foreign trade; foreign trade in such cases is generally in the hands of the manufacturing and commercial nations who hold intercourse with them.

Moderate protection does not grant a monopoly to home manufactures, only a guarantee against loss for those individuals who have devoted their capital, talent, and labour to new and untried industries. There can be no monopoly since home competition takes the place of foreign, and it is open to each member of the state to share in the benefits it offers to individuals. There is merely a monopoly for the inhabitants of one country against those of foreign countries, who themselves possess at home a similar monopoly. But this monopoly is useful, not only because it wakes productive forces lying idle and dormant in the nation, but because it attracts to the country foreign productive forces (material and intellectual capital, *entrepreneurs*, skilled and unskilled workmen).

In the case of many nations of long standing culture the export of raw materials and agricultural products, and the import of foreign manufactures, can no longer benefit their powers of production. Such nations suffer many serious evils if they do not foster their own manufactures. Their agriculture must necessarily be crippled, since, if important home manufactures arose, the increased population would find employment there, and the consequent great demand for agricultural products would make agriculture on a large scale very profitable and favour its development. But in the case supposed the surplus population could only be employed in agriculture. The result would be a subdivision of land and increase of small cultivators which would be most injurious to the power, civilization, and wealth of the nation.

An agricultural population consisting for the most part of peasant proprietors can neither contribute large quantities of products to the home trade nor exercise an important demand for manufactures. In such a case the consumption of each individual is limited for the most part to what he himself produces. Under these conditions the nation can never develop any satisfactory system of transport, and can never possess the incalculable advantages arising from such a system. The inevitable result is national weakness, moral and material, individual and political. These consequences are the more dangerous when neighbouring nations pursue the opposite course, when they advance as we fall back, when yonder the hope of better things to come increases the courage, power, and enterprise of the citizens, while here courage and spirit are more and more depressed by the outlook into a hopeless future. History affords striking examples of whole nations falling into ruin because they did not know how to undertake at the right moment the great task of planting their own manufactures, and a powerful industry and commerce, by which they could insure to themselves intellectual, economic, and political independence.

NOTES TO THE "INTRODUCTION"

Page 293. (1) *Shudders at.* List borrows his phrase from Latin and writes "perhorrescirt."

Page 313. (2) *Scale.* See Memoir, chap. iv. p. 132.

Page 315. (3) *Lion treaties, i.e.* treaties in which one party is in much the stronger position, like the lion of Aesop's Fables.

Page 315. (4) 1768. Probably a misprint for 1786, the date of the Eden Treaty.

LETTER XII

Political Economy is not Cosmopolitical Economy
(Conclusion) †

Reading, July 27, 1827.

DEAR SIR,
After having shown by the two fore-
going letters that the grain growers and the cotton
growers are equally benefited by raising a manufacturing industry, it remains yet to mention that the
shipping and commercial interests in general will not
less gain by this national improvement. I refer to the
preceding expositions of the immense increase of our
internal production and consumption of wollens, cot-
tons etc. which would be effected by fostering domestic
manufactories. The internal exchange of raw materials
and victuals for manufactories would increase in an
equal ratio internal trade, and coast, river, and canal
shipping. To this must be added the increase of our
exports of manufactured goods, and the increase of the
imports produced by our greater exports. *Adam Smith
himself confesses that great manufacturing countries
consume by far a greater quantity of foreign goods*

---

† [Reprinted from Philadelphia *National Gazette*, November
27, 1827.]

*than a poor agricultural country.** A single glance on
England will prove this assertion better than any other
argument. What would the commerce and the shipping
of that country be, if it would only consist in an exchange of raw produce for foreign manufactures? And
what is it now? Great as her external commerce is,
yet it is exceeded by her internal commerce tenfold;
great as her shipping to foreign countries is, yet the
tonnage of her coast, river and canal shipping is of
incomparable greater amount. And are not even all her
external commerce and shipping founded on her manufacturing industry? In one word, to raise the amount
of our tonnage, and our commerce, and our naval
strength equally with the English, there is only one
way, we must bring our manufactories on a level with
the resources of our natural means, and our population.

Why now all this bustle? Why this noise from the
part of the shipping merchants and of the cotton
growers? Why their turbulent meetings, their violent
speeches, their piquant toasts? What a painful sight,
if those, whose duty it is to teach the youth principle,

---

* *Wealth of Nations.* Book III, Chap. III. "No large country,
it must be observed ever did or could subsist without some sort
of manufactures being carried on in it; and when it is said of
any such country that it has no manufactures, it must always
be understood of the finer and more improved, or of such as are
fit for distant sale. In every large country, both the clothing
and household furniture of the far greater part of the people,
are the produce of their own industry. This is even more uni-
versally the case in those poor countries which are commonly
said to have no manufactures, than in those rich ones that are
said to abound in them. *In the latter you will generally find,
both in the clothes and household furniture of the lowest rank
of people, a much greater proportion of foreign productions
than in the former.*" [Italics are List's.]

reason and law, leave their chairs to question before meetings of the people, in the most violent language, *the benefit of the union.*

"Jupiter you put hand to your thunderbolts, you must be wrong!" This is the country of reason and principles, not of terror and menaces—shielded by a threefold shield of reason, they must fall back on your own head. When was ever such language heard in this Union, since the Father of his Country addressed his children for the last time? Was it when the manufacturers were ruined by want of support, whilst the cotton growers floated in superabundance? Was it when the property of the grain growers of Pennsylvania was sold under the sheriff's hammer? No. Such language was never heard before, not even from those who, by the great faults of the general legislature, were reduced from abundance and wealth to poverty and penury.

And what are the cotton growers complaining for? Their present embarrassment is only produced by their overdone cotton production. And what have they to fear from a raising of manufacturing industry? Nothing but deliverance from that embarrassment—a certain and a good market for an infinite time. The cotton growers and shipping merchants can only oppose such beneficial measures, by misapprehending their true interest, from false expositions of such whose intention it is to fish in troubled waters.

Let us, therefore, never oppose passionately; the motion is only on the surface of the sea; the majority of the southern planters themselves will in a short time become our adherents; and the violent—not [considering] the welfare of their country—let alone. There is no class of people which will ultimately lose by the American System, except the English commission merchants; and from this quarter arises all the noise we heard since the American System is in question. First we were frightened with threats that England would declare war. But seeing this would not do, the benefit of the Union is brought in question.

Very respectfully yours,

FREDERICK LIST.

BIBLIOGRAPHY

A. WRITINGS OF LIST.

1817.   System der Gemeindewirthschaft.   (*Württembergisches Archiv*, Band II., Heft 2.)

1817.   Gutachten über die Errichtung einer staatswirtschaftlichen Fakultät.   (*Gesammelte Schriften*, pp. 1–14.)

1818.   Die Staatskunde und Staatspraxis Württembergs.

1818–19.   Contributions to *Der Volksfreund aus Schwaben.*

1819–20,   Petitions, etc., in the service of the Handelsverein. (*Gesammelte Schriften*, pp. 15–62.)

1819.   *Organ für den deutschen Handels- und Gewerbestand.*

1820.   Petition on behalf of his Reutlingen constituents.

1823.   *Themis.* 2tn. Bändchen.   Friedrich Lists . . . ehrfurchtsvolle Denkschrift an Seine Majestät den König von Württemberg.   Zurich.

1827.   Outlines of American Political Economy.   Philadelphia.

Appendix to the Outlines.   Philadelphia.

Speech made at the dinner of the Pennsylvania Society. Philadelphia.

1828.   Correspondence with Josef von Baader published in the *Augsburger Allgemeine Zeitung.*

1829.   Mittheilungen aus Nordamerika.   Hamburg.

1833.   Über ein sächsisches Eisenbahn-System.

1835.   Contributions to the Staatslexicon.   Vols. i., ii., and iv.

1835–6.   *Das Eisenbahn-Journal oder National Magazin.* No. 1–35.

1838. Das deutsche National-Transport (reprinted from Staatslexicon).

1841-2. Das Nationale System.

1843-6. *Das Zollvereinsblatt.*

1846. Memorial concerning an alliance between Great Britain and Germany.

1877. A series of List's letters 1824-5, edited by Wilhelm Roscher in *Nord und Sud*. Band 3.

Contributions to

Révue Encyclopédique, 1831.

Constitutionnel, 1831, 1839.

Augsburger Allgemeine Zeitung, 1837, 1839, 1840, 1841, 1842, 1844, 1847.

Deutsches Vierteljahrschrift, 1840, 1841.

Editions and Translations of His Works.

1850-1. Gesammelte Schriften, herausgegeben von Ludwig Häusse. 3 Band.

    1. Friedrich Lists Leben.

    2. Kleinere Schriften.

    3. Das nationale System. Stuttgart and Tübingen. J. G. Cotta.

1853. Das nationale System der politischen Oekonomie von Friedrich List. Siebente Auflage. Mit eine historischen und kritischen Einleitung von K. Th. Eheberg. Stuttgart. J. G. Cotta.

Ueber ein sächsisches Eisenbahn-System. (With an introduction by O. Brandt.) Philipp Reclam, Leipzig. Universal-Bibliothek, 3669.

1856. The National System, translated with notes by G. A. Matile, with a preface by Stephen Colwell. Philadelphia.

1857. Système Nationale. Translated by Henri Richelot.

1860. Protection as a national system suited for Victoria (extracts from List), with preface by G. W. Cole.

1885. The National System, translated, with brief memoir, by Sampson S. Lloyd. Longmans.

1904. New Edition, with introduction by Professor J. S. Nicholson.

B. Works and Articles on List or containing References to Him.

Allgemeine Deutsche Biographie. Art. List.

Handwörterbuch der Staatswissenschaften. Art. List (by Eheberg).

Schönberg. Handbuch. Art. List (by Hans von Schael).

Dictionary of Political Economy. Art. List (by J. K. Ingram).

History of Political Economy. J. K. Ingram. 1888.

Labor Cyclopædia of Political Science. Art. List (by Joseph Garnier).

Ludwig Häusser. Friedrich Lists Leben. 1850.

Carl Jentsch. Friedrich List. Berlin, 1901.

Julius Weise. Friedrich List, ein Vorlaufer und ein Opfer für der Vaterland. Stuttgart (no date).

Friedrich Goldschmidt. Friedrich List. Deutschlands grosser Volkwirth. Berlin, 1870.

A. Staub. Friedrich List. Munich, 1879.

Arthur Raffalovich. Frédéric List.

Wilhelm Roscher. Zur Erinnerung an Friedrich List. *Nord und Sud.* Band 3. 1877.

Dr. Niedermüller. Die Leipzig-Dresdener Eisenbahn, ein Werk Friedrich Lists. Leipzig, 1880.

Hans Schnurbein. Friedrich List als eisenbahnpolitiker. 1904.

Louis Katzenstein. Friedrich List. Zur Erinnerung an seiner 50-jährigen Todestag. Berlin, 1896.

Dr. Bruno Hildebrand. Die National-Oekonomie der Gegenwart und Zukunft, 1848.

A. Wetzel. Friedrich List als Nationaler Erzieher. Stuttgart, 1898.

Dr. K. Th. Eheberg. Friedrich List. Festrede zur Enthüllung seines Denkmals in Kufstein. Munich, 1908.

Dr. Karl Menger. Article in *Neue Freie Presse*, August 6, 1889.

Georg Stamper. Friedrich List. (Westermann's *Illustrierte deutsche Monatshefte*, vol. 86. August, 1899.

K. H. Bruggeman. Dr. Lists Nationales System der politischen Oekonomie kritische beleuchtet. Berlin, 1842.

K. H. Rau. Zur Kritik über F. Lists Nationales System. Heidelberg, 1843.

John Austin. *Edinburgh Review*, vol. 75. July, 1842.

Henri Richelot. L'Association douanière Allemande. 1845.

Dr. Julius Kautz. Die geschichtliche Entwickelung der National-Oekonomie und ihrer Litteratur. Vienna, 1860.

W. Roscher. Geschichte der National-Oekonomik in Deutschland. 1874.

Eugen Dühring. Die wissenschaftliche Bedeutung Friedrich Lists. (*Deutsche Vierteljahrschrift*, 1867.)

Eugen Dühring. Kritische Geschichte der Nationalökonomie und des Socialismus. Leipsic, 4th edition, 1906.

Gustav Schmoller. Zur Litteratur-Geschichte der Staats- und Sozial-Wissenschaften. 1888.

Wolfgang Menzel. Denkwürdigkeiten. Leipsic, 1877.

Dr. Max Höltzel. Ueber Friedrich List. (Reprint from *Preussische Jahrbücher*, 1903.) Aus der Geschichte der deutscher Eisenbahnen. *Deutsche Eisenbahn-Beamten Zeitung.* August 31, 1905.

Friedrich List. *Neues Tagblatt*, Stuttgart, September 4, 1905.

Dr. Curtius Köhler. Problematisches zu Friedrich List. Mit Anhang. Lists Briefe aus Amerika. Leipsic, 1908.

Dr. H. Losch. Ein deutscher Amerikafahrer, in *Patria*, 1906.

C 1. Works on American Protection, especially bearing on the Period 1816–30.

F. W. Taussig. Tariff History of the United States. (Putnam.)

Ugo Rabbeno. American Commercial Policy. (Macmillan and Co.)

C. L. Elliot. The Tariff Controversy, 1789–1833. (*Leland Stanford Junior University Monographs*, 1892.)

Alexander Hamilton. Report on Manufactures. 1791.

Daniel Raymond. Thoughts on Political Economy. Baltimore, 1820.

C. P. Neill. Daniel Raymond, an early chapter in the history of Economic Theory in the United States. Baltimore, 1897.

Matthew Carey: Many tracts and pamphlets on the tariff controversy.

Niles' Weekly Register, 1819–30.

Congressional Debates, 1827–8.

G. H. Harrower. Alexander Hamilton als Nationalökonom. Halle, 1887.

O. V. Deuster. Die Entwickelung des amerikanischen Zolltarifsystem. Leipsic, 1885.

E. J. James. Studien über den amerikanischen Zolltarif. Halle, 1877.

C 2. On the Relation between List and Henry C. Carey.

Henry Carey-Baird. Carey and two of his recent critics. (*Proc. Amer. Phil. Soc.*, xxix. 1891.)

Knies. Politische Oekonomie, pp. 440 fol.

Gustav Schmoller. Zur Litteratur-Geschichte, etc. 1888.

Eugen Dühring. Kritische Geschichte der Nationalökonomie. 1890.

J. W. Jenks. Henry C. Carey als National-Oekonom. Semmlung Jena, 1885.

INDEX

THE END

PRINTED BY
WILLIAM CLOWES AND SONS, LIMITED,
LONDON AND BECCLES.